Biblical Holism
and Agriculture

Cultivating Our Roots

Biblical Holism and Agriculture

Cultivating Our Roots

David J. Evans, Ronald J. Vos,
Keith P. Wright, Editors

William Carey Library
Pasadena, California

Cover design by Rachel Snodderly
Front cover photo by Ron Storer.
Back cover bottom right photo by Ted Wilcox.

In Chapter 9, permission has been granted to print an adaptation of material originally published in "Change Across Cultures" by Bruce Bradshaw, Baker Academic, a Division of Baker Book House Co., copyright 2002.

Published by

William Carey Library
1605 Elizabeth St.
Pasadena, California 91104

ISBN   0-87808-355-3

Printed in the United States of America

Contents

v

114256

Conclusion

Editors and Contributors

David J. Evans, M.S., is Senior Director of International Operations at Food for the Hungry International in Scottsdale, Arizona, USA.

Ronald J. Vos, Ph.D., is Professor of Agriculture at Dordt College in Sioux Center, Iowa, USA.

Keith P. Wright, M.S., is Director of the Washington Office at Food for the Hungry, USA in Washington D.C., USA.

Wayne A. Kobes, Ph.D., is Professor and Chair of the Theology Department at Dordt College in Sioux Center, Iowa, USA.

Jesse T. Njoka, Ph.D., is Senior Lecturer in the Department of Range Management, Faculty of Agriculture, University of Nairobi, Kenya, East Africa.

Rev. Jim Ball, Ph.D., is Executive Director of the Evangelical Environmental Network in Washington D.C., USA.

Robert De Haan, Ph.D., is Associate Professor of Agriculture at Dordt College in Sioux Center, Iowa, USA.

Harry Spaling, Ph.D., is Associate Professor of Geography and Environmental Studies at The King's University College, Edmonton, Canada.

John H. Kok, Ph.D., is Professor of Philosophy at Dordt College in Sioux Center, Iowa, USA.

Darrow L. Miller, M.A., is Vice President of Wholistic Ministry Resources at Food for the Hungry International in Scottsdale, Arizona, USA.

Bruce Bradshaw, M.A., is Associate Professor of Economic Development at Bethel College in North Newton, Kansas, USA.

Michael Oye, Ph.D., is Vice-Chairman of RURCON, a holistic development agency in Jos, Nigeria, West Africa.

E. John Wibberley, Ph.D., is Visiting Professor, Royal Agricultural College, Cirencester and Visiting Fellow in International & Rural Development, University of Reading, UK.

Kara Unger Ball, MPP, is Former Director of Sustainable Countrysides Programs at the Western Pennsylvania Conservancy in Pittsburgh, PA, USA.

Greg De Haan, M.S., is Mission Partner of the (US) Reformed Church in America, in Gambia, West Africa.

Acknowledgments

It is with deep gratitude that we express our thanks to the many people who helped to make the conference and this book a success. We are greatly indebted to Tetsunao Yamamori, President Emeritus of Food for the Hungry, for his help in organizing the conference, selecting presenters, and advising us on the contents of this book. We also owe a great debt of gratitude to the administration at Dordt College in Sioux Center, Iowa. Without their support, the conference would not have taken place nor would this book have been written. In addition, Heather Moermann, Agriculture Department Administrative Assistant at Dordt, was instrumental in making sure that all the logistics of the conference were in place and functioning well. We *definitely* could not have done this without Heather. We also recognize that many others at Dordt College played a part in making this conference and book a reality. For that we are thankful. We would like to thank Darrow L. Miller who continued to encourage this idea of a conference and book over a period of four long years. We are grateful to the leadership of Food for the Hungry for their strong moral and financial support for this project. We would like to thank AERDO and all those who served on the conference organizing committee. We would like to thank the plenary speakers whose papers comprise the contents of this book. We also greatly appreciate the efforts of Martin Price, David Mann, Scott Sabin, and Frank Louws who served as breakout group presenters at the conference. We greatly appreciate the effort of Tim Smith in videotaping the conference proceedings. We extend special thanks to Cathy Saracco for her able assistance with the conference manuscripts.

We would like to thank the U. S. Center for World Mission and William Carey Library publishers for believing in this project and the contents of this book. Finally, we would like to thank our wives for their encouragement and support during this process. To all these mentioned and many more, we offer our deepest thanks.

Foreword

C. Dean Freudenberger, Ph.D.

Biblical Holism and Agriculture: Cultivating Our Roots addresses the urgent need for constructing a holistic biblical perspective in order to appraise the economic, social, ecological, environmental and spiritual impact of globalization and the unprecedented impact of powerful agricultural technologies and marketing systems. Holistic biblical perspectives reference ancient Hebrew insights about responsible freedom for "keeping" the land by people created in the image of God as representatives commissioned to stewardship and justice.

This book was developed several months prior to the United Nations Earth Summit on Sustainable Development in Johannesburg, August–September, 2002, and published immediately following the conference. It is a most timely piece of work. The essays significantly contribute to the literature on sustainable development as they delineate the spiritual and moral motivation to care about sustainable futures.

In particular, the book identifies three needs in agriculture to be addressed by the churches in mission. The first is to rebuild a new relationship with God, creation and humanity; this is to say, to create a new orientation in the fields of ethics, economics and agricultural science that reflects normative biblical guidelines for the care of land and human communities. The second is to enable leadership of the churches with responsibilities for outreach in mission to comprehend more fully the importance and urgency of the witness and service of agricultural missionaries in the 21st century in response to the negative impact of the globalization of our food system. This prophetic stance of criticizing the status quo in agriculture often leads to isolation from the main stream. The third need is to witness to the vision of justice and care of creation in bringing about a sustainable future for the earth and our agriculture.

The essays in the book complement literature in the field of missiology and agricultural development by demonstrating how biblical holism contributes to a broadened understanding of life's interdependencies, that is, ecological patterns necessary for maintaining and maximizing biological diversity in agriculture and the necessity for creating, in a post-colonial world, a sustainable, or resource regenerative, domestic, self-reliant agriculture. The ethical foundation for this holism is forcefully illustrated in one of the essays about agricultural ethics with the use of Aldo Leopold's land ethic: A thing is right when it contributes to the beauty, integrity and harmony of the biotic community. It is wrong when it goes the other way.

The authors of the essays worked independently in preparation for the Dordt College consultation. One should take note of a most interesting dynamic. There emerges in the writings a consistent identification of elements of biblical wisdom about stewardship in the care of creation and references of the prophetic traditions about social critique.

Several African authors offer stimulating and challenging essays as they demonstrate the unquestionable necessity of consulting indigenous insights about agriculture, its relation to natural ecosystems and to human communities and their value systems. We ignore these insights at our peril!

The need and potential significance of Christian agricultural workers in the 21st century is well articulated. The meaning of servant leadership and prophetic critique is described in the call for the development of a sustainable and therefore just agriculture and food system requiring the evolution of a new paradigm for the way food and fiber must be produced so that humanity serves in God's image for keeping the land. This paradigm emerges from biblical insights about the values of healthy ecosystem functions, human community needs and points to a new agenda for research, testing and modification. These values function as guidelines for the care of all of creation. This challenge suggests a new dimension of Christian discipleship. This work will take us far beyond the limited and frequently destructive mindset of maximizing crop yields for the generation of wealth.

C. DEAN FREUDENBERGER, Ph.D.
Professor Emeritus of Theology
Claremont, California
September 2002

Introduction

Building Consensus for Biblical Holism in Agriculture

David J. Evans and Keith P. Wright

Dating back to the first Lausanne conference in 1974, there has been a growing movement within Evangelical Christianity to minister to the needs of the whole person—spiritual, physical, emotional and social. Various names and/or definitions for this marriage between evangelism and social action have been postulated by several evangelical scholars and activists including Tetsunao Yamamori [symbiotic ministry] (1976, 1987, 1993), and Ron Sider [good news and good works] (1999). In the 1990s, this concept evolved further into what is now referred to commonly as "Biblical Holism." In this more recent iteration, it is important to note that concern is not only directed toward the spiritual, physical, social, and emotional well-being of people, but also toward the non-human part of God's creation. Thus, when one speaks of Biblical Holism, one is usually referring to a triangular relationship between God and humans, God and non-human creation, and humans and non-human creation (Steward, 1994).

A fuller definition of Biblical Holism is God's work, through Jesus Christ, to redeem and restore all things that were created good but became damaged and broken as a result of human sin (see e.g., Colossians 1:20). Expanding upon the key relationships above, Darrow Miller (1999) identifies six key primary and secondary relationships that comprise Biblical Holism:

1

Primary Relationships (vertical):
- God with humanity (Gen. 1:26-27; Gen. 3:6-7; Rom. 5:10)
- God with non-human creation (Gen. 1:1)

Secondary Relationships (horizontal):
- Humans with their individual selves (Gen. 1:26-27; Jer. 17:9; 1 Jn. 1:9)
- Humans with humanity (Gen. 2:18; Gen. 4:8-9; Phil. 2:3-4)
- Humans with the rest of creation [nature] (Gen. 1:26-31; 2:15 & 19-20; 3:17-19; Rom. 8:18-23), and
- Humans with the metaphysical world [especially knowledge, ethics, purpose, and economics] (Gen. 1:26-27; Gen. 1:16)

Building on this definition, Biblical Holism as it applies to agriculture is essentially the healing and restoration of humanity's relationship to God, people and the rest of creation (animals, plants, land, water, air) and, secondarily, the healing and restoration of humanity's relationship to knowledge, ethics, purpose and economics, as those areas relate to agriculture.

The Need:

There is evidence that a fair amount of effort has been invested to date in the area of Biblical Holism in health and that some Christian health development organizations and practitioners are attempting to conduct health development activities from a Biblical perspective (Fountain, 1989; World Relief, 2000). However, the same level of investment and practice has not been achieved in agricultural development. Although there is a growing movement among evangelicals to follow God's Biblical mandate in caring for His creation (DeWitt, 1994; Roberts and Pretiz, 1998; Goedhart, 2001; Vos, 2001), much thinking and work remains to be done in the wider area of Biblical Holism as it relates to agriculture. There is evidence that some early pioneers in this area such as George Washington Carver succeeded in combining their faith and agricultural vocation, but it is the opinion of these authors that many Christians who are practicing, promoting or teaching agriculture throughout the world today have tended to view their work and vocation as separate from their faith. They conduct their "agricultural development" and "evangelism" activities in a non-integrated, parallel fashion. If farmers, gardeners, foresters, ranchers, agricultural missionaries and agricultural development workers desire to live in an integrated manner, *"Coram Deo,"* (before the face of God), then they need to discover what the Bible says about being good stewards of the relationships with which God has entrusted them.

Fostering the restoration of relationships between the agriculturalist and God, the agriculturalist and purpose (including vocation and work), the agriculturalist and his/her fellow humans, the agriculturalist and non-human creation, the agriculturalist and ethics, the agriculturalist and economics, and the agriculturalist and knowledge will require concerted thinking, envisioning, discussion, and action. The Word of God must be the starting and ending point for this proposed exercise. For therein is contained the wisdom, knowledge and understanding necessary for God's intended holism to become a reality in agricultural development throughout the world.

Beginning to Meet the Need:

In order to meet this critical need in the area of Biblical Holism and agriculture, Food for the Hungry International (FHI) and Dordt College partnered together to hold an international conference on Biblical Holism and agriculture that brought together a dynamic mix of researchers, writers and agricultural practitioners from around the world to exchange ideas on this topic. The conference was held at Dordt College in Sioux Center, Iowa, USA in May 2002. Approximately 105 participants attended the conference—representing farmers, pastors, agricultural researchers, professors, missionaries and relief & development workers from four continents. Dordt College proved to be an excellent venue for the conference in that it is one of only a few Christian Colleges in the USA with an agriculture department. More importantly, Dordt has a strong commitment and desire to promote Biblical Holism in agriculture and all other spheres of life. The conference contained a dynamic mix of plenary presentations, small group workshops and activities, and a commitment to action on the part of the participants. Based on the participant evaluations, it is clear that the vast majority of delegates were greatly energized by the conference. Perhaps the most critical short-term impact of the gathering was that it informed, encouraged, and challenged Christians who work in agriculture to do so with a renewed focus on building God's Kingdom through their work.

The major results of the conference can be classified into four areas:

1. *Thirteen conference papers,* which are presented in this book;
2. *Set of devotionals* on themes that link biblical holism and agriculture;
3. *Concordance* of Scripture references based on the conference topics;
4. *Network* of holistic agricultural practitioners who desire to share experiences and resources in the promotion and practice of biblical holism and agriculture that is being facilitated through a listserve and website hosted by Food for the Hungry International.

The chapters that follow in this book are the result of many years of theoretical and empirical research. There are essentially seven thematic areas that are covered herein:

- The Agriculturalist and God
- The Agriculturalist and Humanity
- The Agriculturalist and Non-human Creation
- The Agriculturalist and Knowledge
- The Agriculturalist and Purpose (Including Vocation and Work)
- The Agriculturalist and Ethics
- The Agriculturalist and Economics.

The authors of these chapters hail from several continents and their writings provide the reader with sound principles and recommendations for bringing all agricultural thoughts and actions captive to the obedience of Christ. Many stories are told about the interplay between beliefs and agricultural development. All the chapters are deeply imbued with the scriptural meta-theme of creation, fall, redemption and consummation. It is our hope that you may be challenged by what you read in these pages to make a difference for God's kingdom in the area of agriculture and all other spheres of life.

References

DeWitt, Calvin

  1994   *Earthwise*. CRC Publications.

Fountain, Daniel

  1989   *Health, the Bible and the Church*. Wheaton College Bookstore.

Goedhart, Christian

  2001   "Community: Essential to Sustainable Agriculture." In *Creation Care*, # 12, Winter.

Miller, Darrow L.

  1999   *Discipling Nations: The Power of Truth to Transform Cultures*. YWAM Publications.

Roberts W. D. and P. Pretiz

  2000   *Creation-Care in Ministry: Down-to-Earth Christianity*. AERDO.

Sider, Ronald

  1999   *Good News and Good Works: A Theology for the Whole Gospel*. Grand Rapids: Baker Book House.

Steward, John

  1994   *Biblical Holism: Where God, People & Deeds Connect*. World Vision Australia.

Vos, Ronald

  1994   "Sustainable Farming: A Christian Perspective." In *Creation Care*, # 12, Winter 2001.

Yamamori, Tetsunao

  1976   "Toward a Symbiotic Ministry: God's Mandate for the Church Today." In *Missiology, An International Review*.

  1983   *God's New Envoys*. Portland, Oregon: Multnomah Press.

  1993   *Penetrating Missions' Final Frontier: A New Strategy for Unreached Peoples*. Downers Grove: InterVarsity Press.

The Agriculturalist
and God

Reclaiming a Biblical Vision
for Agriculture

Wayne A. Kobes

At a recent Agricultural Missions Conference held at ECHO in North Fort Myers, Florida, one of the conferees, a Christian development worker, shared his personal frustration. He had committed years of work helping a small group of people in Latin America improve their nutrition through more responsible farming techniques. He stated, "In the name of Jesus Christ we work hard to minister to the hungry and malnourished. But we're always made to feel like 'second-class missionaries' by those who are doing 'real missionary work,' by those 'preaching the gospel of salvation.'" Others in the small group joined their voices to his, making clear that this was no isolated experience.

That conversation has come back to me repeatedly. How could those feeding the hungry—in the name of Jesus Christ—be seen as concerning themselves with secondary issues? How could they be regarded as people engaged in something other than bringing the good news in Jesus Christ? And yet, such a view was obviously widespread!

But should we be surprised? A study of modern approaches to the Christian mission reveals a long-standing debate between an *evangelical* approach that advocates a "word" ministry and an *ecumenical* view that argues for a "deed" emphasis. A helpful overview of the two positions and the confusion and damage they have brought to Christian mission can be found in David Bosch's *Witness to the World: The Christian Mission in Theological Perspective.*

Today one can still find those vehemently defending *either* the *word* or the *deed* emphasis almost to the exclusion of the other—but such are, fortunately, a small minority. Most involved in Christian mission realize that it's not an either/or, but a both/and, even if the emphasis falls somewhat on the one or the other. Most today would argue for the *integration* of word and deed in order to faithfully bring the gospel to the world. Such, of course, gives more validity to the work of Christians involved in activities such as agricultural missions, community development, medical assistance, and hunger relief. It has even begun to legitimatize the idea of biblical holism in agriculture and in other areas of human activity, which, in the past, had been seen as secular, that is, far removed from matters of faith.

In many ways, we have moved closer to a biblical understanding of the gospel and of life, closer to a worldview that calls Christians to "walk in God's ways" in every area of their lives. And yet, a *fundamental problem* remains. To think in terms of integrating *word and deed, faith and life,* or *Christianity and agriculture* still leaves us caught in an unbiblical dualism that prevents the wholehearted, joyful service that God expects of his daughters and sons.

In a significant book, *The Pattern of New Testament Truth,* George Eldon Ladd traces the origins of this dualistic interpretation of Christianity to Greek philosophical influences all too readily embraced by the Christian Church in the past and unwittingly assumed today. He contrasts this widespread interpretation of the Christian faith to the teachings of the Old Testament stating, "The Greek idea that the material world is the sphere of evil and a burden or a hindrance to the soul is alien to the Old Testament" (1968, 31).

Alien or not, it is this Greek dualism that has been uncritically accepted, or more often simply assumed, by generations of Christians. And this has had dire consequences. This unbiblical worldview has functioned like a pair of glasses that Christians have worn as they have read Scripture and as they have looked around at the world God has created. But rather than correcting our sin-weakened eyes so that we could better see what God has revealed in his creation, these improperly ground lenses have further distorted our vision. We look at Scripture, but we don't see clearly. We survey God's creation, but we fail to perceive. And as a result, false problems and crippling tensions arise in every part of the landscape we survey. Are we to preach the gospel or minister to physical needs? Should our emphasis be on word or on deed? Are we to be directed by the Missionary Mandate of Matthew 28 or the Cultural Mandate of Genesis 1:28? Do we feed the hungry and give water to the thirsty as a way of getting a hearing for the gospel message? Do we encourage our youth to enter "kingdom service" or to succeed in secular fields?

Where does such an unbiblical dualism leave the Christian involved in agriculture? At best it relegates the Christian agriculturalist to the position of a son or daughter of the King, as one who seeks to serve God in that which is temporal, passing, of little eternal significance. At worst, it views the Christian agriculturalist as a person who has become sidetracked from the significant, eternal quest and become occupied with what is ultimately irrelevant. To be sure, some Christians are involved in agriculture, a legitimate enterprise that puts food on the table. But the real meaning to life must be found elsewhere, in Christian worship and devotion, in what God is really concerned with.

Deep down I think that most of us sense that there is something inherently wrong with this kind of formulation, with this tension that exists within the Christian community. And yet too often it continues to plague and confuse us and to handicap us as we seek to do Christ's work in today's world. The only way out of this disabling tension is to go to Scripture and to listen to its life-changing, worldview-shaping message. And in doing so we must take care to avoid the temptation to focus only on those verses that reinforce our own particular understanding of the mission God has entrusted to his people while being blind to a fuller vision of the kingdom of God. In fact, it is precisely this bigger picture, this overarching message of God's Word that breaks through the tensions and corrects the distortions in the Church's understanding of her calling. The central thrust of Scripture calls us to a life, individually and communally, that is wholly lived in service of God, the Creator-

King. This bigger picture, this motif of Scripture, must be constantly before us, shaping our thinking and our acting before the face of God. We may summarize this main story line of Scripture in terms of *Creation-Fall-Redemption-Consummation*.

Creation

"In the beginning God created the heavens and the earth." And that beginning is where we must begin to understand God's mission for his people. Standing shoulder to shoulder with the Israelites of long ago we come to know God as the creator, owner, sustainer, and ruler over all of creation. The orderliness and goodness of that universe confront us with a plan and a purpose that God has for every part of his creation, including men and women, his image-bearers whom he has placed to be stewards over what he has formed.

Actually, Genesis one is the beginning of a love story! The relationship between God the Creator and his creation is not a cold, distant connection, but a deep-running love that is witnessed as he meticulously shapes and forms each and every creature, putting it in its proper position in the whole. The recurring theme shouts forth: *"And God saw that it was good!"* He rejoices and takes delight in his creation! And the culmination of that loving creation activity is seen when he forms man from the dust of the ground and breathes into his nostrils the breath of life, and man becomes a living being. Can you picture it? Almighty God stooping down to cradle the human he has formed and like fathers or mothers protectively and lovingly holding their children close to their breasts He breathes life into him! Is there a more loving scene we could witness?

So what do we have at the end of Genesis 2? We have woman and man living joyfully before the face of their Heavenly, loving Father. We have them at home within this beautiful, orderly world, joyfully caring for it and opening up its potential as God intended.

Yes, joyfully caring for and opening up creation's potential! After six days of creating God rested on the seventh, celebrating the goodness of all He created. But this does not mean that the development of creation came to an abrupt end! That the Creator *continues to uphold, guide, and rule* the universe he has called into existence is clearly revealed in the Bible. Furthermore, Scripture teaches that God has placed one part of his creation, man and woman—his image-bearers—within the whole of creation so that they might continue to unfold and develop this beautiful and complex world.

"*God blessed them and said to them, 'Be fruitful and increase in number; fill the earth and subdue it. Rule over the fish of the sea and the birds of the air and over every living creature that moves on the ground.'*" Here we have God's mission for his people. And beginning in Genesis 2 we find an obedient response as Adam and Eve are placed in the garden to fill it and to care for it.

Fall

But the beauty of this love story is soon shattered! The joyful fulfillment of God's command becomes sidetracked! The man and woman whom God lovingly formed determined *to be like God—in fact to replace God as the ruler over all things*. At the instigation of Satan, this rebellion breaks the bond of love and not only is humankind's relationship to God fractured, but brokenness and distortion invade the relationship between the man and the woman and that between them and the rest of God's creation. The God-directed, loving unfolding of creation by Adam and Eve and their children also suffers the devastating consequences of sin. What we witness is tragedy on a cosmic scale! Notice that the evil in the world is not found in it being a material world, it is not a matter of a defect within God's creation, but rather in the rebellion of humankind. Rather than using their existence and their gifts in worshipful, loving obedience to God, humans now turn a deaf ear to God and attempt to manipulate creation for their own destructive purposes. The early chapters of Genesis, in graphic detail, begin to sketch out the horrible creation-wide consequences of human rebellion against God. But we know all about that first hand, don't we. Daily we experience that brokenness at every turn. So much so that it's hard for us to even imagine a world in which shalom prevails.

Redemption/Consummation

God certainly could have immediately wiped out of existence the man and the woman and even the whole of his creation. But he didn't destroy the creation he loves. Already in Genesis 3 we hear the good news of salvation. In the context of words of judgment on the serpent God sends a clear message of hope—a promise of things to come: **"And I will put enmity between you and the woman and between your offspring and hers; he will crush your head and you will strike his heel."** God makes clear that he will not allow Satan to wrest from his hands the creation he has lovingly formed. He will not permit the Devil to own and destroy his image-bearers or any part of his creation.

The rest of the Old Testament and the New reveal to us the Creator God's commitment to his creation, including humankind. The fall into sin has brought catastrophic consequences to women and men as well as to every other creature God had formed. *But for all of that, the Bible never views the world as an alien place for humans as they strive for a heavenly destiny.* Humans and the rest of creation are inseparably bound together—this is the way God intends things to be! This world, apart from the sin that is in it, *is* our home! Redemption is not a matter of escaping to another world, but rather enjoying God's good creation in fellowship with the God who gives them.

This vision of creation regained in the Lord Jesus Christ is the story that looms before us on the pages of the Old and New Testaments *if we but have eyes to see.* In Genesis three, surrounded by words of judgment, the promises take shape—there will be pain in childbirth, but children will be born, life will continue. Cursed is the ground because of you, Adam—through painful toil you will eat of it all the days of your life—but you will eat and live! From the beginning God makes clear that Satan, the usurper, the would-be ruler of God's creation, would not prevail. And throughout history—the history of redemption—the fullness of those promises comes to be seen. The creator God, full of mercy and compassion, forever faithful to his covenant promises, works out the redemption, the restoration of his fallen creation. This is the consistent message of the Scriptures. Salvation is not deliverance from this physical creation God has placed us in, a flight from this world or from bodily existence. Rather, salvation involves the redemption of the whole person and the whole world to which we belong.

Time limits our dealing with the biblical material in great depth, but note the following:

- God's judgment of sin in the days of Noah is also blessing in that he cleanses the earth and preserves a remnant to be his people called to live in obedience. Notice the care he shows to preserve his creatures and also that the covenant God makes with Noah is with the entire creation. (Gen. 9:8-11).

- The promise to Abraham and his descendants involves giving them the *land* in which they might live obediently before Him and become a blessing to the nations.

- Israel is called out of Egypt and established in the promised land to be a light to the nations. God structures their life by his law, pointing them to obedient living. God's laws for them cover the entire range of human life, from social relationships to the care of animals to ways to farm to the proper use of money to the way in which to build houses to the treatment of strangers to foods to be eaten and those to be avoided, etc. Clearly God intended Israel to live in such a way that the message of salvation for sinners became clear but also to live out the meaning of that salvation of humans, i.e., that those redeemed by God lived in a restored relationship with the whole of creation.

- The Old Testament prophets call Israel to covenant obedience in the here-and-now, but also point to a future coming of the kingdom in which the power of sin would be broken and God's good creation restored. Note Joel 2:18-27; Is. 11:7; 65:25.

- From beginning to end the Old Testament sees the destiny of humanity as inextricably connected to life on earth.

- The New Testament brings this to a new fullness in the Lord Jesus Christ.

- Jesus himself embraced God's good creation to the point that he was accused by some "pious" Jews of being a glutton and drunkard.

- At the crucifixion and resurrection note the response of non-human creation to the momentous events.

- Consistently the gospels relate Jesus' promise that when he ascended he would come again to usher in a new earth under new heavens. Such is the clear revelation of Scripture. But some suggest that when we read the New Testament a significant change takes place, namely, that the "Cultural Mandate" of Genesis 1:28 is replaced by the "Missionary Mandate" or "Great Commission" of Matthew 28:19,20: *"Therefore go and make disciples of all nations, baptizing them in the name of the Father and of the Son and of the Holy Spirit, and teaching them to obey everything I have commanded you."* In other words, sin and God's response to sin result in a change of mission for humanity and a rejection of the rest of creation. Now, some claim, the focus is to be exclusively on preaching the gospel to all nations, on baptizing, in the sense of seeking the salvation of souls.

But such an interpretation misses the clear message of both the Old and New Testaments. Simply because Satan, the usurper, makes the claim that he now rules God's creation does not mean that the Creator of heaven and earth simply hands over the world that he has lovingly formed, nor does he retract his mission for woman and man.

Satan's challenge to God is real! The consequences of sin are devastating and extend throughout the whole of creation. But God's response is clearly revealed. Already in Genesis 3 God makes clear that Satan will not succeed, that God is reclaiming his creation—*all of his creation*—from the power of Satan and the destruction of sin. Creation regained!

In the Lord Jesus Christ this is fully accomplished! Through his birth, life, death, resurrection, ascension, and coming again God's promise is fulfilled, creation is regained. That the biblical focus should be on the salvation of woman and man, God's image-bearers, is understandable. Human sin cast the whole creation into darkness and human salvation results in all creation experiencing the light of salvation. Listen to Romans 8:18-21: *"I consider that our present sufferings are not worth comparing with the future glory that* •

will be revealed in us. The creation waits in eager expectation for the sons of God to be revealed. For the creation was subjected to frustration not by its own choice, but by the will of the one who subjected it, in hope that the creation itself will be liberated from its bondage to decay and brought into the glorious freedom of the children of God."

Listen again to the "Missionary Mandate:" "Therefore go and make disciples of all nations, baptizing them in the name of the Father and of the Son and of the Holy Spirit, and teaching them to obey everything I have commanded you." What is the point of this part of the verse that is so often ignored? What has God commanded? It is precisely what He has revealed to us in Holy Scripture! A good creation–a fall into sin that has affected the whole of creation–redemption in the Lord Jesus Christ that has also affected the whole creation–and the consummation of God's redemptive work, his kingdom building that is fully experienced when Jesus returns to establish a new earth under new heavens. Go, preach the gospel of salvation, baptize, and teach what God has revealed is our place in relationship to Him, the proper relationships with other humans, and the proper way to live within the whole of creation–fulfilling the mission God has called us to!

Where does all of this lead us? How do we proceed as people caught up in God's mission in the world? That question is what brings us together in this place. Let me "prime the pump" by simply positing a number of theses:

- The Christian community must examine what is, in fact, driving its thinking and acting. Where and to what extent have we domesticated the gospel and embraced a way of life contrary to the kingdom of God?

- The Christian community must be thoroughly committed to and intentional in developing a distinctively Christian worldview. This must not stop at theoretical formulations, but must be translated into a counter-cultural lifestyle.

- Christians must reject the tendency in modern culture to reduce the kingdom of God to the institutional church

- "Clergy" should not expect or be expected to "give laity" direction in every sphere of life.

- Christian educational institutions must commit to an inner reformation of the sciences, in this way equipping leaders for God's mission in the world. A Christian worldview must be translated into the daily lifestyle of God's people.

- The Christian community must engage its youth early on in this mission.
- Christian organizations (not denominationally determined) are needed to work out the meaning of the gospel in critical areas of our culture.

The specifics of what this means for Christians and agriculture cisely what brings us together this week. It is my prayer that er, led by the Spirit and directed by God's Word, we may to move toward a more faithful response and a clearer to our world.

References

avid.

Witness to the World: The Christian Mission in Theological Perspective. tlanta: John Knox Press.

e Eldon.

Pattern of New Testament Truth. Grand Rapids: Eerdmans.

The Worship of God through Agriculture

Jesse T. Njoka

Introduction

God created Adam and Eve and put them in charge of creation. He also gave them a vocation to be stewards and co-managers with God. The situation changed drastically when they sinned against God and they were then driven out of the Garden of Eden to toil for their upkeep. The consequence of original sin on the broken relationship between man and woman and the Creator has had holistic impacts on other relationships. This paper outlines some foundational principles from the Word of God and proceeds to give an analysis of the character and activities of God in respect to biblical holism and agriculture. The worship of God through agriculture is described including an overview of some references to agriculture in the Bible. This is followed by a brief survey of traditional agricultural practices in relation to acts of worship among the African people. The section that follows discusses the Fall and its consequences from the biblical perspective. The final sections deals with the relationship of the Agriculturalist and God in the context of the unfolding situation of agriculture in relation to current global changes.

Foundational Principles of Biblical Holism and Agriculture

In the words of Benjamin Franklin concerning National Wealth, *"Agriculture—the only honest way wherein man receives a real increase of the seed thrown into the ground, is a kind of a miracle, wrought by the hand of God in his favor, as reward for his innocent life and his virtuous industry.*" (www.biblebell.org/links/farmers.html)

The Bible has much more to say about the relationship between the farmer and God, which many practising agriculturalists and farmers are missing in their vocations today.

The principles listed below are revisited in various sections of this book but a brief overview is helpful to reinforce the teachings relating to agriculture and biblical holism.

1. God is a relational God (Myers, 1999). He created the earth and everything in it. Human beings were created in the image of God—hence we should be in loving, self-giving relationship with one another and with our environment.

2. Stewardship principle: God owns the earth and everything in it. He created male and female and gave them vocation to tend and keep the earth (Genesis 1:27).

3. Ethical principles as developed by Wright and reported in Myers, 1999 are:

   Sharing resources—the land and natural resources are gifts to all mankind and not only to a few. The right for all to use these natural resources is prior to the right of ownership.

   Responsibility to work—Work is a part of being fruitful. God is productive and thus we are also expected to be productive in our initiatives/work and be responsible as well.

   Expectation of growth—God blessed Adam and Eve for a life of fruitfulness and increase. God has provided abundantly in creation so that this is possible. Humankind is endowed with ingenuity and adaptability necessary to create this increase.

4. Sabbath Principle: to be observed for crops, land and animals as well and not just for humankind.

5. Sin or a broken relationship with the Creator leads to poor productivity of land and livestock (Haggai 1:5,6), "Now this is what the LORD Almighty says: 'Give careful thought to your ways. You have planted much, but have harvested

little. You eat, but never have enough. You drink, but never have your fill. You put on clothes, but are not warm. You earn wages, only to put them in a purse with holes in it."

The Character and Activities of God in Relation to Biblical Holism and Agriculture

According to the Westminster Shorter Catechism (Q4) *"God is a Spirit, infinite, eternal, and unchangeable in His being, wisdom, power, holiness, justice, goodness, and truth."* Jesus defines God for us in John 4:24, *"God is Spirit*, and those who worship Him must worship Him in spirit and truth."

In Genesis God is portrayed as a Gardener and it is out of His love that He established the first garden for man as an ideal environment to live in and to enjoy fellowship with him. Man's responsibility to work in the garden and keep it (Genesis 2:15) was not burdensome at this stage, but a way of enriching his well-being in the stewardship of God's creation. God continued to make things grow for the full delight and sustenance of man (Genesis 2:9). God defined the terms and conditions for man in this environment. He was shown the limits of what he could do with what was all the variety of species in the garden. But Satan led him to disobey God's command to stay in the garden and enjoy all the variety of fruits and plants except the forbidden fruit of the tree of good and evil. This act of disobedience led to the fall of man and subsequent eviction from the Garden of Eden; the ground where man was deposed and cursed so that any produce of the ground would always come through toil and hard work. This principle is repeated several times in the Bible. When God's people live within the terms of God's Covenant in the Old and New Testaments, God blesses the land to produce abundantly for man's needs, but when he violates the terms of the Covenant, the ground or land and the produce are cursed as result of man's sins.

Holiness

God is majestic in his holiness as stated in Exodus 19:11. "Who among the gods is like you, O Lᴏʀᴅ? Who is like you majestic in holiness awesome in glory, working wonders?" His holiness is an attribute that characterizes his actions. The Christian agriculturalist is a part of the body of Christ, the Church. The tithe of the produce of the land is holy to the Lord as stated in Leviticus 27:30, "A tithe of everything from the land, whether grain from the soil or fruit from the trees, belongs to the LORD; it is holy to the LORD." Thus tithing of our professional talents as practitioners in agriculture should be informed by our understanding that we are serving a holy God, Who demands the best of what we can offer in His service. First Peter 1:15-16 underscores this point, "But just as he who called you is holy, so be holy in all you do; for it is written: 'Be holy, because I am holy.'" The Christian agriculturalist should lead a holy life in keeping with God's command. We sometimes wonder why we are not effective in our work when we are living unholy lives. Yet we are so enthusiastic to serve before we are set apart for His holy service that we are crusading on issues for our own glory. We should respond to our calling as agriculturalists in humility and in total obedience to His word.

God's Compassion, Long Suffering and Love for Mankind

God's compassion is shown to those who are lost in their sins. He is slow to punish as Jonah attested in Jonah 4:2, "I knew that you are a gracious and compassionate God, slow to anger and abounding in love, a God who relents from sending calamity." Jonah had all along wished that God could punish the enemies of the people of God, but to his surprise He responded to their repentance. We also should not give up on those who seem perpetually trapped in poverty. There are some who see such calamities as famine, starvation and the scourge of HIV/AIDS as the only solution to an overpopulated earth. The debate on whether to give food aid for those who are unable to cope due to drought and poor technological know-how sometimes is characterized by lack of compassion and understanding of our corporate responsibility for undermining livelihoods of others. We should show compassion to those who are unable to cope with modern life and share our skills and abilities with them in addition to fighting the injustices inherent in our agricultural production and marketing systems. Lamentations 3:22-23 underscores this aspect of God's character: "Because of the LORD's great love we are not consumed for His compassions never fail. They are new every morning; great is your faithfulness."

His love for all mankind is revealed through His Son Jesus Christ as John reminds us in John 3:16 and I John 4:9-12, "This is how God showed His love among us: He sent His one and only Son into the world that we might live through Him. This is love: not that we loved God, but that He loved us and sent His Son as an atoning sacrifice for our sins. Dear friends, since God so loved us, we also ought to love one another. No one has ever seen God; but if we love one another, God lives in us and His love is made complete in us." In this passage we are commanded to show love to mankind regardless of their race and ethnic background. This is the love that is spurring our calling to make a difference for Christ in our service to all without discrimination.

God's Providence

It is the character of God in providing for all the physical needs of humankind including through agriculture. *Providence*, defined as "the universal sovereign rule of God," is an assumed principle in the scriptures. Divine providence is the outworking of the divine decrees, which are "the plan of Him who works out everything in conformity with the purpose of His will" (Ephesians 1:11). His providence for nature is well illustrated in the prayer of Nehemiah 9:6, "You alone are the LORD. You made the heavens, even the highest heavens, and all their starry host, the earth and all that is on it, the seas and all that is in them. You give life to everything, and the multitudes of heaven worship You." God is in charge of nature in manifold expression in agricultural activities. The orderly cycles of life on earth are governed by the sun and moon, which are subject to His command (Psalm 104:16-23). God provides the good harvest and rain according to Leviticus 26:4-6, "I will send you rain in its season, and the ground will yield its crops and the trees of the field their fruit. Your threshing will continue until grape harvest and the grape harvest will continue until planting, and you will eat all the food you want and live in safety in your land."

The apparent absence of God's providence in our agricultural practices is more a reflection of our lack of faith and trust in God and also withholding of blessings due to disobedience to His

Covenant. The conflict over productive natural resources in many parts of the world due to human greed is a reflection of our lack of trust in the providence of God for all humankind.

The Lord even extends His providence to cultivated land as indicated in Deuteronomy 11:12-15: "It is a land the LORD your God cares for; the eyes of the LORD your God are continually on it from the beginning of the year to its end. So if you faithfully obey the commands I am giving you today, to love the LORD your God and to serve Him with all your heart and with all your soul, then I will send rain on your land in its season, both autumn and spring rains, so that you may gather in your grain, new wine and oil. I will provide grass in the fields for your cattle, and you will eat and be satisfied." Land productivity is an indicator of God's providence for His creation, both human and non-human creation.

God provided all the bounties of nature for wise use to meet our basic necessities of life (Genesis 1:29-30), "I give you every seed-bearing plant on the face of the whole earth and every tree that has fruit with seed in it. They will be yours for food. And to all the beasts of the earth and all the birds of the air and all the creatures that move on the ground—everything that has the breath of life in it—I give every green plant for food." Jesus reminded us in Matthew 6:26, 30-33 that if God is able to take care of the needs of the birds of the air He is more than willing to take care of our needs. Paul applies the providence principle using the example from agriculture in 2 Corinthians 9:10, "Now He who supplies seed to the sower and bread for food will also supply and increase your store of seed and will enlarge the harvest of your righteousness."

Notwithstanding the degradation of His creation because of sin, God through His providence has promised restoration as prophesied by Ezekiel 36:28-38. Specifically God says in verse 29 and 30 of this portion of the prophecy, "I will save you from all your uncleanness. I will call for the grain and make it plentiful and will not bring famine upon you. I will increase the fruit of the trees and the crops of the field, so that you will no longer suffer disgrace among the nations because of famine."

We should also note that God is doing His part even when we

are ignorant of His ways. If God is going to achieve His purpose of a world where there is peace and prosperity, this will not result necessarily from our own integrity and self-righteousness but from His great love and grace for the fallen creation. In Deuteronomy 9:5, "It is not because of your righteousness or your integrity that you are going in to take possession of their land; but on account of the wickedness of these nations, the LORD your God will drive them out before you." It is important that all of us Christian agriculturalists and farmers from developed and developing countries come together and do something before we stand accused for complacency and inaction.

We should guard against the sin of despondency and apostasy in thinking that our participation in bringing positive change in the world of agriculture is a useless pursuit because the wicked and evildoers have the final word. In Malachi 3:14-15 this was the main sin of the people of God. "You have said, 'It is futile to serve God. What did we gain by carrying out His requirements and going about like mourners before the LORD Almighty?'" Certainly the evildoers prosper, and even those who challenge God escape. We should not give up but patiently do our part as God continues to do His part. Paul reminds us in 2 Corinthians 9:7-11 that God is able to rescue us from our present predicament in agriculture. He promises blessings beyond our imaginations so that in the end we will give thanks to God for His providence. In verse 10, "Now He who supplies seed to the sower and bread for food will also supply and increase your store of seed and will enlarge the harvest of your righteousness."

The Worship of God through Agriculture

Agriculture is the first vocation that God gave humankind according to Genesis 2:15. "The LORD God took the man and put him in the Garden of Eden to work it and take care of it." God knew it was good for man to participate in the management of His creation. The concept of a garden where man would practice his ingenuity in using God's creation for his enjoyment and life support was an important vocation that would enhance communion with God during His frequent visits at opportune time of the day. Good agricultural practices are honoring to God and are an expression of our worship of God. Cain and Abel worshipped God by sacrificing the first produce of their hard work to God (Genesis 4:3-4).

We are also expected to give thanks to God for the mystery of how He makes things grow through His providence (1Corinthians 3:5-7). In Deuteronomy 14:22, 23, we are commanded that we should give a tenth of our harvest to the Lord so that we may revere Him and rejoice in His presence. When we share our produce with others who are disadvantaged in one way or another we show our reverence for God and our joy increases as we come before His presence in worship. The same message is repeated in Deuteronomy 26:2,10,11. "Take some of the first fruits of all that you produce from the soil of the land the Lord your God is giving you and put them in a basket ... 'and now I bring the first fruits of the soil that you, O Lord, have given me.' Place the basket before the Lord your God and bow down before Him." Many Christians have failed to experience the great joy in worshiping the Lord because we have failed to honor God with the first fruits of our labors.

To show our dependence on God's providence, we are commanded to observe Sabbath for people and all animals including the agricultural animals such as donkeys and draught oxen. We reserve the Sabbath day for worship and praise while at the same time we are emotionally and physically rejuvenated to start a new week. Christian professionals have commonly violated this principle as we try to cope with ever increasing responsibilities in different callings. We are also expected to extend the same value of the Sabbath rest principle to the land resources.

According to Leviticus 25:2-6, the Lord instructed Israel through Moses and said to them, "When you enter the land I am going to give you, the land itself must observe a Sabbath to the Lord. For six years sow your fields, and for six years prune your vineyards and gather their crops. But in the seventh year the land is to have a Sabbath of rest, a Sabbath to the Lord. Do not sow your fields or prune your vineyards. Do not reap what grows of itself or harvest the grapes of your untended vines. The land is to have a year of rest." Part of the purpose of this Sabbath observance was to teach God's people greater faith in Him, but the practise also has an ecological justification, (Hoezee, 1998). Allowing land to lie fallow helps to replenish depleted fertility and can reduce erosion. Our motive as Christian Agriculturalists in observing the land Sabbath is to demonstrate love and obedience to God, the creator and the owner of all, and so to affirm our lasting linkage both with Him and His creation (Fred *et al.* 1996).

Agricultural Activities in the Bible

Agriculture in the Bible dates back to Adam who was charged by God to take care of the garden (Genesis 2:15). The first two sons of Adam and Eve were agriculturalists, Cain specializing in crop agriculture, while Abel was mainly on animal agriculture. Abraham, Isaac and Jacob were mainly pastoralists. During their stay in Egypt, the descendants of Israel remained slaves for a period of 400 years, before their deliverance from the slavery through leadership of Moses. The experience in crop agriculture in Egypt prepared the Israelites for livelihood based mainly on crop farming in the land of Canaan. God through His servant Moses gave the children of Israel instructions on how agriculture would be practiced. Farming life was never an easy vocation in Palestine since part of the land was of low productivity. Famine was always a great threat to the survival of the people as in case of Abraham (Genesis 12:10), Joseph (Genesis 41:56) and Ruth and Naomi (Ruth 1:1). In Acts 11:28 we read about a great famine that affected the whole of Roman Empire. "One of them, named Agabus, stood up and through the Spirit predicted that a severe famine would spread over the entire Roman world." The farmer had four main problems: drought, strong winds from the East (the 'Sirocco') which could take away his dry soil, locust plagues, and invading armies (Lion Publishing, 1987).

Crops Grown

Crop agriculture involved production of grain for bread (wheat, barley, spelt and millet), grapes for wine and olives for oil (Exodus 9:31, Deut 7:13, Hosea 2:8). The household also grew some vegetables such as cucumbers, lentils, peas and spices. Fruits included melons, figs, dates, pomegranates, and nuts and these were very useful during the hot summer season. Non-food crops included cotton and flax (Exodus 9:31).

Care for the Soil

Land care was taken seriously as each cultivated piece of land was carefully marked off for each household (1 Samuel 14:14, Proverbs 22:28). Soil fertility was maintained through careful observation of Sabbath rest and fallow periods for the land and by incorporation of livestock and compost manure in the soil. (2 Kings 9:30, Psalm 83:10). Fields were fenced and designated for different crops (Isaiah 28:25); (Isaiah. 5:5; Num. 22:24); (Isaiah 25:10). Synonymous to today when food grown using compost manure in organic farming is preferred in the market than the one grown using chemical fertilizers. Dung, carcasses and blood of animals were used to fertilize soil, (2 Kings 9:37, Psalm 83:10; 8:2, Jeremiah 9:22). Salt either by itself or mixed in the dunghill in order to promote putrefaction, is specifically mentioned as compost (Matthew 5:13; Luke14:34-35). Land was burned to destroy the seed of noxious herbs (Proverbs 24:31, Isaiah 32:13), and was then enriched with ashes. Land preparation was done using a simple wooden plough after clearing the land of stones and thorns (Isaiah 5:2).

Animals

"Cattle" in Hebrew include sheep, goats, oxen and asses, but not pigs. Asses were kept for carrying loads, and oxen for ploughing. Only on special occasions were oxen killed for meat. This is still true among many pastoral tribes who keep cattle mainly for milk production and not for meat. Sheep and goats were most of the time kept together. Sheep mainly provided wool for clothes and for occasional meat, while the goats were kept for meat and milk. Goat hair made coarse cloth and their skins made bottles. God cares for animals as we see in Genesis 9:8-10 where after the flood, God established a covenant with humankind and the rest of creation, including animals. He cared enough to save some of the biodiversity of animals in the Ark. In Psalm 104:17,21,22 the Psalmist tells of the great harmony in nature that includes both domestic and wild animals. Animals have more importance than food, draught and/or transportation.

Traditional Agricultural Practices and Worship of God (African Experiences)

The Character of God

The concept of God being Almighty is easier to grasp than any other attribute. There are many concrete examples from all over Africa, in which people speak of God as omnipotent. Among some peoples, like the Yoruba, Ngombe, Akan and Ashanti, some of the names of God describe Him as 'the All-powerful' or 'the Almighty'. His power is seen in practical terms. The Yoruba might say of duties or challenges, that they are 'easy to do as that which God performs; difficult to God to do as that which God enables not' (Mbiti, 1969). Some of the traditional practices in conservation and management of natural resources support sustainable human livelihoods. Some of these traditional agricultural practices are closely related to biblical views (Romans 1:20).

Among many peoples of Africa, God's omnipotence is seen in His exercise of power over nature. A few examples will illustrate this. In two proverbs the Banyarwanda say that 'the plant protected by God is never hurt by wind', and that 'God has very long arms'. The Kiga refer to God as the one who makes the sun set; and when the Gikuyu make sacrifices and prayers for rain, they address God as the one who makes mountains quake and rivers overflow. The wind, the sun and the rain are beyond human power of control, but not beyond God's power who works through them and other natural phenomena or objects.

The majority of African peoples regard God as essentially good, and there are many situations in which He is credited with doing good to His people. Some, like Akamba, Bacongo, Herero, Igbo, Ila and others, say categorically that God does them only what is good, so that they have no reason to complain. The Ewe firmly hold that 'He is good, for He has never withdrawn from us the good things which He gave us' (Mbiti, 1969).

For some, the goodness of God is seen in His averting calamities, supply of rain, providing fertility to people, cattle and fields. Thus, the Langi consider rich harvests to come from God; and the Nandi invoke God daily to grant fertility to their women, cattle and fields. However, the Katango peoples believe in 'the father Creator Who creates and uncreates'. The Ila show similar difficulties when they consider God to be responsible for giving and causing to rot. Some people hold that God is capable of showing anger; and death, floods, drought, locusts and national calamities are interpreted to be manifestations of His anger (Mbiti, 1969).

Providence and Sustenance

Rain is the most widely acknowledged token of God's providence. To the African peoples rain is always a blessing, and its supply is one of the most important activities of God. For that reason, God is known as 'the Rain Giver' or 'Water Giver', among the Akan, Ila, Ngoni, Mender, Tswana, Akamba, Tiv and many others. Some of these even say that rain is God's spittle, this, in African societies being the vehicle of blessing, so that formal pronouncing of a blessing is often accompanied by gentle spitting. The spittle symbolizes prosperity, health, happiness and good welfare.

It is also widely believed that God shows His providence through fertility and health of human beings, cattle and fields, as well as through the plentifulness of children, cattle, food and other goods. Many societies therefore pray for these items. Thus, the Nuba performs a ceremony at which they pray for the increase of cattle, saying:

God, we are hungry
Give us cattle, give us sheep!

When making their sacrifices, the officiating elder prays:

God, increase cattle,
Increase sheep, increase men!

The Worship of God

Example of Sacrifices and Offerings. The Dinka regard every event or occasion as suitable for sacrifices; and for them 'every bull or ox is destined ultimately for sacrifice. Animal sacrifice is the central religious act of the Dinka, whose cattle are in their eyes perfect victims'. The Nuer also have many occasions when they sacrifice to God. Cattle are the usual animals for this purpose, and on important occasions the people make long invocations, (Mbiti, 1969). The Turkana for example pray in their sacrifice rituals, "this is your animal, take it. This is your ox, take him." Then they continue, "Give us life, health, animals, grass, rain and all good things" (Barret, 1998).

Prayers. The Galla make frequent prayers and invocations to God. They pray in the morning and in the evening every day, asking Him to protect them, their cattle, crops and families. The Ila people are said to pray for special needs, soliciting God's help. When there is a drought, they come together and join in singing and invoking God saying, *"Come to us with a continued rain, O God, fall!"*

Before they start sowing their seeds the Lozi assemble at sunrise, under the leadership of the local headman who erects an altar of sticks and clay. A dish is placed on this altar into which every household puts some seeds, hoes and axes. The headman prays on behalf of the community asking God to bless the people and the agricultural implements, as well as the seeds, so that by His power the people may use them beneficially. After this ceremony is over, planting now start, (Mbiti, 1969).

Example of Two Gikuyu Prayers

a) The Prayer for Rain—Threat of Drought and Famine.

During times of drought and threats of famine, the Gikuyu elders (*Njaama*) arranged for public prayers where a sacrifice for the rain was offered to God. The Chief Elder while holding the two calabashes facing *Kirinyaga*, (Mt Kenya) uttered the following prayers:

> *"Revered Elder (God) who lives on Kere-nyaga, (Mt Kenya) You who make mountains tremble and rivers flood; we offer to you this sacrifice that you may bring us rain. People and children are crying; sheep, goats and cattle (flocks and herds) are crying. Mwene-Nyaga (God), we beseech you, with the blood and fat of this ram, which we are going to sacrifice to you. Refined honey and milk we have brought for you. We praise you in*

the same way as our forefathers used to praise you under this very tree,
and you heard them and brought them rain. We beseech you accept this,
our sacrifice, and bring us the rain for prosperity. (Chorus or response):
Peace, we beseech you Ngai, peace be with us."

It is reported on many occasions the rain would come almost immediately. If there was failure of quick response to their prayers, the elders would repeat the ceremony while trying to find out exactly what would have gone wrong on the part of the people. Normally the conclusion would be that there were some unconfessed offences that God is not happy with and they would implore him for forgiveness and appeal to his providence and mercy. The Gikuyu people believed in a living God who is all-powerful and in control of natural forces.

b) The Prayer of Thanksgiving.

The purpose of this prayer was to acknowledge God's providence during the harvest season. Nobody was allowed to taste the new harvest before thanksgiving prayer in form of a special ceremony. The people also exercised self-control by restraining to use the harvest until the thanksgiving ceremony was performed. The elders then slaughtered a ram, melted the fat of the ram for use in sprinkling the gardens, granaries, pots and fireplaces. In the process of sprinkling, the elders would be reciting the following prayer:

"*Ngai* (God) we bring you this fat to implore you to bless and to allow us to use the grains of this crop without any fear of war or of sickness, as you alone are the Giver of all good things," (Wanjohi, 1997).

This prayer is an instance of the Gikuyu praying during prosperity to express appreciation to God for the harvest. This expression can be related to Psalm 103:1-5, where David blesses the Lord for satisfying him with good things.

The various examples cited above concerning African spiritual world view in relation to agricultural practices affirms Romans 1:2 that, "For since the creation of the world God's invisible qualities— His eternal power and divine nature—have been clearly seen, being understood from what has been made, so that men are without excuse." Although the African traditions are being transbull or formed by modern agriculture at a rapid rate, the cultural and religious values on various agricultural practices would be a good entry point for establishing biblical holism in agriculture. Currently, the breakdown of these traditional values and lack of biblical view of the world is the major cause of many conflicts due to injustices of accessing the land and sustainable livelihood based on natural resources management. The Christian witness to these peoples should seek areas of similarities in upholding social justice issues in agricultural practices. While in most African traditions, land was held in community trust with well defined rights of access for cropping or grazing, currently, the capitalism disease in an environment of poor and weak legal regulatory framework of many postcolonial governments, the marginalization of the majority of people from access to productive resources is increasing unabated.

The Fall and Its Consequences on Biblical Holism and Agriculture

The account of how sin entered the world is given in Genesis 3 when the great deceiver, Satan, in the body of a serpent, deceived Adam and Eve to disobey God. The pronouncement of the curse on the ground signified hard work for humankind as far as agricultural based livelihoods are concerned. The fall of humankind from grace of God was holistic in its impact on the whole creation and in all human endeavors. The era of peace and harmony between Humankind, God and the environment was marred by sin. Man who was created in God's image lost his dignity and identity. The human development in all aspects of this world is marked by the original sin and therefore it is characterized by injustices and broken relationships with God, society and his environment. Instead of pursuing positive relationship with God, humankind has been on their own journey to find meaning and value of their existence but without much success (Myers, 1999).

Haggai 1:5-6 clearly indicates that because of our sinful nature that we have not been reconciled with the Creator, our harvest is never enough from our fields or our vocation. We are always complaining that what we get is never enough because we do not ox is actually work for God but for our own selfish ends. "Now this is what the LORD Almighty says, 'Give careful thought to your ways. You have planted much, but have harvested little. You eat, but never have enough. You drink, but never have your fill. You put on clothes, but are not warm. You earn wages, only to put them in a purse with holes in it.'" In Galatians 6:7-10 we are reminded of the law of sowing and reaping. When one sows to please his/her sinful nature one reaps destruction.

Leviticus 26:20 specifically focuses on the loss of soil fertility and futility of our hard work. "Your strength will be spent in vain, because your soil will not yield its crops, nor will the trees of the land yield their fruit."

Christian Farmers commentary (www.Iccc.net/intl-en/info/html/cf/cf.html) suggests that there are forces that are at work to undermine the foundations for the freedom and independence of a nation to achieve self-sufficiency in food production, thus creating unhealthy state of dependence. Such concerns were among the reasons for the disruption of the World Trade Organization (WTO) Ministerial Conference, Seattle in November 1999. One of these international NGOs, ActionAid, expressed concern over the three key agreements under WTO which has special relevance to food security for the poor: The agreement on Agriculture (AoA), the Trade Related Intellectual Property Rights (TRIPs); and the Sanitary and Phytosanitary Measures (SPS). Issues related to AoA include reduction of trade distortions in agricultural trade, reduction in domestic subsidies and provision for minimum market access.

One of the campaign brochures says, "The World Trade Organization is prescribing food insecurity." The NGO has launched an international food rights campaign to safeguard poor peoples' right to food. It is expected that the final outcome of this campaign will ensure that international agricultural trade benefits the poor and protects farmers' rights to seed and the plant resources. There is need for fair international laws that support poor farmers' rights and enable developing countries to achieve food security for all by addressing the issues of the impact of genetic modification and patenting of genetic resources for food and farming among others.

God has promised abundant blessings for humankind if we obey and carefully follow all the commands in His word. Deuteronomy 28 outlines the promised blessings accompanying this obedience. "You will be blessed in the city and the country. The fruit of your womb will be blessed, and the crops of your land and the young of your livestock, the calves of your herds and the lambs of your flocks" (verse 3 and 4). The productivity of our agricultural enterprises will increase even those that may seem a bit remote from our immediate concern. God also promises food security, "Your basket and your kneading trough will be blessed … the Lord will send a blessing on your barns and on everything you put your hand to … the Lord will open the heavens, the storehouse of His bounty, to send rain on your land in season and bless all the work of your hands" (verse 5, 8 and 12). The refrain on these promises is based on our obedience to his will. For prosperity and peace of a nation, we must implement policies and actions that glorify God. The Christian agriculturalist is usually working within national policy frameworks that are not in keeping with God's command.

On the contrary, humankind disobedience to God has its dire consequences. In James 4:17, he who knows the good he ought to do and doesn't do it, sins. God is angered when He blesses the agriculturalist with bountiful harvest and the increase of his flocks and herds, but instead of recognizing and honoring Him, agriculturalists boast of their own wisdom and effort. This is what is happening in the world today. Humans think they have made it because of their hard labor, use of modern technology and agricultural intensification, in most of which God is not acknowledged. Instead of worshiping God, man worships himself, his work and the fruit of his labor, which brings a curse upon him and all that he does (Deuteronomy 8:14, 17, 19). Hosea 2:8-9 says, "She [Israel] has not acknowledged that I was the one who gave her the grain, the new wine and oil, who lavished on her the silver and gold which they used for Baal. Therefore I will take away my grain when it ripens, and my new wine when it is ready. I will take back my wool and my linen, intended to cover her nakedness." This is a clear indication to man that the fruitfulness of his agricultural work is entirely dependent on God.

The relationship between the fruitfulness of crop and animal husbandry practices and God's blessing is a well-acknowledged fact even among the African people as shown in the above accounts.

Sin is the major explanation of meager crop yields in our farms. "A ten-acre vineyard will produce only a bath of wine, a homer of seed only an ephah of grain" (Isaiah 5:10). "They will sow wheat but reap thorns; they will wear themselves out but gain nothing. So bear the shame of your harvest because of the Lord's fierce anger" (Jeremiah 12:13). "The fields are ruined, the ground is dried up; the grain is destroyed, the new wine is dried up, the oil fails. Despair, you farmers, wail, you vine growers; grieve for the wheat and the barley, because the harvest is destroyed" (Joel 1:10-11). Crop failure, poor harvest and destruction of crops in the field either by unfavorable weather and/or pests are some of the dire consequences of sin that the Christian Agriculturalist has to contend with. No wonder our agricultural development initiatives do not have much impact because we are operating in unjust socio-political systems.

The Relationship of the Agriculturalist and God in the Context of Current Issues in Agriculture

Rationalization of Global Trade Liberalization

The summary of common ideas on trade which have an impact on the national policy and which form the basis of the WTO Agreement on Agriculture with a member country are listed as follows: (Dasgupta 1998)

- Trade benefits for every participant; though some benefit more than others.
- The productivity and efficiency of a country's economy are linked with outward orientation.
- The theory of comparative advantage determines what a country can produce and export.
- Any barrier to trade in the name of self-sufficiency based on a strategy of substituting promotes inefficiency.

- Even if import liberalization results in the closing down of some lines of domestic production, it is inevitable and is welcome as it helps to determine which of the domestic products are or are not in tune with comparative advantage.

- Subsidies distort allocation of resources and do not allow market forces of demand and supply to equalize and thus determine the desirable levels of price and output at which the market is cleared.

- The world trade is, on the whole, free and competitive, and the prices ruling in the world market emerge from the inter-action of the forces of demand and supply and hence, are rational and objective, and reflect the scarcity values of the products in question.

Theological reflection on both short-term and long-term impacts of this rational thinking on agriculture needs to be addressed urgently. If most of the reasoning is based on economic rationality and no other aspects of agriculture are considered at this stage of international policy formulation, many people will only find livelihood in agriculture as employees of large agribusiness, transnational and national corporations.

Agriculture Policy Challenges within the Framework of WTO Agreement on Agriculture

Current discussions/negotiations on the domestic and international policy reforms and the influence of WTO agreement on Agriculture sector is an important entry point for advocating the adoption of policies that contribute towards transformational development agenda (Myers, 1999). The issues that are on the table for discussion include impact of global agriculture and food policies on food security at national and household level in the face of growing human population that is straining sustainable use of the earth's resource and carrying capacity. The core issue is how the agriculturalist can facilitate appropriate technology transfer to meet the projected food deficit especially in Sub Sahara Africa.

Finally we need to advocate for the multifunctional aspects of agriculture from a holistic perspective that appraises the economic, social-cultural, spiritual and environmental conservation perspectives. (Reza Lahidji, Wolfgang Michalski and Barrie Stevens, 1998)

Environmental Concerns

The state of environment in the world is currently a matter of international concern. The nations of the world are deeply concerned with the dilemma of achieving sustainable development without compromising on environmental quality. The United Nations Environment Programme was established in 1972. In 1992 the Earth Summit meeting on Environment and Development in Brazil produced Agenda 21 to guide the nations of the world on the integration of environment and development issues. Notwithstanding all these international initiatives, the agricultural industry ranks as one of most serious threats to the global environment. We as Christian agriculturalists should draw lessons from the biblical holism and agriculture to inform the ongoing debate that the major root cause of this problem is human rebellion against God's wisdom and commands.

Human Development Concerns

The 225 richest people in the world had a combined wealth of over $1 trillion—equal to the annual income of poorest 47% of the world's people (2.5 billion) (Human Development, UNDP Report, 1998). How can the Christian agriculturalist use his/her vocation to improve the human development situation in the world? Agriculture has the greatest potential for providing dignified livelihood if we can enhance its viability by improving the technology and marketing possibilities. Many small-scale farmers are not just practising agriculture for subsistence but also as an income generating opportunity to meet their basic needs of education, health and social obligations. Reduction of poverty and vulnerability of poor people to famine and disease is more preferred than the fire brigade type of response to emergency situations and humanitarian involvement. Improvements of the welfare of the poor will also minimize conflicts rooted in prevalence of poverty. Jesus reminds us in Luke 12:15, "Watch out! Be on your guard against all kinds of greed; a man's life does not consist in the abundance of his possessions." We are called to be modest in our lifestyle and we should support a development model that does not lead to accumulation of wealth at the expense of the others.

References

Alexander, Pat
>   1987   *The Lion Encyclopedia of the Bible Life and Times, Meaning and Message, a Comprehensive Guide*, Special Edition. Lion Publishing Company.

Barrett, Anthony Joseph
>   1998   *Sacrifice and Prophecy in Turkana Cosmology*. Nairobi, Kenya: Paulines Publications Africa.

Exell, Joseph S.
>   1963   *Biblical Illustrator, Genesis*, Volume 1. Grand Rapids: Baker.

Hoezee, S.
>   1998   "Bearing God's Image in the Creation." In *Remember Creation—God's World of Wonder and Delight* (pp. 61-73). Grand Rapids: Eerdmans.

Lahidji, Reza, Wolfgang Michalski, and Barrie Stevens,
>   1998   "The Future of Food: An Overview of Trends and Key Issues." In *The Future of Food: Long Term Prospects for the Agro-food Sector*. OECD publication.

McGauchie, Donald, President, National Farmers Federation, Australia
>   1998   "The Future of Agricultural Production Structures." In *The Future of Food: Long Term Prospects for the Agro-food Sector*. OECD publication.

Mbiti, John S.
>   1969   *African Religions and Philosophy*. Nairobi, Kenya: Heinemann Educational Books Limited.

Myers, Bryant L.
>   1999   *Walking with the Poor: Principles and Practices of Transformational Development*. Maryknoll, New York: Orbis Books.

Scott, Hoezee
>   1998   *Remember Creation—God's World of Wonder and Delight*. Grand Rapids: Eerdmans.

Tablino, Paul
>   1999   *The Gabra: Camel Nomads of Northern Kenya*. Nairobi, Kenya: Paulines Publications Africa.

Unger, Merrill F.
    1980   *Unger's Bible Dictionary*, 3rd Edition. Chicago: Moody Press.

United Nations Development Programme
    1998   *Human Development Index.*

Van Dyke, Fred, David C. Mahan, Joseph K. Sheldon, and Raymond H. Brand
    1996   *Redeeming Creation—The Biblical Basis for Environmental Stewardship.*
            Downers Grove: InterVarsity Press.

Wanjohi , J. Gerald
    1997. *The Wisdom and Philosophy of the Gikuyu Proverbs; The Kihooto World
          View.* Nairobi, Kenya: Paulines Publications Africa.

Zondervan N.I.V. Bible Library, Zondervan Publishing Company.

The Agriculturalist
and Humanity

Social Principles for 'Good' Agriculture

Ronald J. Vos

Introduction

Followers of Jesus Christ are not constrained by the culture in which they live. In fact in many ways they should transcend the culture in which they live (James 4:4, 2 Corinthians 5:17, Romans 12:2). In this chapter I will be focusing on the "culture" of agriculture. Although often unrecognized, there is a culture associated with how food and fiber is grown and how it is consumed or utilized. By using the term culture, I am referring to a people's whole way of life. This consists of all the ideas, objects, and the ways things are done by humans and how humans interact with each other. Another way that culture can also be described is as the sum total of ways of living built up by a group of people that is then transmitted from one generation to another. It is also interesting to note that the word "culture" can also mean the action or practice of raising plants and animals. All of these aspects of culture are important as the culture of agriculture is examined. However, today in North America, the word agriculture is often replaced by a relatively new term, "agribusiness." Currently, this term is being widely used in other parts of the world. The implication of the term agribusiness is that there is no longer a culture associated with agriculture, that all dealings with agriculture are reduced to economic issues, and that economic cost is the only way to assess the success of agriculture.

If Christians are to live out their lives before the face of God, where should they look for guiding principles in how to conduct agriculture? While it is easy and thus tempting to look to the modern culture in which Christians live for answers, the first place they should look to is the Bible, not the prevailing culture in which they live. Although there are many items in human culture that are noble and worthwhile, there are also many that under close scrutiny are not consistent with Scripture. Since Christians profess that they are followers of the Bible, that is the first place they should go for guidance and insight. However when using Scripture, one must be careful in how it is interpreted. Instead of just seeking out one or two proof texts to reinforce an already held position by the individual, one should look to the whole of Scripture in an organic, complete manner to look for guiding principles.

The second source that Christians should explore for guiding principles is the rest of creation. If one wants to find out more about the Creator, one of the best places to seek this out is to observe His creation. Allow me to give an illustration. If I want to find out more about some of the great European painters, the best way for me to do this today is to search out as much of their creations that I possibly can. In order for me to find out more about Rembrandt or Van Gogh, I will need to seek out their paintings. Not only will I have to seek out their paintings, I will need to study the paintings extensively. I will also need to find out as much as I can from any of the painters' own written records that might exist in addition to other items which historians have written about them. Rather than just a rapid perusal, finding out more about the painters will involve extensive study and reflection. Similarly, the writings of the famous painters are analogous to God revealing himself in Scripture and their artworks are analogous to God revealing Himself in creation. It is through both of these that Christians can obtain guidelines on how they are to interact with other humans in the area of agriculture.

The following example illustrates how this relates to agriculture. It is obvious from Scripture that God delights in the diversity of what He made (Job 38–42, Genesis 1, Psalm 19). He delights in things that humans may ignore or think are insignificant. If we examine what He created, we also see rich diversity. One can draw the conclusion from both of these sources that diversity in creation is normative. Consequently, humans then have the responsibility to encourage diversity in agriculture. This then becomes a social principle for agriculture. Policies and practices that promote diversity should be encouraged because this is consistent with what we see in Scripture and creation.

Types of Agriculture

This raises an interesting question. Should all forms of agriculture be endorsed by Christians? In reality, Christians do practice any and all types of agriculture. But to be consistent with Scripture and the revelation in creation, Christians should endorse certain types of agriculture. If one takes seriously the concept of Biblical Holism regarding agriculture, then there are many types of agriculture that should be rejected and relatively few types that should be considered by Christians. The type of agriculture that I believe should be promoted by Christians is Sustainable Agriculture. This type of agriculture I believe is most consistent with a theocentric view of creation.

However, more probing questions need to be raised. As redeemed Christians, what is our role in the area of agriculture? Do evangelicals believe that Christianity is merely a personal experience that applies only to one's private life and therefore has no application to agriculture or how we live out our lives before the face of God? Is it the idea that people can follow popular culture during the week and then worship God on the special day that He set apart at the beginning of creation? That idea needs to be rejected as being incomplete. The prophet Jeremiah had harsh words addressed to the people of Judah who practiced this type of dualism. Jeremiah 7:9-11 states "Will you steal and murder, commit adultery and perjury, burn incense to Baal and follow other gods you have not known, and then come and stand before me in this house, which bears my Name, and say, 'We are safe'—safe to do all these detestable things? Has this house, which bears my Name, become a den of robbers to you? But I have been watching! declares the Lord." (See also Jeremiah 7:1-8, 12-15, Isaiah 56:7, Matthew 21:13, Mark 11:17 Luke 19:46.)

Many Christians think that doing the proper thing on Sunday is extremely important, as if that is all that the Lord requires of us. What is done on the other days is less important in their minds. Church worship, prayer, and saving souls are of utmost importance. They do not worry about what happens outside of church and leave the world to the devil. Others believe that their faith is only a personal matter between them and God. These ideas are not complete. Instead, what is needed is a complete transformation of a prevalent (agri)cultural situation. This requires special discernment for humans, who are created as God's image bearers. We need to return to the practice of the early Christians. Tom Sine describes how Christians of the first century were not engaged in Roman culture during the week and then church on the weekend. There was no dualistic, compartmentalized faith for them (Sine, 2000). Instead there was a complete, radical change in how they reacted to the contemporary culture.

Creation, Fall, Redemption

From the book of Genesis, we know that God is the Creator of all things. Even though God created everything good, sin through the disobedience of humans has destroyed the perfect relationship that existed between humans, between God and humans, and between humans and the rest of creation. However, because He loved the world (John 3:16) that He had made, God in the person of Jesus Christ came into this world to pay the penalty for all sin. Through his suffering, death, resurrection, and ascension, Christ has redeemed His people and all of creation (Colossians 1:15-20). In gratitude for our redemptions, with the help of the Holy Spirit and by the use of Scripture we are called to spread this good news and seek to reform human activities to be in accord with the original mandate. Chuck Colson and Nancy Pearcy note that salvation does not consist simply of freedom from sin; salvation also means being restored to the task that we were given in the beginning— the job of creating culture. Christians are saved not only *from* something (sin) but to something (Christ's lordship over all life) (Colson and Pearcy, 1999).

As a result of the Fall, every part of creation was subjected into enmity toward God. And yet God established a covenant with humans and the rest of creation (Genesis 9:8-11, 22) that He would never destroy the world again with a flood. It is obvious from this convent that God delights in the other parts of his creation as well as humans. This is in stark contrast to the modern utilitarian view that the value of creation is determined solely by how it can benefit and be utilized by humans. This places great responsibility on Christians in how we interact with creation and humanity. For while the natural world obeys God's laws without any choice in the matter, in culture and society God rules indirectly, entrusting to humans the tasks that need to be done. For example, all of creation is subject to God's law of gravity and will suffer immediate consequences by ignoring it. However, humans can often and do rebel against God's created order and moral law assuming that they can escape the consequences.

As stated previously, God delights and enjoys the great diversity that he has created. This fact has great implications for how we practice agriculture and the value that humans place on creation as the following examples illustrate. Weeds are not some evil plants that have been planted by the devil, but plants that are growing in places where humans wish they were not growing. A weed is simply a plant that is out of place from a human view-point. This plant still functions as God intended. It prevents soil erosion by anchoring with its roots and reducing the impact of raindrops on soil with its leaves; produces carbohydrates as a result of photosynthesis; and can serve as a source of food and protection for other creatures. Domestic animals are not just objects that produce something to be utilized by humans. Animals are part of God's creation and their diversity apparently gives Him great pleasure. An animal gives praise to God by allowing it to be the animal that God intended it to be. Humans must remember this fact as we raise our animals for food and fiber. Christians especially need to remember that they are dealing with something that is not theirs. creation is a gift given to them by the Creator Himself. This fact should instill in Christians a sense of awe and respect. How we deal with weeds and animals should first of all not depend on what the popular culture around us tells us to do, but we should seek out the proper response based on guidelines from Scripture and creation.

Historical Setting for Sustainable Agriculture

The term, "Sustainable Agriculture," is a relatively new one in North America, as Ron Vos and Del Vander Zee have noted (Vos and Vander Zee, 1989). It is an outgrowth of the mid 1980s farm crisis. Its birth came as a result of a wrenching period in North American agricultural history when bankruptcies were high as a result of management trends of the late 1970s. Its birth name was Low Input Sustainable Agriculture (LISA) but a few years after its conception it took the name Sustainable Agriculture. It is that name that is widely used today.

While the industrial model of agriculture is very prominent today, the Sustainable Agriculture model is gaining acceptance as Vos and Vander Zee point out in their chapter on Sustainable Agriculture in the book, *Signposts of God's Liberating Kingdom* (Vos and Vander Zee, 1998). The definition of Sustainable Agriculture defined by Vos and Vander Zee in the late 1980s is as follows: *Sustainable Agriculture is an agriculture that is economically viable, resource efficient, environmentally sound, promotes justice to both the human and non human creation, and builds community while providing food and fiber for humans for long periods of time.* While many agricultural producers would probably agree with this definition in the abstract form, it is not practiced to the fullest extent possible for a variety of reasons. One of the main reasons is that federal government policy generally does not encourage its practice. A very practical application of social principles for agriculture is to support public policy that seeks to encourage Sustainable Agriculture.

I now want to focus on why Sustainable Agriculture is most consistent with a theocentric worldview; how this is consistent with the theme of creation stewardship; and why Christians especially should promote and practice it. Some of my thoughts on this topic have been mirrored in an article by Roger W. Elmore, in the *Journal of Production Agriculture*, Volume 9, No. 1, 1996. The very fact that his article appeared in a scientific publication at all may be the result of the Cyrus principle (see 2 Chronicles 36:22, 23 and Ezra 1:1-4 for the details). The Cyrus principle refers to the fact that God may use unbelievers to accomplish His will as He did with King Cyrus in the Old Testament.

People's relationship with the ecosystem does affect their perception of Sustainable Agriculture. If we live according to our worldview, either God, the rest of creation, humans, or something else is exalted. We are not passive observers of the ecosystem. Humans are directly involved in the ecosystem and like the rest of creation are created by God. For example, we derive our food and the air we breathe from the ecosystem and we add wastes to it. How we react with the rest of creation is largely a spiritual matter. In fact what we call the ecosystem reflects how we view it. It is often referred to as nature but the more correct term is creation. We must ask ourselves if our own individual philosophy when extended to its logical conclusion leads to the practice of Sustainable Agriculture.

A biocentric person exalts the ecosystem over humans. Humans are often seen as a pathogen that threatens the health of the planet. While exalting the rest of the creation may appear unselfish, people who believe this either tend to worship creation or remove themselves from it in order to conserve resources for the good of the ecosystem. It is pointless to discuss the sustainability of this worldview if people are removed from the world however good this might be for environmental quality. If humans are allowed to exist under a biocentric worldview, their food and fiber needs as well as the economic viability for agricultural producers would have little, if any, priority. Many people reject this view as being outlandish. However, when non-Christians perceive Christians as being anthropocentric, many turn to biocentrism as a corrective to anthropocentrism.

A worldview that is commonly held by people is the anthropocentric view that exalts humans. This view places people above the rest of creation and assumes that people are accountable to no higher authority for their treatment of the rest of creation. Everything created is made for humans and nothing has intrinsic value. Things only gain value if humans decide they are valuable. Land is worth only the amount of the income it will produce for its owner. Therefore the best use of land is what brings in the most income. Forests or prairies only have value and should be preserved because they can provide us with a plentiful supply of oxygen; or because there may be some plant species that could serve as future sources of medicine or food for humans. The anthropocentric view puts the forests' and prairies' economic value above its intrinsic value. An anthropocentrist will often speak against short-term greed and selfishness while advocating long-term greed and selfishness. Since creation exists solely for human benefit, according to this worldview, all technology is good technology because it hastens the human exploitation of creation for human good.

Fallen humans, including many Christians, often embrace this worldview, largely because of the misinterpretation of Genesis 1:28. Christians who recognize that humans are created in God's image often think this gives them the right to use their power to do as they please, rather practicing the servant leader model as exemplified in Jesus Christ. It is our selfish human nature that is exhibited most in this worldview. The results of this concept were illustrated by G. Hardin in the late 1960s in an animal-grazing example (Hardin, 1968). In a grazing area that is open to all herders, everyone will work together for their mutual benefit until the carrying capacity of the land is reached. At that point each herder may consider the cost and benefit of adding one more animal to his herd. This person may soon discover that his benefit is one more animal and that the cost of the additional animal is divided among all herders. As each individual herder seeks to add more animals, the commons is ruined and tragedy ultimately results. "Ruin is the destination toward which all men rush, each pursuing his own interest in a society that believes in the freedom of the commons. Freedom in a commons brings ruin to all" (Hardin, 1968).

Richard Young has stated that there is another dimension that permeates how Christians view reality. He calls this worldview theanthropocentric, in which everything revolves around God and humanity (Young, Chapter 6). This he says is a result of the reformer's concentration on justification by faith, because humanity's relation to God was the primary focus and nature was just a backdrop to salvation history. Luther and Calvin believed that humans are to be responsible stewards, but also that everything created was made for the sake of humans. Because of wide spread acceptance, theanthropocentrism is presumed to be a universal truth today among Christians. Yet all forms of anthropocentrism ultimately are the result of humanity's rebellion in the garden.

An anthropocentric view does not promote Sustainable Agriculture. Under this view, some people, but not all, will have food; some people, but not all, will have a reasonable quality of life; and some, but not all agricultural producers, will be economically viable. This is considered a normal economic process because there is a "survival of the fittest" mentality driving this worldview. There is no place for justice in this worldview except that which humans decide is just. The first herders to take advantage of creation had the most economic gain before the commons area collapsed as described by Hardin. Destruction of creation is driven by human greed and selfishness.

Theocentrists believe God is in charge, that people were created in part to be faithful stewards of the ecosystem, and that every part of creation belongs to Him. They acknowledge that there is a separation between God the Creator and His creation and thus the creation is not equal to God. Theocentristics believe that everything exists for the sake of God and to serve His purposes. While people like Berkeley historian Lynn White often blame Christians for the environmental crisis and the exploitation of creation, it is a misinterpretation of the Biblical message that is more likely the cause. Evidence of severe environmental problems in the former Soviet Union indicates that huge problems do exist in non-Christian societies. However some Christians who hold an anthropocentric view have added to the environmental crisis by emphasizing the spiritual— saving the soul and getting to heaven—and therefore see nothing in nature beyond consuming it or using it to prove the existence of God. This however should not be used to blame Christians because of their Christianity. It is because of their failure in Christianity. The theocentric theme is repeated often in the Scriptures (Romans 12:2, 2 Corinthians 10:5, Philippians 2:5).

Because of Adam's sin, humans have separated themselves from God. We have exercised our place in creation wrongly. We are rebels who have tried to make ourselves the center of the universe. This was not part of God's original plan but it is symptomatic of the selfishness and greed common to all humanity apart from God. God sent His son Jesus Christ as a sacrifice for this sin and separation. By His death and resurrection He has conquered sin. As redeemed Christians we now have the freedom in Christ to exhibit the theocentric view of creation and to acknowledge that the Lordship of Christ extends to every cubic centimeter of creation. Christians, of all people, should not be destroyers and exploiters of creation, but should treat creation with overwhelming respect. Our role as servants in creation should be to care for it with compassion and humility. We are called as faithful stewards of creation that God loves.

Theocentrists exalt God over creation, including humans. This means that they reject anthropocentrism and seek not to be controlled by their own egos. Following the example of Christ as servant leader, they have the ability to put others above self and see humans as caretakers of creation accountable to God. This view is consistent with Sustainable Agriculture and will promote good environmental stewardship and sufficient food production. It results in a reasonable quality of life for humans and allows the non-human creation to flourish. This will also promote the long-term sustainability of creation.

A concept appropriate to these issues is that of "usufruct." This concept should be a guiding principle in how we should practice agriculture. Usufruct is a word that is rarely used in modern culture; in fact most modern dictionaries do not have it listed, probably because the concept is no longer considered relevant in our modern economic climate. Usufruct literally means to "use the fruits of" or, is the right to utilize and enjoy the profits and advantages of something belonging to another so long as the property is not damaged or altered in any way. In response to the concept of usufruct, author and farmer Wendell Berry stated in a presentation in the 1980s: "To receive the gift of creation and then to hasten directly to practical ways of exploiting that gift for maximum production without regard to long term impacts is at best ingratitude and at worse blasphemy (the act of claiming for ones self the attributes and rights of God)." May God guide us as we seek to do His will in terms of how we practice agriculture.

Indigenous Knowledge Is Important (Equality Vs. Egalitarianism)

God cares about the whole person, not just souls. Jesus took on a bodily form and the resurrection of Jesus' body reaffirms this. The idea that spiritual is more important than the physical is a concept more closely identified with Plato than Scripture. Plato characterized the material world in negative terms, as a realm from which we need to escape to enjoy an ideal existence in the non-material realm of the spirit up there somewhere. Tom Sine notes that Francis Bacon in the 16th century reinforced this Platonic dualism. On one side is the Word of God dealing with the world of the Spirit. This is for theologians. On the other side is the work of God, the natural world. Bacon divided the spirit from the body, evicting the Creator from the creation and created a dualistic worldview that pervades modern culture (Sine, 2000).

The roots of western agriculture go back to the Enlightenment period when belief in progress and human reason dominated western society and agriculture became a science. Eating was reduced to obtaining needed nutrients in order to live instead of a sacred act of sharing the goodness of the land. People in the western tradition automatically assumed that they should spread this enlightened view to other "under developed" people.

The arrogance of developed (western) nations in the belief that their ways of doing things are the best or the only way, often adds to the problem of sharing the good news that Christ's redemption affects all of creation, including how we practice agriculture. The belief that western culture, agriculture, technology, practices, and knowledge are innately better than that of other cultures is at best, misguided. While there may be some items that can be transferred to agriculture in other countries, the idea that all knowledge resides in the western or developed countries is erroneous. The concept that western culture must be spread around the world by Christian missionaries is to make the mistake of thinking the western way is the equivalent of the Christian way. This mistake is made even worse when it is thought that this is the Christian gospel that needs to be shared instead of the Gospel of Jesus Christ.

Ironically, many non-western people don't suffer from the

dualism that was mentioned previously. They have a holistic view of reality albeit one not centered around the God revealed in the Bible. Tom Sine mentions that when his wife was working in Ghana, she noted that the spirituality of the people she worked with affected every facet of their lives (Sine, 2000). There are some branches of Christianity that do not suffer from the western dualism. My own experiences with the Russian Orthodox Church bear this out. Bringing a dualistic gospel to people who already have a holistic view, adds an unnecessary level of confusion to the process. All cultures need to be examined in the light of Scripture and all need the redemption of Jesus Christ.

The typical western model of transfer of agricultural knowledge is a top down model. This model assumes that the great knowledge that resides at the upper level needs to be extended to the lower level where little knowledge exists. This is another example of dualism, where those with the training of the mind have higher value than the work of producers. While there are a few positive benefits of the typical western model, it may not be the most appropriate one in all parts of the world. However, it should not be imposed, even unknowingly, as part of the good news of redemption in Christ. A more appropriate model assumes that all players are at the same level, all possess valuable unique knowledge, and the exchange of information occurs between all players equally. A social principle of Biblical Holism in agriculture is participation. All stakeholders must have representation in the process.

Community and Cooperation Vs. Competition

One of the characteristics of modern industrial agribusiness is the idea that agricultural producers are in competition with one another in the production of their products. Neighbors are no longer valued because of their contribution to building community, but instead input suppliers tell producers that they should view their neighbors as their competitors. This situation is especially true of producers who raise undifferentiated, bulk commodities that are undistinguished from one another. It is less frequent among practitioners of Sustainable Agriculture who often produce for niche markets. Nonetheless, producers today repeatedly lament the fact that excessive competition is prevalent in the culture of modern agriculture. For example, farmers featured in the book *Caretakers of Creation: Farmers Reflect on Their Faith and Work* (1990) repeatedly mentioned that generally farmers feel pressure to use cutthroat methods to beat out their neighbors by a few bushels per acre. Competition in the past between farmers, they noted, was limited to a friendly game on the softball field during the evening or holidays. The concept of competition seems to be a character-istic of the culture in agriculture. During the farm crisis of the 1980s in North America, it was often said that farmers were more interested in their neighbor's land rather than in their neighbors as people in a community. In general, among people involved in agriculture, there is a feeling that competition is much more prevalent than it used to be.

Unbridled competition is not consistent with a theocentric view of agriculture. Competition is a result of the Fall and dis-obedience of Adam in the Garden of Eden. Competition may be a powerful motivation for the average person because in our fallen human nature we suffer from a competitive nature. Redeemed Christians however should not encourage human action that is built on a human weakness that is a result of sin. Instead compassion and cooperation should be emphasized. In Christ's teachings, He did not encourage people to try to get ahead of another person or to view other humans as competitors. Instead we see the opposite behaviors praised in Scripture (Sermon on the Mount, in the Bea-titudes, and in the fruits of the Spirit listed in Galatians 5).

If Christians are indeed new creations in Christ, our actions should be shaped by the mind of Christ not by what the worldly culture is telling us to do. By following the mind of Christ people involved in agriculture will not try to get ahead of their neigh-bors, they will reach out to them (Matthew 25:35-6, 40). Instead of competition, there will be cooperation and sharing. Instead of concealment and hiding, there will be transparency and openness to help the neighbors.

Some interesting developments can often be observed among Christians involved in agriculture when they serve as volunteers. Many of these people become involved in mission trips that take them away from their homes as volunteers; often to rural places to assist others struggling with agriculture. This is a noble thing and should be encouraged. One item is the tendency of Christian agriculturalists to expect the people they are assisting to then become competitive towards others around them involved in agriculture, even though this may not be a prominent part of the indigenous culture.

The other item that often happens is just the opposite. Even though while living in their home culture Christian agriculturalists may treat their neighbors as competitors, these same Christians take mission trips to assist others in agriculture far away from home. This is type of assistance is something they would ordinarily not do in their own competitive culture. This is yet another example of dualism instead of Biblical Holism. Because mission trips are connected to church, or what happens on Sunday, this seems to make it a special situation whereas the everyday activities are done according to what popular culture is informing us. Again, Biblical Holism demands consistency in all of life and neither of these examples are compatible with Biblical Holism.

Poet and farmer Wendell Berry summarizes the results of over competitiveness very well in an essay that appeared in *Harpers*, April, 2002. "The 'law of competition' does not imply that many competitors will compete indefinitely. The law of competition is a simple paradox: Competition destroys competition. The law of competition implies that any competitor, competing without restraint, will ultimately and inevitably reduce the number of competitors to one. The law of competition, in short, is the law of war" (Berry, 2002). This warlike attitude of conquering has also been taken to how agricultural land is used and viewed. Instead of trying to imitate natural processes in agriculture, there is an attempt to mine or conquer the natural processes. I will not address that issue here since others are doing that elsewhere.

Examples of the effect of competition in North American are readily seen. Mary Hendrickson and William Heffernan report that the top four firms control 81% of the beef packing industry, 59% of the pork packing industry, and 46% of the pork production industry, (Hendrickson and Heffernan, 2002). The top four firms control 61% of the flour milling industry and 80% of the soybean crushing industry. Many of the same firms show up in different categories. For example: Tyson, ConAgra, and Cargil are among the top four beef and pork packers.

The effects of competition concerning the use of agricultural technology have been noted for decades. Agricultural economist Willard Cochrane used the term agricultural treadmill to describe how early adopters get higher than normal profits, (Cochrane, 1958). But as more farmers use the technology, the supply of product produced by the technology increases and forces down the price. Later adopters run the risk of falling hopelessly behind. As supply increases faster than demand, farmers will either adopt or be forced out of business. The effect of competition is to put more farmers out of work.

Competition, with its warlike attitude of conquering, should not be the cultural model that drives how Christians live. There are many examples of Christian farmers who are very willing to share their successes with others. Richard and Sharon Thompson of Boone, Iowa, members of Practical Farmers of Iowa, are excellent examples of this. Beginning in the early 1980s, they have hosted thousands of people at their farm. The Amish are a unique Christian community that exhibit a love for people and creation and as a result have thriving rural communities. Cooperation and sharing among community members is emphasized instead of competition.

A recent phenomenon has occurred in North America beginning in the 1990s as a reaction to the current system of agriculture. It is called Community Supported Agriculture (CSA). CSAs are membership driven and operate on a local scale. Members pay the producers money at the beginning of the growing season for produce they will receive later. This allows a relationship to be established between the grower and the consumer early in the season. It also means that the grower often doesn't need to borrow money to put the crop in the ground because of cash received early in the season. CSAs encourage active participation by all parties involved. There is an awareness of how the food is grown and the benefits of the system stay in the community. In CSAs growers literally and directly are their brothers keeper. Growing food in a backyard garden is another way to subvert the conventional system of agriculture.

Encouragement and Empowering Vs. Extraction and Exploitation

One of the most important historical events that should be examined in order to understand the present agricultural situation is the fact of Western colonialism. Colonialism was practiced from around the 14th century until the last half of the 20th century. C. Dean Freudenberger, in his book, *Global Dust Bowl* (1990), defines colonialism as the "occupation of peoples, their cultures and land, by other peoples and other cultures from other lands. The primary purpose of colonial occupation is to generate wealth and to extend political power. The outsiders who occupy the land want to bring another region into their economy" (p. 79). The colonies were not considered equal to the mother country since the purpose of acquiring the colony in the first place was the exploitation of the colony's people and goods by the mother country for its utilization.

By not considering the colony as an equal, the mother country was absolved of any moral obligation to educate the indigenous people in the liberal arts. Courses like social ethics, history, or government were seldom taught. Instead, the indigenous people were trained in ways that continued to support the colonial system. They were trained largely as workers in enterprises that continued to support the mother country by providing it with the goods that it wanted. The mother country had little care for what was happening to the culture, social structures, or land in the colony as long the goods kept flowing to the mother country. In fact, there was good reason not to educate the people of the colonies in subjects like history and political science. If people in the colonies were educated in these things, they might recognize the injustice of the system that they were working under and rebel. This would be disastrous to the mother country because then the goods of the colony would stop flowing.

People were treated badly under the colonial system. Many of the people of the colonies were slaves. The main reason for the existence of people under the colonial system was to plant the crops, mine the ores, and in general do what ever the mother country thought was appropriate in order to get the goods it wanted. Families were broken up and males often separated from the rest of the family in order to work the colonial enterprises. Humans, as well as the land, were exploited in the colonies for the benefit of the mother country.

The legacy of colonialism still haunts current agricultural systems. While the intent of modern systems of agriculture may not be the same as the colonial system, many of the results are the same. In North America and around the world, the present system of agriculture encourages exploitation of people and the land. Instead of owners being operators of agricultural enterprises, owners may be large corporations that have their headquarters hundreds or thousands of miles away from the operations. Workers in these operations are usually uneducated in the liberal arts but instead are narrowly trained in the jobs that are needed to make the current system work. Goods are taken from one region and brought to another in order to benefit the owners living hundreds or thousands of miles away.

While slavery is no longer practiced, the workers usually get paid substandard wages often without medical benefits. The brightest and best of the people in the rural communities often leave these areas in order to escape this unjust system. This problem goes largely unnoticed in urban areas because there is little concern for what happens in the rural areas as long as the goods keep flowing. In fact some economists use phrases like "this situation frees up people to pursue better jobs in urban areas." Few people question if that is what the displaced people really want, or if this is a just system. In many countries the urban areas are overflowing with poor people displaced by the agricultural system that was just described and the last thing that is needed is to have more people moving to the cities.

Redeemed Christians need to promote a system of agriculture that empowers people to develop to their fullest God-given potential. This may mean that government policy needs to be changed to encourage these types of systems. For those not directly involved in agriculture, it means becoming aware of the situation that exists and taking whatever steps are needed to correct the situation. Banning packer ownership of livestock, requiring owners to live near operations, paying livable wages, encouraging education not just training for farm workers, finding out where and how the food we eat is grown are just a few of the examples of ways that people can have an impact on the food system to make it more just.

Another legacy of the colonial mentality is biopiracy. Biopiracy can be described as the taking or patenting of genetic material and traditional knowledge without proper informed consent and agreed terms. Western nations, because of intellectual property rights, facilitate piracy of indigenous knowledge and biodiversity of developing nations. Some in the developing nations charge that biopiracy robs these countries of their biological and intellectual heritage just as in the colonial era European countries robbed non-European countries of their land and gold (Freudenberger, 1990). Christians need to encourage systems of agriculture that promote justice in this area also, even though this may be different from what popular culture promotes.

Servant Leader and Prophetic Critic

In summary, the role of the redeemed Christian who seeks to promote Biblical Holism is twofold: To be a servant leader and a prophetic critic. In Jesus Christ we have the ultimate example of servant leadership. Christ who knew no sin was made to become sin on our behalf (Romans 8: 1-4). This certainly is a model for followers of Christ to emulate as we deal with Biblical Holism as it relates to agriculture.

But Christ was more than just a nice, meek, floor mat type person. To His accusers He was a dangerous threat to the popular culture of the day. He was considered a dangerous firebrand. He insulted respected religious leaders of the day by calling them hypocrites! He referred to King Herod as a fox. He assaulted tradesmen selling their wares in the temple and threw them and their belongings out. He cast out demons by sending them into other people's hogs. He was counter-cultural to the extreme!

And so redeemed Christians have another role to play. We are no longer to live according to our sinful nature but rather to live in accordance with the Holy Spirit (Romans 8:5-17). This means that we need to speak out against injustice and seek to promote agricultural systems, especially among Christians, that are just, sustainable, and consistent with Biblical Holism. We need to encourage people to become participants in the creation of a new society based on justice. This may mean at times that we will be unpopular; about as unpopular as the Old Testament prophets were when God used them to call His people back to Him. His prophets were usually from among the common people and they were called to prophesy to these same people. This is analogous to what we are called to do as we seek to bring Biblical Holism to a "Christian" culture that believes what one does on Sunday in a faith setting has little connection to what one does during rest of the week.

We need to build community among like-minded Christians to support one another in this endeavor. As Ben Franklin said in another context: "Either we hang together or we hang separately." This may be one of the tasks that local churches can be doing. We need to support each other in the academic area, in the area of missions, in the area of food production, and in the public policy area. By building community we will get to know our "neighbors," we will hold each other accountable, knowledge will be shared, and the summary of the ten commandments given by Christ to "love God above all and to love our neighbor as ourselves" will become reality. These communities will be counter cultural but supportive. As we seek to move ahead on this endeavor let Micah 6:8 be our guide: "What does the Lord require of you? To act justly, to love mercy, and to walk humbly with your God." Soli Deo Gloria!

References

Berry, Wendell

    1985   Quoted by Wes Jackson in a presentation given at a Theology of Land Conference. Collegeville, MN: St. Johns University.

    2002   "The Idea of a Local Economy." *Harpers*, p. 18. April.

Cochrane, Willard

    1958   *Farm Prices: Myth and Reality*. Minneapolis: University of Minnesota Press.

Colson, Charles and Nancy Pearcy

    1999   *How Now Shall We Live?* Carol Stream: Tyndale House.

Elmore, Roger W.

    1996   "Our Relationship with the Ecosystem and Its Impact on Sustainable Agriculture." *Journal of Production Agriculture*, Volume 9, Number 1.

Freudenberger, C. Dean.

    1991   "Get Along, But Don't Go Along." *Caretakers of Creation*. Minneapolis: Augsburg Fortress.

    1990   *Global Dust Bowl*. Minneapolis: Augsburg Fortress.

Hardin, G.

    1968   "The Tragedy of the Commons." *Science* 162: 1243-1248.

Hendrickson, Mary and William Heffernan

    2002   *Concentration of Agricultural Markets*. Department of Rural Sociology, University of Missouri. February.

Shiva, Vandana

    2000   "North-South Conflicts in Intellectual Property Rights" p. 50. *Peace Review* 12:4.

Sine, Tom

    2000   *Mustard Seed Versus McWorld*. Grand Rapids: Baker.

Slattery, Patrick, editor

    1990   *Caretakers of Creation: Farmers Reflect on Their Faith and Their Work*. Minneapolis: Augsburg Fortress.

Vos, Ron and Del Vander Zee

    1989   "Trends in Agriculture: Sustainability Pro Rege." Sioux Center, IA: Dordt College Press.

    1998   "Sustainable Agriculture: Signposts of God's Liberating Kingdom." Pretoria, South Africa: Potchefstroome University Press.

White Jr., L.

   1967   "The Historical Roots of Our Ecological Crisis." *Science* 155:1203-1207.

Young, Richard

   1994   "The Biblical Perspective: Anthropocentric, Biocentric, or Theocentric." *Healing the Earth: A Theocentric Perspective on Environmental Problems and Their Solutions.* Nashville, TN: Broadman & Holman.

"Behold I Give You":
A Christian Perspective on Farming

Rev. Jim Ball

> *The earnest student has already learned that nature does not expend*
> *its forces upon waste material, but that each created thing is an indis-*
> *pensable factor of the great whole, and one in which no other factor*
> *will fit exactly as well.*
>
> – George Washington Carver.

Introduction

This chapter will focus on three interrelated questions: What is the role of the agriculturalist from a biblical perspective, what is his/her relation to humanity today, and what is the church and society's relationship to the agriculturalist today? I approach these questions from my training as a biblical theologian and ethicist concerned with justice, as well as from my calling as a creation-care advocate, which is itself based upon a biblical foundation.

The Role of an Agriculturalist from a Biblical Perspective

Image of God; Image of Christ. All human beings are created in the image of God (Gen. 1:28). In other words, we were created to image God, to be a reflection/representation of God on earth and in our dominion of the earth; we are to "tend and keep" (Gen. 2:15) the earth as God would. To image God or do God's will means that we have to know something about the character of God through revelation (Scripture and the Incarnation). Unfortunately, the Fall warped the image of God within humanity and inhibits humanity from imaging God in our relation to others and in our care of the earth. Christians know, however, that the true image of God is Jesus Christ (Col. 1:15), the supreme revelation of God's character. Empowered by grace and guided by the Holy Spirit, Christians are to strive to image the true Image, Christ. As Philippians 2:5-11 proclaims, we are to follow Christ in his servanthood. We are to be servants of the Suffering Servant intent on fulfilling the Great Commandments to love God with all our heart, soul, mind, and strength, and love our neighbor as ourselves (Mt. 22:34-40; Mk. 12:28-31; Lk. 10:25-28; cf. Rom. 13:9; Gal. 5:14; Jas. 2:8; Dt. 6:4-5, Lev. 19:18). In their relationships to the rest of humanity, future generations, the land, and to God's other creatures, agriculturalists who confess Jesus Christ to be Savior and Lord are called to image God in Christ with an attitude of humility and service, to have the mind of Christ (1 Cor. 2:16), and be his ministers of reconciliation towards the whole of creation (2 Cor. 5:18; Col. 1:20).

Servant Stewardship and the Agriculturalist

In looking at biblical themes and texts that relate specifically to agriculture, those seeking a Christian approach to agriculture should interpret these texts not as detached observers or as self-interested actors in a free market, but as disciples of Jesus Christ, striving to view them through the mind of Christ as presented in Scripture. Those who profess Christ as Savior and Lord are to have a Christocentric hermeneutic. With that in mind, we will highlight four biblical themes: ownership and stewardship; distributive justice; future generations; and, God's provision for the rest of Creation.

1. Ownership & Stewardship

The Bible makes clear that it is the Creator that owns the land and its creatures and cares for it. Ps. 24:1 states it succinctly: "The earth is the Lord's, and everything in it" (cf. 1 Cor. 10:26; see also Ex. 9:29; Dt. 10:14, 11:12, 1 Chron. 29:11; Job 41:11; Ps. 50:9-12).

Colossians 1:16b identifies more specifically who the Lord is. It is Jesus Christ: "all things were created by him and **for** him." Christ is, as Heb. 1:2 puts it, the "heir of all things."

Lev. 25:23 not only proclaims that the land belongs to the Lord, but describes humanity's status: "'The land must not be sold permanently, because the land is mine and you are but aliens and my tenants.'" Human beings are not owners, but caretakers or stewards who are to image God in their relationship to the earth and the other creatures. In the words of Gen. 2:15, they are to "tend" and "keep" the Garden and the soil from which they themselves come (v.7). Finally, v.23 begins by saying that tenants or stewards of a demarcated piece of land could not sell it permanently, "because the land is mine ...".

Given that God is the Owner, anything produced from the land belongs to Him. This is made clear in the Old Testament through the sacrificial system (Dt. 15:19; Lev. 1-7), tithing (Dt. 14:22-29; Lev. 27:30-33; 2 Chron. 31:2-8; Mal. 3:8-12) and the three major festivals (Passover, Weeks, and Tabernacles).

Thus, the Christian agriculturalist is to treat the land and the animals under his stewardship with Christ-like care, since Christ is the owner and the Christian agriculturalist is His follower.

2. Justice & Mercy

This idea of a Loving and therefore Just Creator as Owner leads into the next theme, justice and mercy. In Lev. 25's description of the Jubilee, distributive justice is clearly articulated. Every 50th year, the Year of Jubilee, all land was to return to the families to whom it had been distributed at the time when the Israelites entered the Promised Land (Lev. 25:10,13). If someone had to "sell" God's land apportioned to them and they or their family members couldn't buy it back, it would revert back to them on the 50th year (vv.25-28). This procedure is to ensure that land distribution doesn't get too concentrated; that everyone would have the land necessary to support their families. Lev. 25 requires distributive justice of the land, or of the means to produce food or support one's family with the basic necessities of life, because God is a loving God and therefore wants justice. This naturally follows if one assumes that the true owner is Jesus Christ who has reconciled all things through His blood, shed on the cross (Col. 1:20). Lev. 25 does not imply equality, but rather mandates limits to societal inequality. Legitimate differences in ownership can result from capability, but there is to be a limit to these differences. At a minimum, there is to be sufficiency for all. The maximum level of land/wealth accumulation should be before bonds of community break such as when someone else's wealth puts someone else in a situation of insufficiency.

Implicit in Lev. 25 is the idea that land and wealth distribution will become lopsided. As does Jesus (Mk. 14:7), Dt. 15:11 recognizes this explicitly: "There will always be poor people in the land. Therefore, I command you to be openhanded toward your brothers and toward the poor and needy in your land." God commands this because he loves them, too.

Mt. 25 proclaims that Christ loves the disenfranchised so much he identifies actions towards them as actions done to Him. "Then the righteous will answer him, 'Lord, when did we see you hungry and feed you, or thirsty and give you something to drink? … 'whatever you did for one of the least of these brothers of mine, you did for me'" (vv. 37, 40).

While some might be tempted to make judgments as to who is worthy to benefit from food from the land, Jesus' teaching that God sends rain on the just and the unjust (Mt. 5:45) suggests that the essentials of life such as food and water should never be withheld from anyone, even the unjust.

Over-concentration of land in the hands of a few at the expense of others to provide sufficiently for themselves is clearly contrary to the teachings of Scripture, as is the denial of food to anyone. Righteousness, a pro-active stance, requires that we provide food for everyone. Fulfilling such obligations is not charity (i.e. something at the whim of the giver), but the requirements of biblical justice commanded by the God who loves everyone.

3. Future Generations

When it comes to loving all generations, God shows no temporal partiality. Christ died for all generations. Christian agriculturalists are called, therefore, to love neighbors across time through the servant stewardship of their land and animals. This, too, is part of the ministry of reconciliation. However, the Bible makes it clear that the sinfulness of the present generation can impact themselves and innocent future generations. In Jer. 4:18-20 the Lord states: "'Your own conduct and actions have brought this upon you. This is your punishment. How bitter it is! How it pierces to the heart! ... Disaster follows disaster; the whole land lies in ruins...'".

Thus, servant stewardship of the land requires the type of care that ensures its fruitfulness for the sake of future generations.

4. God's Provision for the Rest of Creation

Closely related to maintaining the fruitfulness of the land for future generations via proper stewardship is the biblical requirement of a **Sabbath year for the land**. "'When you enter the land I am going to give you, the land itself must observe a Sabbath to the Lord ... The land is to have a year of rest'" (Lev. 25:2, 5b). "'I will send you such a blessing in the sixth year that the land will yield enough for three years'" (Lev. 25:21). Second Chronicles 36:21 makes it clear that there would be consequences to not allowing the land a Sabbath. Israel's exile into Babylon allowed the land to have the rest that was withheld from it. In light of this, Christian agriculturalists cannot be "soil robbers" as George Washington Carver put it.

In addition to the Sabbath year, the 4th commandment states that the animals under a biblical agriculturalists' care are to enjoy the Sabbath day of rest just like the human beings (Ex. 20:8-11; Dt. 5:12-15).

The earth was not only created for humanity, but for **God's other creatures as well**. In Genesis 1, God blesses the other creatures (v.22) and states that vegetation is for both humanity and the other creatures (vv.29-30). Noah's Ark is a picture of the fact that humanity and all the other creatures are in the same boat, and that God ensured that all creatures would survive. The Noahic Covenant, where God promises to never destroy the earth again, is with all the creatures (Gen. 9:9-11, 15). Ps. 104 describes the balance in provision that God provides for all His creatures: He makes grass grow for the cattle, plants for humanity to cultivate—bringing forth food from the earth: wine that gladdens the heart of man, oil to make his face shine, and bread that sustains his heart. The trees of the Lord are well watered ... there the birds make their nest ... You bring darkness and it becomes night, and all the beasts of the forest prowl. The lions roar for their prey, and seek their food from God. The sun rises and they steal away; they return and lie down in their dens. Then man goes out to his work, to his labor until evening ... These all look to you to give them their food at the proper time (vv. 14-17, 20-23, 27).

Thus, as tenants or stewards of Christ's land and animals, Christian agriculturalists are to keep the soil and their animals healthy by not pressing them beyond their limits and by providing adequate rest. In addition, as human creatures, we are to use our fair share of God's provision, but not more than our fair share, so that all of our fellow creatures may also enjoy God's blessing of life.

These texts on God's provision for His other creatures, when combined with Lev. 25 and other passages on caring for the poor, provide us with a biblical picture of what God desires for all His creatures: sustainable sufficiency.

The Agriculturalist and Humanity Today

Given the biblical understanding of the agriculturalist's role as laid out in this paper, what should be the relationship between the agriculturalist and humanity today? Four goals will be explored: service; health; stewardship of the land and care for animals; and distributive justice. We should recognize up front that the ability of Christian agriculturalists to achieve these goals could be complicated by a lack of ownership of the land he/she tends, government policies, the role of capital investments, and other countervailing forces. In the next section I will briefly address some of these forces.

A. Service

As followers of Jesus Christ, the true *imago dei*, those called to be Christian agriculturalists are to have an attitude of service that infuses all activities and decisions related to this high calling to feed those God loves. This is the opposite of acting solely in one's self-interest, as is assumed by economic theory since Adam Smith.

B. Health

In keeping with this attitude of Christ-like service, the Golden Rule (Mt. 7:12; Lk. 6:31), the commandment to love our neighbors as ourselves, concern for future generations, and respecting God's provision for other creatures, Christian agriculturalists should implement practices that enhance rather than detract from the health of human beings, God's other creatures, and the land, both now and in the future. When looking at water quality, so-called "non-point source" pollution is now the major problem, and agriculture is generally considered the largest contributor to these sources, which include sediment and pollutants attached to it, nutrients from fertilizers, and harmful pathogens. The use of pesticides and herbicides should be reduced and if possible eliminated. Nutrient management programs should be implemented.

In the U.S. it is especially the case that the practices of factory farms or "confined animal feeding operations" (CAFOs) can have serious health impacts. Waste lagoons from factory farms should be eliminated, given that they produce harmful gases (hydrogen sulfide), and can break, leak, or overflow, sending nitrate pollution, harmful microbes, and antibiotics into the water supply. Threats associated with such pollution can result in death.

It almost goes without saying that the practices of factory farms in the U.S. are unhealthy for the animals, which is a main reason why they are treated with massive amounts of antibiotics. This, in turn, can have serious impacts on human health. About 25 million pounds of antibiotics are fed every year to livestock for growth promotion and disease prevention, almost eight times the amount given to humans to treat disease. The Centers for Disease Control, the American Medical Association, and the World Health Organization have called for an end to the use of antibiotics as growth promoters in agriculture that we depend on in human medicine. Antibiotic-resistant bacteria are on the rise. Patients of serious medical problems may now have to try three or more antibiotics before they find one that works. As overuse of antibiotics in agriculture continues, this trend promises to get worse. Christian agriculturalists need to act by reducing use of antibiotics in order to fulfill their responsibility to provide for the health of others.

C. Stewardship of the Land and Care for God's Other Creatures

If one properly cares for one's animals and for the soil by keeping it healthy and preventing soil erosion, then many of the health impacts just mentioned could be reduced and possibly eliminated. Farm animals belong to Christ, and as His servant stewards Christian agriculturalists should provide them with a decent life. This also argues against factory farms and any other practices where animals are not treated humanely. Measures to prevent soil erosion, such as low-till or no-till, should be taken. Soil regeneration techniques such as composting, crop rotation, and cover crops should be implemented. As a general rule crops and techniques should be compatible with the local situation. Given that our food stock is dangerously simplified from a genetic perspective, Christian agriculturalists should grow heirloom stock (both plants and animals) as well as diversify the plants and animals they grow and raise.

Christian agriculturalists should farm in a way that is compatible with local conditions. They have a responsibility for stewardship of other lands and economies specific to their local conditions. They should attempt to eliminate adverse impact on their streams, implement sustainable forestry practices, and minimize habitat fragmentation on their land. For example, a farmer with creek frontage should employ practices (such as leaving a buffer) that eliminate or reduce pesticides, nutrients, and sediment loadings in the creek in order to provide for the creatures that live in the water.

A final consideration is development. Good land stewardship practices are rendered meaningless if the land is converted to other uses. Such deals can be lucrative. Besides being lost to farming, land converted from farming to development can reduce groundwater recharge, increase air and water pollution, and be a tax burden on the community. Christian landowners thus need to consider impacts on their neighbors, future generations, Christ's other creatures, and the land when making such an important decision. We must remember Isa. 5:8 "Woe to you who add house to house and join field to field till no space is left and you live alone in the land."

D. Distributive Justice

Lev. 25 and Mt. 25 make it clear that God wants everyone to have food and no one is to go hungry. Some might suggest that this trumps all other considerations (such as the health and stewardship issues outlined above) and justifies almost anything to boost production in the near term, such as factory farms, massive use of pesticides and chemical fertilizers, neglect of good long-term stewardship practices, etc. This false "lesser of two evils" argument would say that we are forced to choose between competing biblical admonitions.

But Lev. 25 addresses poverty by propounding a system that ensures that generation after generation of families will be able to support themselves instead of having to depend on the whims of charity, while at the same time enhancing the soil by providing for "rest." This points towards families and communities worldwide being able to support themselves. All communities now and in the future should have the potential to grow a food "safety net"—something they can produce themselves. This is the type of distributive justice that Lev. 25 points us towards. It also implies that the biblical concept of sustainable sufficiency applies to agriculture.

What about agriculturalists in the U.S. who want to help those in other countries that struggle with sufficient production to feed their populations? Those who work small farms in a manner that promotes health and good land stewardship could become short-term missionaries and share what they have learned—and in the process learn from those they are trying to help.

The Relationship of the Church and U.S. Society to the Agriculturalist Today

While the agriculturalist serves humanity, the Church and society are called to support the agriculturalist in faithful service. agriculturalists are brothers and sisters in Christ, are our neighbors, and could be those in need. The basic goal for the Church and for Society should be to make it easy—not difficult—for the producers and consumers of agricultural products to do the right thing. Right now in the U.S. it is much too difficult. We should make it easy to do good, not hard.

Assuming that small farms and true family farms will be more successful at fulfilling the five biblical goals outlined above, how can Church and society truly support small farms and family farms? The following suggestions are illustrative, not exhaustive.

A. Individual Christians

Stimulate demand by asking for and buying organic and local produce grown by small farms at the grocery store. Be willing to pay more for it. Become a member or support a local Community Supported Agriculture (or CSA) farm (preferably Christian, but not ones associated with an alternative religious perspective). Support organizations like Food for the Hungry to help address food concerns in other countries. Seek out a variety of produce grown locally, especially items indigenous to the area. This will help support those who grow/supply them and help maintain genetic diversity of our food systems.

B. Local Churches, Denominations, & Parachurch Organizations

Local churches could organize to support local farmers, including local Community Supported Agriculture (CSAs) farms. Denominations and/or parachurch organizations could educate their members about the biblical approach outlined in this paper. They could promote CSAs and provide their own CSA accreditation. Or denominations and organizations could work together to form a national Christian Organic Food Cooperative. Denominations should support Christian educational institutions that teach agricultural practices in keeping with the biblical, Christ-centered vision outlined above. In poor countries, they should support the creation of the food "safety net."

C. The Nation—Policy Principles & Recommendations

1. Support True Family/Small Farms

Currently over 60% of U.S. federal farm subsidies go to large producers, while many small farmers receive nothing. It appears the 2002 Farm Bill will not change this basic situation. This is hastening the decline of the true family farm in the U.S. Biblically, as we have seen, this is completely backwards. If we are going to have a subsidy program, then federal policy should reverse the current situation and provide the lion's share—if not all—of subsidies to small farms.

2. Support Local and Regional Distribution

Give locally produced agricultural products that are distributed locally and regionally tax credits that reflect the reduced environmental impacts of these products.

3. Regulate Factory Farms

Factory farms are industrial facilities and should be regulated accordingly. They should be required to obtain permits, monitor water quality and pay for cleaning up and disposing of their wastes.

4. Help Educate in Sustainable Practices

A recent poll by Gallup found that over half of all large conventional farmers have considered sustainable alternatives—but over a third say they don't know how. Provide funding to educational institutions and suitable non-governmental organizations to educate farmers. Educate all state and federal employees of agriculture agencies on sustainable practices and new organic regulations. Teach sustainable agriculture in private and public colleges and universities with agriculture programs.

5. Support Organic Research & Development

Regulations arising out of the Organic Foods Production Act of 1990 have been promulgated and implementation of the program is underway. It is now a critical time to provide additional support to ensure that all farmers are able to benefit fully from the National Organic Program at the USDA created by this legislation. FY 2001 USDA allocations for organic agricultural research and extension are estimated at about $5 million, or less than 0.3% of total federal agricultural research funding. Domestic and international markets for certified organic foods continue to grow at rates well above 10% annually. We should boost current federal research and development funding to $50 million.

6. Curb the Use of Antibiotics

The Federal Drug Administration (FDA) should ban or severely limit the use of antibiotics for nontherapeutic purposes such as growth promotion or disease prevention. This is especially the case for antibiotics used for human health.

7. *Approve GMOs on a Case-by-Case Basis*

As of the summer of 2001, there were 40 genetically engineered foods on the market. In keeping with the Great Commandments, the Golden Rule, concern for future generations, and God's provision for other creatures, genetically modified organisms or GMOs should be proven safe on a case-by-case basis by government agencies, not assumed safe until proven otherwise. There must be strong regulation of genetically engineered plants and animals once in use, and clear and prominent mandatory labeling of genetically engineered foods. All things need to be considered, including the effects of these products on nearby organisms (e.g., the BT corn was killing nearby monarch butterflies and other moths and butterflies).

Conclusion

To image Christ, Christian agriculturalists must approach their calling with an attitude of humility and service, striving to live a life of righteousness by creating sustainable sufficiency for all of God's children and creatures. Individual Christians and the Church collectively are to support them in their calling by purchasing their products and helping to structure society so that it is easy for everyone to do the right thing.

References

Bhumbla, Devinder K.

  n.d.   Agriculture Practices and Nitrate Pollution of Water. West Virginia University Extension Service.

Ferrell, John S.

  1995   *Fruits of Creation: A Look at Global Sustainability as Seen through the Eyes of George Washington Carver.* Shakopee: Macalester Park Publishing.

James, Frank

  2002   "Subsidies Grow in Farm Bill." *Chicago Tribune.* 27 April.

National Resources Defense Council and Clean Water Network

  2001   "Cesspools of Shame: How Factory Farm Lagoons and Sprayfields Threaten Environmental and Public Health." July.

Ongley, Edwin D.

  1996   "Control of Water Pollution from Agriculture," FAO Irrigation and Drainage Paper#5. *Gallup Poll: Trends in Agriculture 2000.* Core Results, p.7.

The Agriculturalist
and Creation

Production Principles for 'Good' Agriculture

Robert De Haan

Introduction

As a Reformed professor in the Agriculture Department at Dordt College, I tell my students that God calls them to transform agriculture so that it is more in line with what He desires. The first time they hear this, the majority of my students respond by saying (or sometimes just thinking) 'I really don't see much wrong with the status quo, and even if there are a few things that should be changed, I don't know what a Christian alternative would be!' The agriculture students at Dordt College are quite representative of the broader Christian community, and their attitudes are a strong indication that many Christians are poorly equipped for the task of transforming agriculture. This was brought home to me one day when I took a class on a field trip. As we were driving through the countryside, I asked the students to study the farm places we were passing by and tell me how old the farmers were. The students warmed to the task, and began to guess the ages of the residents. They looked at whether there were swing sets on the yards, motorcycles parked on the lawn, or well-worn driveways and found that they could guess the ages of the people quite accurately. I then asked the students to guess whether the residents were committed Christians or not. The student's voices quieted down as they began to look for clues. They studied the passing farm places closely, looking for things that would indicate who the resident's Lord and Master was. After several minutes, they stated that they just couldn't tell. They said that they didn't know what signs to look for; they didn't know what features in the agricultural landscape would set the believer apart from the non-believer, and they had no idea which farm belonged to a Christian and which did not.

The fact that Christians in many parts of the world produce food in the same way as their non-Christian neighbors, and don't have a clear sense of what they should be doing differently, highlights the importance of taking a serious look at food production from a distinctly Christian perspective. If Christians are to work effectively in the area of agriculture, the Christian community must begin to wrestle with what God would consider 'good' agriculture. We need to communally develop a vision, an ideal, which we can then work towards and implement. The goal of this paper is to provide some suggestions that can move us along on this journey.

How can we really know what God considers 'good' agriculture? I believe that God communicates with His people through the Bible, the book of creation, fellow Christians, and at times directly through the Holy Spirit, and that God does not hide the truth from those who search for it. As I have searched for wisdom in the area of agriculture, I have unearthed several principles that I believe can be used to help the Christian community develop a Christian vision for agriculture—an agriculture that truly brings glory to God. The first five principles apply to the Christian life in general, and set the stage for the production principles, which deal directly with agriculture.

Foundational Principles

The earth is the Lord's. The cosmos was created by God and belongs to him. Genesis 1 and 2 clearly state that God created everything, and that there is nothing here that we can call 'ours'. Psalm 24:1 says "The earth is the Lord's and everything in it, the world and all who live in it." It is all His. The land we live on is God's. The livestock and wild animals, the crops and trees, the buildings and equipment, the water, the air, the neighbors, the finances, the insects and birds; everything belongs to God (Job 41:11). People cannot own creation, and should not act as if they do. In Leviticus 25:23 God reminds the Israelites, and us, that "The land must not be sold permanently, because the land is mine and you are but aliens and my tenants." Christopher Wright's 1993 essay provides a helpful overview of this topic.

The purpose of creation is to give praise, honor, and glory to God. God clearly delights in the creatures he has made, and they give him praise and honor by living as He created them to live. Christians, therefore, are to view forests, for example, as eco-systems designed to give God praise, rather than as raw materials for the construction of houses or furniture. Understanding that all of creation gives God praise and honor and glory is fundamental to a Christian view of agriculture, and is clearly illustrated in passages such as Job 39 and Psalm 104. The real value of creation is not its human utility, but its ability to give praise, honor, and joy to God the Creator (Van Dyke, Mahan, Sheldon, & Brands, 1996, pp. 45-55)

God created people to care for, or 'shamar', His creation. Genesis 2:15 says "God took the man and put him in the Garden of Eden to work it and take care of it." The Hebrew word for 'take care of' is 'shamar', the same word used in the priestly blessing found in Numbers 6:24. In this passage the priests are told to bless God's people by saying "The Lord bless you and keep (shamar) you" … Like the rest of God's creatures, we give God praise, honor, and glory by living as He created us to live. We were created to keep creation as God keeps us. It is important to note that the word 'creation' is used in a comprehensive way in the Bible, and in the preceding sentences. Creation includes everything that God has made—rocks, people, plants, fish, bacteria, water, and everything else. Nothing is left out. Nothing is to be uncared for.

Ruling really means serving. God rules by serving His creation, and we are to rule by doing likewise. In fact, we image God by ruling as He rules. In Luke 22:25-26 Jesus says "The kings of the Gentiles lord it over them; and those who exercise authority over them call themselves Benefactors. But you are not to be like that. Instead, the greatest among you should be like the youngest, and the one who rules like the one who serves." This concept is clearly illustrated in John 10:11, where Jesus says, "I am the good shepherd. The good shepherd lays down his life for the sheep." Once we understand God's definition of ruling, we see that when God instructs Adam to rule over creation (Genesis 1:28) he is really telling Adam to serve creation. This is a critical concept, and one that Satan has worked overtime to twist and distort. This topic is addressed in detail in the book *Redeeming Creation* (Van Dyke, 1996, 89-101).

God will redeem the entire creation. After God created the cosmos, sin entered the world, breaking relationships and distorting God's good creation. God, however, didn't abandon his creation. Instead, he made plans to defeat Satan and rescue creation from the effect of sin (Genesis 3:15). God's victory over Satan will be complete and will include the entire creation. Nothing will be left out. Nothing will be left under Satan's control. God's intention to redeem all of creation is seen already in Genesis 9:9-11 where He says to Noah after the flood "I now establish my covenant with you and with your descendants after you and with every living creature that was with you ... every living creature on earth." Noah is acting as creations' representative, but the covenant is clearly with all of creation. Paul picks up on this theme in Romans 8:19-21 where he writes that "The creation waits in eager expectation for the sons of God to be revealed ... in hope that the creation itself will be liberated from its bondage to decay and brought into the glorious freedom of the children of God." The apostle John completes the picture in Revelation 21:5a where he says "He who was seated on the throne said, 'I am making everything new!'"

Because of our pivotal role in shepherding, guiding, and caring for creation, and our ability to choose good or evil, we were and are prime targets for Satan's attacks. Once he persuades creation's servant-caretakers to separate themselves from God and rule selfishly instead of serve, the creation under their care is affected as well, and the praise and honor and glory that all creation gives to God is diminished. God, however, is not willing to give up on creation, and so through his own sacrifice has made it possible for us to once again have a close relationship with him, and to function once more as his servants in this world. We are then able to see that Satan's goal is to destroy God's creation, while God is working to sustain and uphold it in all its' beauty and complexity. Our challenge is to determine how we can work with God to uphold (and in many cases restore) the beauty of creation as we do agriculture. It is my hope and prayer that the following principles will help the Christian community meet this challenge.

Production Principles

The Bible is full of seemingly impossible commands. If you and I take a close look at the ten commandments (Exodus 20:1-17) and then evaluate our lives, we quickly realize that we sin (miss the mark) each day. Jesus is even more demanding. He tells us that we are to love our enemies and pray for them, and then says that we should be perfect as our heavenly Father is perfect (Matthew 5:43-48). When we look at these commands we have a choice: we can either dismiss them as unrealistic and impossible, or we can affirm their truth and ask our Heavenly Father to help us follow them, knowing that he is willing to forgive when we fall short of his expectations. Our call as Christians involved in agriculture is to discern God's desires and intentions for this aspect of creation. His desires for us in agriculture, as in all of life, are likely to be very demanding, and perhaps even seem unrealistic and impossible. We then have a choice to make. One might even call it a crisis of faith. We can either decide that it is just too difficult to do Christian agriculture and we won't bother trying, or we can make a conscious decision to forge ahead in faith, confident that God will give us the grace to follow him in this area of life. The principles I have outlined below are certainly challenging. In fact, it is probably impossible to fully implement them in our world today. Does that reduce their value or make them useless? Definitely not—in fact, principles like these are precisely what Christians in agriculture need. We need a target, something to aim for. We need a Christian framework that we can use to critique the status quo, and we need some principles to guide us as we work to create an agriculture that truly gives praise, honor, and glory to our heavenly Father.

The list of production principles described below is not meant to be exhaustive. In the Agriculture Senior Seminar class that I currently teach, students are asked to write an essay in which they describe and support three or four Christian agricultural production principles. Collectively, the students came up with 31 distinct principles this past semester, and each of them had merit. I can't possibly cover all of that ground in this paper. My intention is to describe and support a few broad principles that I believe are particularly important in today's world, and then give some examples of agricultural practices that are consistent with these principles.

Real needs for food and fiber are met. People are called to be God's representatives on earth and image him by nurturing and caring for his entire creation. We need food, shelter, and clothing to fulfill this task. A good agricultural system will produce a sufficient supply of delicious food that promotes human health (Genesis 2:9). It will also meet societies' needs for other biological products such as clothing, building materials, and renewable energy.

God has given humans permission to eat seed-bearing plants, fruits, and anything that lives and moves (Genesis 1:29, 9:1-3). In other words, God expects us to harvest some of creation's bounty so that we can serve him here on earth. However, God also gave the birds of the air and the creatures that move on the ground every green plant for food (Genesis 1:30). It quickly becomes obvious that our food production practices must meet real needs, and not cater to our every whim and fancy. As servant-leaders we will want the rest of God's creatures to be able to meet their nutritional requirements, and we may even be called to sacrifice so that their needs are met. As Christians we need to encourage the production of staple food items rather than items for export that don't meet real needs. Current U.S. food policy, which promotes overproduction of livestock feeds, obviously runs contrary to this principle. As consumers, Christians will resist the temptation of gluttony (Proverbs 23:20-21) as it is expressed in over consumption and in the desire for excessive choice and convenience. The accumulation of unnecessary material possessions, such as large houses and multiple vehicles, each of which is ultimately obtained from creation, also runs contrary to this principle and is frequently condemned in Scripture (1 Timothy 6:3-10). God intended the production of human food and other biological products to be done in a way which meets human needs and simultaneously encourages all of creation, both human and nonhuman, to flourish.

Our family lived in Nigeria from 1986 to 1989, while I managed a large Nigerian farm. Many of our Nigerian friends followed this principle to a large extent, but for most it was a matter of necessity, and was not a conscious choice. Few North Americans choose to produce or purchase food that meets real needs, but the increasing interest in seasonal, locally produced foods in North America and Europe is an important exception (Gussow, 2002). The growing popularity of food production and distribution via community supported agriculture organizations (CSA's) is an encouraging development, and one that Christians can enthusiastically support.

Diversity is valued. Agriculture designed to give praise and honor to the Creator will be diverse. It will exhibit diversity within crop and livestock species (genetic diversity), involve many different species (species diversity), be composed of different assemblages of organisms from one region of the world to the next (ecosystem diversity), involve people with different backgrounds and traditions (cultural diversity), and it will change from year to year (diversity through time).

God clearly delights in diversity. According to Genesis 1:20-22, God created a world teeming with creatures, and then pronounced it 'good'. The account of Noah illustrates God's desire to maintain the diversity that he created. It would have been much easier for Noah to build a boat for just a few of the species, but he was commanded to provide space for all of God's creatures (Genesis 6:11-22).

The book of creation also provides strong support for this principle. God has made this world so that there is genetic diversity within each species; with few exceptions, each individual organism is unique. God created many different species, each of which fills a specific role in the ecosystem in which God placed it and called it to flourish. The plants, animals, microbes, and physical environments that make up ecosystems also show incredible diversity, so that no two landscapes are identical. People and people groups (cultures) are amazingly diverse. In addition, landscapes are continually changing, creating diversity over time. A couple of specific examples clearly illustrate the astonishing diversity that God has created on earth. Beetles are incredibly rich in species diversity. To date, researchers have identified about 400,000 species of beetles, and they estimate that there may be up to 30 million species still unidentified (Erwin, 1991). Bacteria are probably even more diverse. Several Norwegian scientists collected one-gram soil samples from two different environments, and estimated that each sample contained 4,000 different species of bacteria (Torsvik, Goksoyr, & Daae, 1990; Torsvik, Salte, Sorheim, & Goksoyr, 1990).

Farmers have applied this principle for generations to minimize risk, adapt food production to the specific piece of land that they farm, and keep their diets and production systems interesting. Today, however, industrialization and globalization are exerting tremendous pressure on producers to abandon this principle and adopt standardized farming practices producing genetically uniform products for a mass market. For example, plant breeders select for widely adapted cultivars that can be marketed to a large geographical area, egg production in North America is controlled by a handful of companies desiring uniform eggs, and in the less industrialized countries one banana cultivar makes up the bulk of exported bananas. Diversity definitely runs counter to agricultural trends in both industrialized and less industrialized countries today, and it is a challenge to put this principle into practice.

Stephen Gliessman, in his 1998 book, *Agroecology—Ecological Processes in Sustainable Agriculture*, does an excellent job of defining and describing agricultural diversity, and provides some practical strategies for increasing diversity in agroecosystems. He mentions strategies such intercropping, multiple cropping, strip cropping, cover cropping, alley cropping, using border plantings, reducing tillage and chemical use, and employing complex crop rotations. Additional opportunities for increasing diversity include the use of genetically diverse plant and animal cultivars, production of heirloom or specialty food products, and the maintenance of plant and animal gene pools unique to specific communities (land races).

God-given characteristics are celebrated. God has given each living organism on earth a unique set of characteristics, and a unique role to play in his creation. Christian caretakers recognize and celebrate these distinct characteristics. They take joy in seeing each of God's creatures living as God designed them to. Chickens, for example, were designed by God to obtain their food by foraging for young plants, seeds and insects. They are also created to form social relationships, to mate, to nest, and to raise their young. Christians are called to recognize these characteristics, recognize their value in giving glory and praise to God the Creator, and celebrate them in the way in which they manage poultry production. Recognizing and celebrating the amazing characteristics and abilities that God has given to chickens, pigs, cattle, goats, sunflowers, strawberries, and all other organisms harvested by humans is fundamental to a Christian view of agriculture (Hoezee, 1998).

God clearly takes joy in seeing his creatures live as he created them to. This is particularly obvious in the book of Job. In Job 39:1-4 God says, "Do you know when the mountain goats give birth? Do you watch when the doe bears her fawn? Do you count the months till they bear? Do you know the time they give birth? They crouch down and bring forth their young; their labor pains are ended. Their young thrive and grow strong in the wilds; they leave and do not return." There is much about creation that Job does not understand, but God sees it all and enjoys watching his creatures. This perspective clashes head-on with most people's view of creation. As sinful people we tend to put our desires first, and we often treat plants and animals as food production machines rather than as God's creatures; creatures that he has lovingly fashioned and continually watches over (Matthew 10:29). The industrialized poultry, swine, and row crop production practices common in North America are prime examples of a failure to recognize and practice this principle. Loren Wilkenson gave a graphic description of the end result of this approach in a lecture he gave at Dordt College in the late 90s. He said that if we view pigs simply as protein producing machines, then they really don't need to be able to hear, see, reproduce naturally, or even walk. If protein is the only goal, then a 'pig' that reproduces asexually and is little more than a blob of protein with the ability to take in nutrients and convert them efficiently to meat will be the end product. I don't think any of us want to end up there, but that is where a human-centered worldview will end up taking us.

As difficult as it may seem to follow this principle, there are some farmers who take it seriously, and have tried to design their production systems in a way that encourages animals to function as God intended. In his book, *You Can Farm*, Joel Salatin describes how he makes use of the natural rooting and feeding activities of hogs to turn his compost pile, and how he allows chickens to forage for dropped fruit and debug his garden (Salatin, 1998, pp. 265-280). *The Power of Duck* (2001) by Takao Furuno describes a fascinating duck and rice production system in which the ducks' natural swimming and feeding activity is promoted, and has positive effects on the rice. Management intensive grazing for cattle and Swedish farrowing systems for hogs are also practices that are in tune with this principle.

Environmental quality is maintained and/or restored. This is a broad principle, and applies to many aspects of agriculture. In order to follow this principle, agricultural practices need to maintain ground and surface water quality, soil organic matter levels, and topsoil depth. But that is just the beginning. They should also maintain air quality, and not contribute to (or perhaps even mitigate) the buildup of greenhouse gases in the atmosphere. Agricultural chemicals (pesticides, antibiotics, fertilizers, fuels, lubricants, and others) need to be environmentally safe. The equipment, buildings, and facilities used in agriculture need to be recyclable, and energy should come from current sources (solar, wind, biomass, etc). Nutrient cycles need to be closed, maintaining adequate nutrient concentrations in agricultural areas, and preventing the buildup of nutrients in other regions (typically those with high human and livestock populations).

This production principle is based squarely on the foundational principles of care for creation and ruling as service, which were outlined previously in this paper. At its core, it is the living out of Jesus' summary of the law. In Matthew 22:37-40, Jesus says "Love the Lord your God with all your heart and with all your soul and with all your mind. This is the first and greatest commandment. And the second is like it: Love your neighbor as yourself. All the Law and the Prophets hang on these two commandments." If we truly love God above all, we won't degrade or destroy what he has made, and if we love our neighbors, both present and future, we won't endanger their health or diminish the beauty and wonder of their future home.

Current agricultural trends are a mixed bag when it comes to following this principle. Soil erosion rates in North America have declined with the widespread adoption of conservation tillage practices, but we are becoming increasingly aware of the water quality problems associated with the leakage of pesticides and nutrients from agricultural land into surface and ground water (Carpenter, S., et al., 1998; U.S. Geological Survey, 1996). Cropping practices in both the industrialized and less industrialized countries of the world have reduced soil organic matter and soil quality. Agriculture in less industrialized countries still makes relatively good use of current energy sources in the form of human labor and animal traction, but agriculture in the industrialized countries depends heavily on fossil fuels. Most industrialized countries contributed substantially to the global concentration of greenhouse gases when they removed the natural vegetation and replaced it with annual crops, and the same thing is happening in many less industrialized nations today. The massive regional and global movement of staple food sources such as rice, corn, soybeans, and wheat results in open nutrient cycles and the accumulation of nutrients in some regions of the world and the depletion of nutrients in others. It is also heavily dependent on fossil fuels.

The development of local food production and distribution systems has the potential to alleviate some of the nutrient cycling and fossil fuel consumption problems, and is being advocated by Iowa's Leopold Center for Sustainable Agriculture (Pirog, Van Pelt, Enshayan, and Cook, 2001), among others. The ideals of organic agriculture also fit well with the principle of maintaining and/or enhancing environmental health. According to the 2001 OCIA International Certification Standards (p. 9), certified organic producers are required to develop and implement "a conscientious soil-building program designed to enhance organic matter and encourage optimum soil health."

Natural ecosystems and wild creatures are cared for. As Christians, called to be caretakers of God's creation, we are to value and care for the native plants, animals, insects, fish, fungi, and eco-systems that God created. This means that agriculture needs to be done in a way that enables us to meet our needs without destroying the integrity and beauty of the creation. We are called to work with God to enable all of creation to flourish. God expects our agricultural practices to work in harmony with the nonhuman creation. In order to do this, we need to become familiar with the native plants and animals that God has placed in our communities. We must learn their names, find out what they eat, and begin to understand how they interact with the rest of God's creatures. If we are to succeed in our task we will need to set aside some areas for non-domesticated species, but that is not enough. We also must manage agricultural landscapes for the benefit of 'wild' plants, birds, animals, insects, microbes, and other creatures. We need to rule by simultaneously serving the nonhuman creation and our neighbors.

As Christians, we are to view natural ecosystems and the plants, animals, and other organisms that God has placed there, as a sacred trust. God made them, repeatedly called them good (Genesis 1), and then instructed us to care for them as he cares for us. For Christians, the value of God's creation is not left to human discretion or the market economy. It is assigned by God, and based on the joy, praise, and honor that it gives to him. In Genesis 2:16 God gives people permission to eat of the fruit of the land. However, He never gives humans permission to destroy or obliterate his creation in their attempts to feed themselves. That is the prerogative of the owner of creation, not its tenants. Instead, he commands Adam to name all the creatures (Genesis 2:19-20). God had Adam name the creatures because Adam couldn't care for what he didn't know. Christians in agriculture are called to know, value, and care for 'wild' ecosystems and creatures, just as they know, value, and care for the parts of the landscape that produce harvestable goods. We image God by valuing what he values and caring for what he cares for.

Another challenging principle! One of the effects of sin is that it sometimes leaves us with only poor choices. In much of Asia, parts of Africa, and other parts of the world, poor social and economic policies, cultural traditions and other factors have lead to such high human population densities that meeting human nutritional needs is difficult, let alone meeting the needs of the non-human creation. Christians working in such areas are forced to focus on meeting people's short-term nutritional needs. In many parts of the world, however, there are good opportunities to live out this principle. Where land is being converted from wildlife habitat to agricultural use, we can push for restricted development and the establishment of conservation areas. Christian farmers in the U.S. can, and do, put land in the conservation reserve program. They can also manage their harvested land in ways that benefit wildlife and native species (Jackson and Jackson, 2002). Even city dwellers can manage their small lots with an eye for creation care (Wilkinson and Wilkinson, 1997). Finally, we can support conservation organizations like the Nature Conservancy (2002) that are identifying and preserving endangered ecosystems and using easements and other creative approaches that enable farmers to receive financial compensation for managing agricultural land in ways that benefit native species.

Creation as a model. This principle is simple and straightforward, but powerful enough to completely change the way we look at agriculture and natural ecosystems. The central idea is that the plants and animals God placed in a particular location are well adapted to the physical and climatic conditions of that environment, and therefore are a good indication of the type of plants and animals best suited to the area. It follows that this assemblage of species also illustrates important ecosystem functions and processes. The natural ecosystem in a given area of the world, then, becomes the model for the structure and function of a good agroecosystem in that part of the world. When this principle is put into practice, farmers may conclude that the best way to do agriculture in some areas is to leave the ecosystem essentially intact and simply harvest a portion of its production for human use. In other situations farmers may find it necessary to mimic the structure and function of the natural ecosystem using domesticated species. The latter strategy has been described in some detail for both forest (Ewel, 1986) and prairie ecosystems (Jackson, 1985, 93-115).

As Christians we need to learn from, and value, what God reveals to us through his creation. Psalm 19:1-4 says "The heavens declare the glory of God; the skies proclaim the work of his hands. Day after day they pour forth speech; night after night they display knowledge. There is no speech or language where their voice is not heard. Their voice goes out into all the earth, their words to the ends of the world." Paul echoes these words when he writes in Romans 1:20 "For since the creation of the world God's invisible qualities—his eternal power and divine nature—have been clearly seen, being understood from what has been made, so that men are without excuse." The Psalmist and Paul both understood that creation not only testifies to God's existence, it also helps us to understand him better. When we have eyes to see and ears to hear, (Matthew 13:10-17, 43) pasque flowers and plains bison have much to tell us about their maker. On a broader scale, we need to understand that God is inviting us to study his creation, learn from it, and model our agroecosystems after the ecosystems the he himself has lovingly fashioned. In reality, natural ecosystems are blueprints for truly good agriculture, printed on the landscape and custom-designed by God himself for each square inch of his creation.

Following these blueprints takes work. The first step is learning to read them. We have to become biologically literate and learn the plant and animal species native to our area, and how they interact. In many cases, ecologists have already done this basic work and a trip to the library or bookstore can be very helpful. The second step in the process is to take a good hard look at the human population in the region, and determine what sorts of products we really need to produce. Are carbohydrates in short supply? Do people need a dependable protein source, certain vitamins, raw materials for clothing, building supplies, fuel for cooking? Once we understand how the ecosystem functions and what the communities needs are, we can begin to assemble the necessary species to create a productive, diverse, agroecosystem that mimics natural ecosystem structure and function, maintains environmental quality, and enables us to care for the native creatures that are a part of the landscape. Given the limits of human understanding, our initial attempts at agroecosystem design are likely to leave room for improvement, and the final step in the implementation process is ongoing research, testing, and modification.

The basic concept of using nature as a model for agroecosystem design has been promoted for more than twenty years by Wes Jackson and others at the Land Institute in Salina, Kansas (Jackson, 1985). Dr. Jackson and his colleagues have focused on designing a perennial polyculture of seed-producing plants, patterned after the prairie ecosystem native to central Kansas. Although a long-term project, efforts such as this certainly deserve our support. Bill Mollison, the founder of the permaculture movement, has been promoting agricultural systems based on natural patterns since the 1970's, and has written several books on the topic (Mollison, 1988). On a more modest scale, many people in agriculture have the opportunity to implement some aspects of this principle right now. Getting to know the plants and animals God originally placed in a given area is often just a matter of picking up a guide to wild flowers, birds, trees, or mammals, and then actually 'seeing' these species when you run across them. Most of us have a pretty good idea of what people in our community need, but economic policy, social constraints, or simply fear of change keep us from adjusting our production practices. As a general rule, native ecosystems are dominated by perennial plants, and agroecosystems are dominated by annual plants. This major structural and functional change typically results in reduced environmental quality and diversity in agroecosystems. In North America, producers might look for ways to incorporate perennial forage crops into their rotation as one way to live out this principle. In less industrialized countries with diverse agricultural systems, there are often many opportunities to incorporate tree, shrub, or vine crops into the production system, and capture some of the environmental benefits of perennial systems. As with the other principles, we need to be constantly looking for ways to implement this principle, and then take advantage of the opportunities that God brings our way.

It is my prayer that we will communally accept our Heavenly Father's invitation to join with him in caring for all of creation as we do agriculture. If we are willing follow the blueprint that God has outlined in the Bible and embedded in creation, we can develop a truly Christian vision for agriculture, and begin to create a system that meets our needs, is diverse, celebrates the unique characteristics of each of God's creatures, maintains environmental quality, and enables us to preserve the beauty and integrity of God's handiwork.

References

Carpenter, S., N.F. Caraco, D.L. Correll, R.W. Howarth, A.N. Sharpley, and V.H. Smith
   1998   "Nonpoint Pollution of Surface Waters with Phosphorous and Nitrogen." *Issues in Ecology*, 3, 1-11.

Erwin, T.L.
   1991   "How Many Species Are There?: Revisited." *Conservation Biology*, 5, 330-333.

Ewel, J.J.
   1986   "Designing Agricultural Ecosystems for the Humid Tropics." *Ann. Rev. Ecol. Syst.*, 17, 245-271.

Furuno, Takao
   2001   *The Power of Duck—Integrated Rice and Duck Farming.* Tasmania, Australia: Tagari Publications.

Gliessman, S.R.
   1998   "Agroecosystem Diversity and Stability." In *Agroecology—Ecological Processes in Sustainable Agriculture* (pp. 227-247). Chelsea, MI: Ann Arbor Press.

Gussow, J.
   2002   "Home Foods." *Mother Earth News*, 191, 68.

Hoezee, S.
   1998   "Bearing God's Image in the Creation." In *Remember Creation—God's World of Wonder and Delight* (pp. 61-73). Grand Rapids: Eerdmans.

Jackson, D.L. and L.L. Jackson
   2002   *The Farm as Natural Habitat.* Washington: Island Press.

Jackson, W.
   1985   *New Roots for Agriculture.* Lincoln, NE: University of Nebraska Press.

Mollison, Bill
   1988   *Permaculture: A Designer's Manual.* Tasmania: Australia: Tagari Publications.

Organic Crop Improvement Association International, Inc.
   2001   International Certification Standards. Lincoln, NE.

Pirog, R., T. Van Pelt, K. Enshayan, E. Cook
  2001   "Food, Fuel, and Freeways: An Iowa Perspective on How Far Food Travels, Fuel Usage, and Greenhouse Gas Emissions" [On-line, June]. Leopold Center for Sustainable Agriculture, Ames, IA. Available WWW: http://www.leopold.iastate.edu

Salatin, J.
  1998   *You Can Farm.* Swoope, Virginia: Polyface, Inc.

The Nature Conservancy
  2002   [On-line]. Available WWW: http://nature.org/

Torsvik, V., J. Goksoyr, and F. Daae
  1990   "High Diversity in DNA of Soil Bacteria." *Applied and Environmental Microbiology*, 56, 782-787.

Torsvik, V., K. Salte, , R. Sorheim, , and J. Goksoyr
  1990   "Comparison of Phenotypic Diversity and Dna Heterogeneity in a Population of Soil Bacteria." *Applied and Environmental Microbiology*, 56, 782-787.

USDA
  2001   The Alternative Farming Systems Information Center [On-line, December]. Available WWW: http://www.nal.usda.gov/afsic/csa/

U.S. Geological Survey
  1996   "Pesticides in Ground Water." U.S. Geological Survey Fact Sheet FS-244-95. U.S. Government Printing Office.

Van Dyke, F., D.C. Mahan, J.K Sheldon, and H.B. Raymond
  1996   *Redeeming Creation—The Biblical Basis for Environmental Stewardship.* Downers Grove, IL: InterVarsity Press.

Wilkinson, L. and M. Wilkinson,
  1997   *Caring for Creation in Your Own Backyard.* Vancouver, BC: Regent College Publishing.

Wright, C.
  1993   "Biblical Reflections on Land." *Evangelical Review of Theology*, 17, 153-167.

Enabling Creation's Praise:
Lessons in Agricultural Stewardship from Africa

Harry Spaling

Introduction

Biblical stewardship is not fundamentally about caring for creation for the purpose of meeting human needs such as food, clothing, shelter and livelihoods. This inverted view accepts humans as the object of stewardship, placing creation in a subservient role. In contrast, biocentricism, an increasingly popular ethic embedded in most environmental education curricula today, presumes nature is at the center and that humans are to preserve it. Both anthropocentric and biocentric understandings of human-nature relationships are objectionable from a biblical perspective. The scriptures teach that the Creator is the first and foremost object of stewardship. All of creation, including humankind, is to praise and worship the Creator. Stewardship is a divine mandate to humans to care for creation in such a way that the Creator is acclaimed, revealed and glorified. This basic premise underlies a biblical framework for understanding the relationship between agriculture and creation.

Human cultures also have sources of knowledge and insight about God, humanity and nature that may enrich the biblical notion of stewardship. For example, holism is embedded in most African cultures. The spiritual and physical dimensions of reality are intertwined, with fluid boundaries between them. Africans generally view life religiously where all phenomena are associated with God, and humans and nature interact materially and spiritually. God, humanity and creation are integrally connected. Tellingly, the term "environment" has no direct translation in many African languages because to distinguish it is to separate it from life (Gitau 2000).

African holism is also under threat. The dualism of western thought has infiltrated most African development policies and practice, which now shun the spiritual realm. Individualism is promoting material accumulation for a few self-interested African elite and eroding communal mechanisms for more equitable distribution of wealth. Globalism based on economic, political and institutional monism is displacing the rich cultural diversity of the continent. African holism is even threatened by Christian missions, especially evangelicalism, focused primarily and often exclusively on spirituality and personal piety. This skewed gospel message has seriously weakened a Christian communal response to widespread poverty, injustice, poor governance and environmental degradation in Africa (Kinoti 1997). These forces have generated considerable interest in rediscovering traditional African wisdom of holism, including within Christian thinking.

This chapter explores biblical teachings and traditional African wisdom about creation in order to develop a set of principles for agricultural stewardship. The paper begins with a typology of perspectives on the relationship between agriculture and nature, outlines a biblical framework for stewardship, describes traditional creation wisdom of the Kikuyu and Masai peoples of Kenya, and demonstrates principles for agricultural stewardship with brief cases from Africa.

Agriculture-nature Relationships

Humanity's relationship with nature is clearly manifested through agriculture. The way in which agriculture transforms abiotic and biotic resources into food and fiber reveals significant insight into how humans view nature and relate to it. This relationship may be understood from three perspectives.

Nature as Storehouse

The first sees nature as subservient to the needs of agriculture. Sunlight, water and soil may be freely used, and plants and animals readily domesticated, for agricultural production. Resources with high agricultural productive potential (fertile land, high-yielding varieties, fast-growing breeds) are selected and continuously improved through technological or genetic manipulation. Creation is viewed as a vast storehouse supplying the increasing demands of a global, industrial agricultural system.

This is the prevailing agricultural ethic of western society. It is predicated on the commodification of resources, especially land but increasingly also genetically modified organisms. The value of a resource is determined by its utility for agriculture. Resource value, expressed as a price, is set by an exchange between buyer and seller in the market. Transfer of ownership and property rights is presumed in the exchange. National policies (liberalization) and global institutions (World Trade Organization) rigidly protect commodification and ownership of resources.

Nature and Agriculture in Equilibrium

An equilibrium perspective acknowledges that agriculture is dependent on the continual provisions of nature. Thresholds in biophysical systems are explicitly recognized and even managed to maintain productive capacity (soil fertility, moisture, crop rotation). The aim is sustained rather than maximum production. An example is shifting cultivation practiced by subsistence farmers in many African countries. Farmers typically clear a small plot, grow crops for two or three years, usually by intercropping, and then abandon the site for several decades, allowing natural revegetation to replenish soil fertility. Traditionally, shifting cultivation balanced intense land use for a short period with long-term nutrient replenishment. However, population pressure and production-oriented agricultural policies have reduced the length of the fallow period in many systems, resulting in shorter cycles and increased environmental stress (depleted nutrients, soil erosion). Other systems that traditionally balance resource use include pastoralism, ranching and mixed farming.

An equilibrium perspective is apparent in contemporary notions such as sustainable agriculture, organic farming and agroforestry. This view recognizes the limits of natural systems and adapts agricultural systems to accommodate them. Agriculture and nature are regarded as a partnership, each taking from and giving to the other (Ebenreck 1983).

Nature in Control

A third view accepts nature as the dominant force. Agriculture is fully dependent on nature's provisions and ultimately controlled by them. Exceeding the capacity of natural systems degrades the resource base, adversely affecting agricultural productivity. For example, continuous cropping may decrease soil fertility, monoculture may increase pest populations, overgrazing may contribute to desertification and global climate change is likely to impact where and how farming is practiced in the future. In all these examples, natural forces constrain agriculture. These forces even have the potential of destroying entire agriculture systems (Mesopotamia). This perspective, rooted in radical biocentricism holds that nature is all-powerful and in control and that humans are subject to it.

Valid but Limited Perspectives

The three perspectives are not mutually exclusive. A production system at the farm, regional or national scale may manifest any of the three views over time. For example, a farm may practice intensive agriculture (storehouse perspective), periodically take land out of production due to low commodity prices or adopt soil conservation measures in response to public policy (equilibrium perspective), and occasionally experience drought (control perspective). In reality, farmers trade-off the three perspectives in their pursuit of the multiple goals of maintaining economic viability, managing the resource base and adapting to extreme natural events. These trade-offs are legitimate realities of daily agriculture.

More fundamentally, each perspective is a recognized and integral part of a larger whole. Each plays a valid and important role in shaping the overall agriculture-nature dynamic:

1. The storehouse view acknowledges the availability of natural resources for the production of life-sustaining food,
2. The equilibrium perspective restricts exploitation of the resource base upon which agriculture depends, emphasizing management and conservation of resources, and
3. The control view recognizes the limits and potential hazards of natural systems.

Notwithstanding the contributions of each perspective, there are two conceptual problems. First, there is a risk that one perspective will dominate the others. This is a problem because the dominant perspective may become the normative framework for trade-offs, skewing farm decisions. For example, the storehouse perspective dominating industrial agriculture has contributed to resource degradation that has adversely affected the viability of some farming systems (wind erosion during the dust-bowl thirties, salinization from irrigation, depletion of the Ogallala Aquifer). Thus, the whole is at risk from one of the parts.

A second problem is that each perspective is ultimately self-serving. The storehouse perspective views nature as subservient to agriculture. Anthropocentrism and utilitarianism permeate this view. In contrast, nature is served in the control perspective, reflecting biocentrism. The equilibrium view tries to serve both humans and nature based on its assumption of ontological unity. These perspectives are self-serving because relationships are confined to the human-nature realm, which is presumed to be merely biophysical.

An alternative is to develop an integral perspective based on biblical norms. This means that neither humans nor nature determines the norms for the other; only God as Creator does. These norms include acknowledging a divine Creator; realizing praise is the primary function of creation, and recognizing humans as stewards of creation on the Creator's behalf. Normative claims based on scripture radically alter the structure and purpose of an agriculture-nature relationship, re-directing it toward biblical holism.

A Biblical Framework for Stewardship

The biblical framework for stewardship proposed here builds on the triangular model of Creator, creature (humans) and creation (non-humans) by characterizing six reciprocal relationships (the 6 S's). The Creator-creation relationship is defined by God "sustaining" creation (Col. 1:17, Is. 27:3) and the creation responding in "song" (Ps. 96, 98, 148). God knows his creation intimately (Ps. 50:10-11) and extends to it his loving care (Matt. 6:26).

God created humans uniquely in his own image on the "sixth day" (Gen. 1:26-27, Ps 8) and humans "serve" in obedience (Heb. 9:14), exemplifying the Creator-creature relationship. Humans occupy a special position in the created order (Ps. 8:5-8).

The creature-creation linkage is defined by "stewardship" (Gen. 2:15), which is a call to manage the praise-ability of creation that, if faithfully exercised, results in creation's abundant "sustenance" or provision for humankind (Lev. 26:3-5). Stewardship is a delegated responsibility with authority limited by divine ownership (Ps. 24:1, Jer. 27:5). Humans may enjoy the fruits of creation but may not destroy its fruitfulness (*shamir* in Hebrew) (Deut. 22:6). This biblical edict is applicable to all primary production systems (agriculture, forestry, fisheries).

Human sin has distorted these relationships, alienating humanity and creation from each other and from the Creator. Humans are no longer welcome in the Creator's presence as symbolized in the expulsion from the Garden (Gen. 3:23). Humanity and creation are now in tension. Creation yields its provisions reluctantly, requiring great human toil, only for humans to end up in creation's dustbin (Gen. 3:17-19). God even altered his own relationship with creation by cursing the ground, wild and domestic animals, and plants (Gen. 3:14, 17-18).

Like humanity, an alienated creation longs to be redeemed (Rom. 8:20-22). Biblical evidence shows that God is actively restoring relationships among himself, humanity and creation. A land covenant with Abraham promised creation's blessings of milk and honey (Gen. 17:8, Ex. 3:8). An ecological covenant after the flood pledges life to not only Noah but to all creatures (Gen. 9: 8-17). In the New Testament, many of Jesus' parables have agrarian themes that emphasize stewardship. For example, God is depicted as an absent landlord who hands over his vineyard to stewards that subsequently abuse their delegated responsibility (Lk. 20:9-16).

Jesus' earthly life of humility and contentment model a way of life for faithful stewards that should thwart materialistic resource consumption and imitate God's love for creation.

Redemption is finally promised through Jesus Christ who is Creator, Sustainer and Redeemer. Christ created all things (Creator), sustains the entire cosmos (Sustainer) and, through his death and resurrection, will redeem the whole creation (Redeemer) (Col. 1:15-17, 20). Ultimately, God will dwell again with his people in the new creation, where all relationships will be restored (Rev. 21:1-3). In anticipation of this final redemption, God's people are to proclaim and bring about Christ's Kingdom in all areas of life, including agriculture.

These biblical teachings about creation have several implications for agriculture. At its most basic level, agriculture involves the transformation of creation's resources into life-sustaining food and fiber (growing tobacco or crops for illicit drugs fall outside this norm). Cultivating plants and tending animals are clear expressions of the cultural mandate (Gen. 1:28-29). God is pleased with a diverse, flourishing creation that provides sustenance for humanity (DeWitt 1995).

Stewardship in agriculture means transforming creation for human benefit in such a way that the Creator is praised. This occurs in two ways. First, God is praised when humans transform the productive resources of creation into daily nourishment. Second, praise emanates from the creation itself, independent of any human alteration. Beams of sunlight, the water and carbon cycles, soil formation, photosynthesis and reproducing animals all praise the Creator directly. The elements and processes of creation have inherent worth. Agricultural stewardship entails developing and preserving the praise-giving task of creation. This is the ultimate measure of faithful stewardship.

Creation discloses the Creator. Agricultural activities that indiscriminately destroy or degrade creation shroud the Creator and tarnish his character as Creator, Sustainer and Redeemer. Destroying a species or exploiting a resource is, metaphorically, like tearing out a page of scripture (UCS 1996). All elements of creation give praise. Agriculture must protect the gifts of creation as a source of God's revelation. Just as creation leads humans to God, so should humans enable creation to praise its Creator.

This biblical framework for stewardship is enriched by traditional African wisdom.

African Contributions to Stewardship

> "Christians need to understand and appreciate the African spirituality which views life in its totality for proper stewardship towards nature – where all creatures are meant to live having positive influences on each other." (Gitau 2000: 162)

As a non-African, I am severely handicapped for this section. I am gratefully indebted to Samson K. Gitau, whose work proposes an African Christian theology of nature based on a synthesis of traditional values of the Kikuyu and Masai peoples, and biblical teachings on creation. African contributions to stewardship are discussed below with particular reference to the conceptions of God, humanity and nature among the Kikuyu (agriculturists) and Masai (pastoralists) peoples of Kenya (Gitau 2000).

Kikuyu and Masai Perspectives

Both the Kikuyu and Masai claim that God is Creator of all things. God is divine, distinct from the created elements and more powerful than creation or humans. Kikuyu names for God include *Ngai* (to distribute), *Nyaga* (brightness, referring to Mt. Kenya) and *Nyene* (owner of all). Masai names for God include *Enkai* (unseen one) and *Enkai Narok* (black God—from dark clouds that bring rain and life). God is the source of all that exists for both groups. God is omnipresent in creation and manifested in it, especially in sacred places such as Mt. Kenya and dark clouds, but these are not worshipped as deities; only God is divine.

Africans are acutely aware that humans depend on God for essentials of life. As agriculturists, the Kikuyu know that the Creator sends rain, makes crops grow and gives grass to cattle. The pastoral Masai believe that God gave them all the cattle in the world and that, as primary custodians their right to cattle supercedes that of all other cultures. Cattle are loved, provide the basics of life and are central to Masai culture. Both groups believe that the Creator is continuously active in his creation providing for human needs.

Creation is seen as God-given. It belongs to God but is a gift to humans. Unlike western culture, where giving gifts is a one-way relationship from giver to receiver, African gift giving implies a reciprocal relationship, indebting the receiver back to the giver. Thus, the gift of creation to humanity includes obligations. Land is a gift to the Kikuyu farmers that must be cared for. Cattle are a gift to the Masai, which are tended lovingly.

Both groups viewed humans as part of creation, not masters of it. Traditional Kikuyu agriculture and Masai pastoralism represented a relatively stable balance with nature. Farming and grazing co-existed with natural areas. Kikuyu sacred places (Mt. Kenya) helped to conserve ecosites that provided micro-climates, protected habitat for flora and fauna, and isolated catchment areas for water supply. Indigenous knowledge of land, plants and animals was very important to Masai under-standing of a balance between humans and nature. Young Masai boys may know 20 varieties of grass, but not even know their grandmother's name. Unfortunately, traditional Masai knowledge is being eroded because of an "ecological apart-heid" that has evicted the Masai from game reserves. Ironically, this is to let in tourists who impact these fragile ecosystems to a much higher degree through development of infrastructure (road, hotels) and services (waste disposal, game drives) (after Mbiti 1969 in Gitau 2000 p. 123).

African Wisdom and the Scriptures

Traditional African conceptions of God, humanity and creation are remarkably similar to those of the ancient Israelites—a divine Creator is the source of all that exists, God's presence is manifested in specific elements of creation (Mt. Sinai and Mt. Kenya, burning bush and sacred trees), and rituals, ceremonies and sacrifices that involve elements of creation. This does not idealize traditional Kikuyu or Masai relationships with nature. In fact, bush and grass fires, used by both cultures to clear land and rejuvenate grasses, sometimes burned out of control destroying huge areas. From a bib-lical viewpoint, notions of redemption and eschatology are absent from each culture. However, traditional African wisdom and biblical perspectives intersect at several points:

1. Both confess a divine Creator who is distinct from, but in relationship with, humanity and creation. The Creator sustains creation and humanity.

2. Humans are unique in, but also part of, creation. The biblical account of God creating humans on the sixth day parallels many traditional narratives that tell of a distinct origin for humanity. However, uniqueness in the created order does not separate human beings from it. Scriptures teach that humans depend on creation's provisions and are to serve (abad in Hebrew) it on behalf of the Creator. African wisdom views humanity as a partner with nature, striving to live in harmony with it.

3. Creation is a gift from God. Its provisions are God's blessings for his people. Like God's other gifts (grace, mercy, forgiveness), the gift of creation is also an invitation to a relationship. The wisdom of African gift giving parallels the biblical idea.

4. The Bible and African wisdom teach that God is revealed through nature. Both acknowledge sacred places (Mt. Sinai, Mt. Kenya) and interpret natural phenomena as metaphors for God's presence (thunder, burning bush, fig trees) but neither apply divine or moral status to nature.

5. The African perspective on humans in community resonates with biblical views of social relations. This perspective includes hospitality, social equity and communal ownership of natural resources (land, water, forests). Traditional wisdom viewed wealth as being important not for its production but its distribution, emphasizing the meeting of basic needs and communal security (Gitau 2000). This focus on the collective good echoes the biblical principles of justice and contentment and provides a social basis for communal care of creation.

In summary, traditional African views on God, humanity and nature are not all useful or even biblical, but there is sufficient wisdom to help formulate principles for agricultural stewardship.

"If we are to develop a realistic, praxis-oriented Christian ethic aimed at the liberation of nature/creation, *we have to probe the wisdom of Africa, and seek the intuition that has lain at the roots of earthkeeping in African traditional religion and philosophy all along.*" (Daneel 1991: 100, italics in original)

Applied Principles for Agricultural Stewardship

The above biblical framework and traditional African wisdom are used to develop a set of principles for agricultural stewardship. These are focused at the farm level since producers are the primary transformers of resources. Some attention is also given to structural justice and security, especially as these relate to stewardship. Each principle is illustrated with a brief narrative from Africa.

1. Diverse, flourishing agricultural landscapes give praise to the Creator (Gen. 1:28, 29).

Variations in rainfall, temperature, elevation, soils, plants and animals have resulted in an amazing variety of farming systems. God loves this agri-cultural diversity. God is pleased when human culture and the resources of creation are transformed in an integrated way, each affecting and developing the other.

An example is Machakos District, a semi-arid region of eastern Kenya that has been transformed into a diverse, productive landscape by local soil and water conservation practices (Mortimore 1998, Tiffen et al. 1994). Annual rainfall averages about 700 mm, much of it lost to runoff and evaporation. The District has experienced 90 seasonal droughts during the last century, many for two or more consecutive seasons (Hughes 1999). Soils are nutrient deficient and easily eroded. In the 1930s, a British colonial report concluded, "every phase of misuse of land is vividly and poignantly displayed in this Reserve, the inhabitants of which are rapidly drifting to a state of hopeless and miserable poverty and their land to a parching of desert, stones and sand (Maher 1937 quoted in Mortimore 1998, p. 162). Since then population has increased more than six times.

Despite limited rainfall, recurring droughts, poor soils and population growth, the District has achieved remarkable agricultural potential. This is primarily attributable to water conserva-

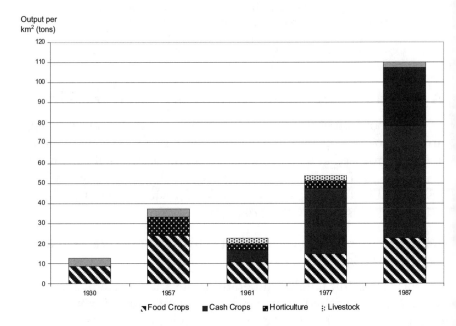

tion practices, especially bench terraces constructed by throwing the soil up slope (*funya juu* in Kiswahili). These reduce runoff, increase infiltration and trap eroded sediment, resulting in improved yields of maize, the staple, and market crops such as coffee and vegetables, especially in drier years. Terracing gradually replaced shifting cultivation. A key social factor behind its success was the use of traditional work groups (*mwethya* in Kiswahili), which rotated pooled labor among individual farms. Other on-farm innovations included plowing with oxen, using manure for soil fertility management, harvesting fodder in place of free grazing, and tree farming for fuelwood and fruit sales.

Farm output has increased significantly even though the amount of arable land per person has declined with population growth and inheritance has decreased farm size. Since the negative colonial assessment, the farmers of Machakos have reversed trends in land degradation, intensified agricultural production and created a sustainable rural landscape. Agricultural systems that conserve the resources of creation, use cultural management practices and intensify production for human needs honor and praise the Creator.

2. Enjoy the fruits of creation but do not destroy its fruitfulness (Gen. 2:15).

Humans are to conserve the productive potential of climate, land, plants and animals. Creation's fruitfulness even may be improved through science and technology, but these are humble tools relative to God's provisions.

In West Pokot District of western Kenya, farmers have transformed the Darau River valley into a highly productive irrigated system, but population pressure is straining the catchment's water and land capacity. Traditional irrigation has been practiced for generations in this valley. Water is extracted from the river at an elevation strategically selected to facilitate flow through a hand-dug furrow that follows the contour for several kilometers. A series of intakes and furrows irrigate plots at various levels along the slopes. A complex system of social organization governs water extraction from the stream and its distribution among plots. This small-scale irrigation provides subsistence production for the household and occasionally income from market crops (onions, tomato, kale). These indigenous systems offer valuable lessons for sustainable water and land use, and social organization for effective resource management, especially for introduced irrigation schemes.

Despite its success, the valley has reached its productive capacity. All intake points along the stream have been developed and available land irrigated. Population pressure from natural growth and in-migration is increasing the demand for land. Some upper portions of the valley are already being cleared for shifting cultivation despite a local by-law. This is threatening the catchment's water supply. Local leaders recognize the dilemma but have not yet devised a long-term solution.

One possible alternative is to develop an adjacent valley along similar lines. However, this is a medium-term solution. Population growth needs to be addressed. When human population strains creation's fruitfulness, both creation and humans suffer, and it is humans that must respond.

3. The Sabbath is for creation too (Lev. 25:2-5).

Creation requires rest from the stresses of agricultural production (declining soil fertility, erosion, overgrazing). This is especially the case where agriculture must adapt to very narrow environmental thresholds. An example is the Turkana of northern Kenya, a pastoral society highly adapted to erratic rainfall and sparse vegetation (Cullis and Pacey 1992). Seasonal movement of livestock is the most important strategy for avoiding drought and maintaining grazing areas. The Turkana have a complex system of allocating rangeland throughout the year based on rainfall patterns, biomass productivity and water for livestock. Grazing areas are accessed in a predetermined pattern generally progressing from grasslands on the plains during the rainy season to higher pastures where grass is more plentiful in the long dry season. This system of rotational grazing rejuvenates moisture reserves and rangeland for the next season.

Pastoralism depends on seasonal sabbaths for the land. Other systems use different lengths of time for restoring productive capacity ranging from multi-year crop rotations to decades for shifting cultivation. Scriptures teach that sabbath keeping is a necessary condition for creation's provisions, and that the Creator will grant the creation its Sabbath if humans do not (Lev. 26: 3-4, 34).

4. Some parts of creation are not for agriculture (Ps. 104).

God also loves natural biodiversity. Agriculture may not indiscriminately destroy the praise-ability of natural systems. Crop or livestock production does not belong in places where farming resources are marginal, ecological functions are critical (aquifer recharge, migratory routes) or biodiversity is high, and especially not where only a few remnants of God's creatures remain. A Kenyan example is the encroachment of cultivation into wildlife habitat. Land clearing for farming and rural settlement has resulted in loss of habitat and decreased food supply. Wildlife, particularly elephants, has invaded fields, destroying crops and killing people. Human-wildlife conflicts, and a perception that wildlife is a higher priority, have generated a negative attitude to wildlife conservation among many rural people.

Another example is the excision of forests for agriculture. Only five percent of Kenya's land area is classified as forests and woodlots (IEA and SID 2001). Almost 356,000 hectares of forest have been lost to all uses since independence in 1963. Less than one half of this area has been excised by state sanction, the remainder illegally. Many excisions are for conversion to farming, tea plantations and flower production. Beneficiaries include the President and churches (Opala 2002).

Africa is endowed with some of the largest intact natural ecosystems on earth (savannah, tropical forests, mangroves, deserts). These praise and manifest the Creator in ways that agriculture cannot. Crop and livestock production may not indiscriminately detract from these tasks.

5. Stewardly agriculture treads lightly on the creation (Ezek. 34:18, 19).

Impacts of agriculture on creation need to be systematically identified and managed. Africa is replete with rural development projects that failed to consider basic environmental factors. Examples include the ZAMCAN Wheat Project (Zambia) that ignored local soil conditions, the Bura Irrigation Scheme (Kenya) that ran out of water because of a shift in the course of the river, and the Fish Ponds at Kasinthula (Malawi) that were unsuccessful because a large population of fish-eating birds cleared the ponds (Kakonge 1995). These projects demonstrate the consequences of ignoring environmental factors when planning agriculture projects.

Environmental assessment is one way of evaluating and managing the environmental sustainability of agricultural projects (Spaling et al. 2001). An example is the Muhanga Mixed Agricultural Project of the Church of Uganda that trains farmers in 'modern agricultural practices' to increase household food production. Located in southwestern Uganda, the region boasts rich volcanic soil and a suitable climate. Despite favorable environmental conditions, intense population pressure from the influx of refugees from Rwanda and the Democratic Republic of Congo and the migration of Ugandans to the region has contributed to land scarcity, soil erosion and shortages of fuelwood and water.

An environmental assessment of the project analyzed local trends in population growth, soil fertility, erosion and fuelwood availability—four indicators of environmental change chosen by the community. These trends were reconstructed from resident's memories and oral history. Results show that population growth and soil erosion have increased and soil fertility and fuelwood supply have declined over the last 30 years. Reasons for the changes include climate variability, population dynamics and land management. The assessment raised awareness within the community on the sustainability of local agricultural practices and provided useful input for project design.

Culturally adapted and participatory tools may contribute to productive and stewardly use of land, water and other resources, helping agriculture to tread lightly on creation.

6. Effective agricultural stewardship requires justice and security (Lev. 25:18, 19, 1 Kings 21, Is. 5:8).

Structural barriers to stewardship in Africa include conflict over access to communal resources (e.g., water, grazing land), land grabbing, commodification of land, and unjust international food relief policies. Violent disputes over land and access to the River Tana in Kenya have resulted in more than 100 deaths and 1000 displaced families since February 2001 (Nation Team 2002). Two ethnic groups, the Orma pastoralists and Wardei farmers, have resorted to arms over water and riparian land rights. The conflict has recently escalated because of a decision by authorities to issue individual title deeds for prime communal land in the riparian zone. This parceling and commodification of land, primarily for the farming elite, has threatened river access and livestock watering for the pastoralists.

Another type of injustice negated last year's good harvest in several districts of Kenya. Fake fumigants were sold to many unsuspecting farmers who subsequently lost their harvest to storage pests (Mugo 2001). The chemical was diluted with chalk, flour or dust and packed in standard packages complete with counterfeit labels.

Injustice also has an international face. Relief aid from industrialized countries is usually conditional on the purchasing of food (grains, legumes, cooking oil) from the donor country. Imported food aid has been distributed in Turkana District, Kenya for the past two years during a prolonged drought. However, the Morulem irrigation scheme has successfully produced crops in the District for the same period. Tons of surplus maize and sorghum sit idle in the scheme's warehouse because aid policy does not permit the purchase of locally available foods. Imported food aid has distorted local markets and systems for re-distributing food within Kenya.

> *A poor man's field may produce abundant food, but injustice sweeps it away. (Prov. 13:23)*

7. Indigenous stewardship knowledge can empower communities (Num. 14:6-9, Deut. 11:1-18, Josh. 18).

> "Stewardship is absolutely essential for the empowerment of the rural poor." (Ajulu 2001: 53)

Knowledge of local resources and traditional farming culture are powerful tools of empowerment for creation-care. Many agriculture projects have ignored this local wisdom. Its importance is demonstrated in a personal case involving "recovered" indigenous rice culture in Sierra Leone.

As a Christian agriculturist working among the Krim farmers in the river rain flood plains of southern Sierra Leone, I had introduced improved varieties of flood-tolerant floating rice and also demonstrated the potential of irrigated rice production during the dry season. Despite highly visible demonstration plots, field days, extension services and even a harvest guarantee, both introduced ventures failed.

One day Tommi Somaila, a local master (elder) farmer, took me across the flooded plain by canoe to a small rice plot in the transition zone between wetland and upland. I did not immediately recognize this particular type of rice. Following his advice, I bit into a ripe kernel and observed a distinct reddish husk that I had not seen before but knew was characteristic of indigenous African varieties (*Oryza glaberrima*) (NRC 1996). These were historically displaced by *O. sativa* varieties imported from Asia for a mechanical cultivation scheme operated by the colonial British for rice export. Known locally in Mende as "puu mbei" (white rice), these imports were characterized by fuller grains and a longer maturation period that matched the needs of mechanical cultivation. The monocultural need for synchronized seeding and maturation disrupted the indigenous risk-reducing strategies of using multiple varieties, staggered seeding dates and planting at various elevations to ensure at least some harvest each season. Yields of imported *"puu mbei"* were higher but only under minimal flood conditions. These conditions were rarely met, generally only once in every three years, resulting in frequent harvest failures and an extended hungry season. Displacement of indigenous *O. glaberrima* also resulted in the loss of its culture such as the names, characteristics and seeding dates of individual varieties. Tommi Somaila was one of the very few farmers who had retained this knowledge because of taste preference and as a buffer against the frequent failure of the "puu mbei" harvest. He agreed to use a portion of his harvest for seed multiplication and, with a few other master farmers, to train those interested in this indigenous rice culture. The next year, farmer response exceeded expectations. After decades of failed harvests, collapsed cultivation schemes and other introduced agricultural projects, local farmers took a sudden and great interest in the re-discovery of their own rice culture.

This case shows the value of indigenous agriculture that comes from long experience of adapting to local environmental conditions. This experience shapes a specific culture of knowledge, skills and organization that can empower local communities for agricultural stewardship.

Conclusion

This paper has proposed an integral framework for agriculture and creation based on biblical teachings and traditional African wisdom. Scripture's story of creation, fall and redemption fundamentally affect how agriculture and creation relate to each other and the Creator. African wisdom provides insight into the wholeness, manifestation and provisions of the created order. Both acknowledge an agriculture-creation relationship centered on the Creator.

The suggestion that traditional African wisdom and biblical teachings may inform an integral framework runs the risk of syncretism. This charge is rebutted on several fronts. First, the Christian doctrine of general revelation is exemplified in traditional African wisdom, which explicitly confesses a divine Creator. Creation's manifestation may be incomplete with respect to the fall and redemption, but no less important to a people searching for God. Second, the framework assumes a pluralistic notion of stewardship that accepts the complementarity of various perspectives on holism (Barrett and Grizzle 1999). It does not deny the centrality of the scriptures but recognizes that human constructs about creation, including biblical understandings, are often limited to specific times and places. A pluralistic approach acknowledges and celebrates the variety of stewardship perspectives and approaches of various cultures. Finally, interfaith dialogue does not mean religious relativism. Each faith may contribute positively to another. For example, holism and redemption of creation are shared concepts that may enable both African and western cultures to better fulfill the biblical call of stewardship (Daneel 1999).

Caring for creation is a necessary but not sufficient normative task for agriculture. Human structures govern ownership of and access to resources (e.g., land, water, genetic material), technology and capital, and exert control over markets and trade. There is often conflict over land, water and even food, resulting in landlessness, displaced people, and violence. Kingdom-building in agriculture also calls for justice for the producer and consumer, and peace for all.

Agricultural stewardship is fundamentally about enabling creation's praise. Praise may emanate from rain falling on parched soil, fields of ripening grain or a new, genetically modified organism. Agriculture must preserve the praise function by not over-exploiting, degrading or polluting resources. God promises to bless faithful agricultural stewardship through the abundant and continuous provisions of creation (Lev. 26:3-6, Joel 2:18-27, Amos 9:13-15). Farming households and rural communities that preserve and develop creation's praise are promised the Creator's blessing. This is the hope for African agriculture.

Acknowledgement

This paper received sabbatical support from The King's University College, Edmonton, Canada and Daystar University, Nairobi, Kenya. The Christian Reformed World Relief Committee and

World Vision Canada, and their African partners provided first-hand insight into agriculture projects. Anja Buwalda, Dwein Hodgson, John Hiemstra and Tom Post contributed constructive and encouraging comments.

References

Ajulu, D.
>   2001   *Holism in Development: an African Perspective on Empowering Communities.* Monrovia, CA: MARC.

Barrett, C. and R. Grizzle
>   1999   "A Holistic Approach to Sustainability Based on Pluralism Stewardship." *Environmental Ethics* 21: 23-42.

Cullis, A. and A. Pacey
>   1992   "A Development Dialogue: Rainwater Harvesting in Turkana." London: Intermediate Technology Publications.

Daneel, M.L.
>   1991   "The Liberation of Creation: African Traditional Religious and Independent Church Perspectives." *Missionalia* 19: 99-121.

Daneel, M.
>   1999   "Earthkeeping Churches at the African Grass Roots." *In* D. Hessel and R. Radford Ruether (eds.) *Christianity and Ecology: Seeking the Well-being of Earth and Human.* Cambridge: Harvard University Press.

DeWitt, C.
>   1995   "Ecology and Ethics: Relation of Religious Belief to Ecological Practice in the Biblical Tradition." *Biodiversity and Conservation.* 4: 838-848.

Ebenreck, S.
>   1983   "A Partnership Farmland Ethic." *Environmental Ethics* 5: 33-45.

Gitau, S.
>   2000   *The Environmental Crisis: A Challenge for Christianity.* Nairobi: Acton.

Hughes, S.
>   1999   "The History of Food Security in Ukambani." Unpublished Paper Prepared for the Christian Reformed World Relief Committee, Nairobi.

Institute of Economic Analysis (IEA) and Society for International Development (SID).
2001 *Kenya at the Crossroads: Research Compendium.* Nairobi: Iea, and Rome: Sid.

Kakonge, J.O.
1995 "Dilemmas in the Design and Implementation of Agricultural Projects in Various African Countries: The Role of Environmental Impact Assessment." *Environmental Impact Assessment Review* 15: 275-285.

Kinoti. G.
1997 *Hope for Africa and What the Christian Can Do.* Nairobi: International Bible Society

Mortimore, M.
1998 *Roots in the African Dust: Sustaining the Drylands.* Cambridge, MA: Cambridge University Press.

Mugo, W.
2001 "Fake Farm Chemicals Hurt Food Security in Rural Areas." Nairobi: *Daily Nation*, December 27.

Nation Team
2002 "Four Killed in Tana Attack." Nairobi: *Sunday Nation*, January 13.

National Research Council (NRC)
1996 *Lost Crops of Africa.* Volume 1: *Grains.* Washington: National Academy Press.

Opala, K.
2002 "How the High and Mighty Shared Kenya's Heritage." Nairobi: *Daily Nation*, January 21.

Spaling, H., J. Zwier, and D. Kupp
2001 "Earthkeeping and the Poor: Assessing the Environmental Sustainability of Development Projects." *Perspectives on Science and Christian Faith* 53: 142-151.

Tiffen, M., M. Mortimore and F. Gichuki
1994 *More People, Less Erosion: Environmental Recovery in Kenya.* Chichester: Wiley.

Union of Concerned Scientists (UCS)
1996 "Keeping the Earth: Religious and Scientific Perspectives." Video. Cambridge, MA: New Wrinkle Inc. and the National Religious Partnership for the Environment.

The Agriculturalist
and Knowledge

Affinity, Dominion, and the Poverty of Our Day:

Calling and Task of Agriculture in a World That Belongs to God

John H. Kok

Introduction

The BHA conference dealt with a number of foundational issues and wrestled with many important questions. Although few of us present were philosophers, we had, in a way, all been philosophizing: uncovering and addressing basic assumptions and implicit presuppositions regarding agriculture as well as biblical holism. Philosophers usually take great delight in doing just that: reflecting on underlying foundations and overarching frameworks. And being a philosopher, that is what I look forward to doing with you in this chapter.

Foundations, of course, are just below or, sometimes, well below the surface of cultural activities and results—be that a scientific theory, a theatrical production, an architectural style, a political structure, or industrial and agricultural practices. Foundations and frameworks too often go unquestioned; they have become so second nature to us that they go without saying. I would have you consider that when we ask authentic questions about these kinds of things, what goes unquestioned (at least for

123

the moment) constitutes one's position or perspective—the pivotal components or dimensions of which may be referred to as one's *worldview*: "one's comprehensive framework of basic beliefs about things."

Everyone has one—however bifurcated or fragmented one's framework, one's worldview, might be. And every worldview is ultimately rooted in some final allegiance that has the "last word" in one's life—be it the (financial) "bottom line" or a (hedonistic) peaceful feeling, the (social security) of "friends" or the (lifestyle) dictates of the Koran. In other words, Christians are not odd fellows out when it comes to hanging on to an authoritative word (revelation). As one matures, this allegiance and an ensuing framework—habits of the heart for one's hearing and doing—become so much "second nature" that it usually goes without saying during the usual course of everyday.

In dealing with foundational issues philosophers try to ferret out some of the differences between "first" and "second" nature, between what is given and what we have made of what is given. In so doing they seek to make explicit what often "goes without saying," not only as regards the structures of society, but also when it comes to cultured ways of doing things (like agriculture, industry, and ecology). In this paper I will briefly analyze two models of farming and the holism to which contemporary ecology lays claim. Then I'll suggest a framework that might help us better to find our way among the questions that need asking concerning what tilling the earth and keeping it (Gen. 2:15) requires of us today.

Contemporary Agriculture: Two Models

When it comes to foundational issues in contemporary agriculture, a common distinction is between a production or industrial paradigm—an economic model of farming—and an ecological model of farming. I will use Keller and Brummer (2002) to summarize these two models, and in doing so endorse their claim that "the amount of attention given to the underlying values of agriculture is inversely proportionate to the environmental impact of agricultural activity" (p. 264).

The Economic/Industrial Model

Contemporary (western/industrial) agriculture rests on a conception of nature as causal nexus. Implicit to many of its practices is a mechanistic view of the world. Nature is seen as a grand and exquisite machine that functions according to the universe-wide laws of nature. Given the uniformity of nature, it can be analyzed, explained, and manipulated in terms of logically independent factors that are causally, and hence predictably, related. Nature as *explanadum* has as such no intrinsic value. As John Locke puts it: our labor adds the value to nature as we transform the latent resource value of land into property and products. This value-added view of nature tends to promulgate an economic model of human-nature interactions, also when it comes to working the land.

Today agriculture is industrialized in order to reliably produce the most (plant and animal) "product units" while minimizing labor inputs. By infusing manufactured components (fertilizers, pesticides, and technology), the agriculturalist manipulates the land to make it amenable to the industrial process, to increased productivity. Continuing scientific research leads in turn to the development, production, and implementation of new technology: "The prevailing philosophy is one of a *component approach* to crop production, whereby the producer focuses on individual farming practices and methods" (Acquaah 2002). As Francis Bacon would put it: after first submitting ourselves to nature we through our knowledge will come to control it: knowledge is power (and—Frederick Taylor will add—just like in industry, productive efficiency is the only way to make working the land financially feasible).

The economic/production model of farming could be summarized as maintaining a clear Subject—Object (Man—Nature) framework; with an adjacent fact value [is/ought] dichotomy, such that "values are epiphenomena of human subjectivity and human activity; they are not embedded in the land" (Keller and Brummer 2002, 265). Nature is "object" with no inherent value. The physical and biological constraints are methodically removed or controlled in order to increase productivity with a minimum of labor and a maximum of efficiency to guarantee a high degree of security and uniform quality.

The Ecological Model of Farming

The ecological model, in principle and practice, is often embraced in response or reaction to the industrial model. Some react to the financial stakes, others to an implicit one-size-fits-all attitude. Still others lament that the simplified, mono-cultural, scientifically transparent systems of modern, industrial agriculture bear little resemblance to highly complex natural ecosystems and insist, "many factors relating to the ontology of agro-ecological systems are not amenable to quantification" (Keller and Brummer 2002, 267).

Since the 1930s ecologists have done what they could to show the broader public that in natural ecosystems, various biotic and abiotic elements form an intricate network of interactions—with types of value above and beyond economic value alone (e.g., the value of wetlands for migratory bird habitat)—allowing the systems to be both functional and adaptive under a wide range of conditions. The ecological model of farming tries to heed ecology's word. Farms do have to produce food, but ecologically sensitive farmers often consider the land to be a living thing, including not only soil but also the plants and animals living on it and the water and energy flowing through it. This model, though diverse in practice, could well be characterized as a much more co-operative Subject—Subject approach. "[As] a *whole systems* perspective [it] emphasizes the need for producers to conduct their agricultural activities in harmony with the biosphere. This holistic system model promotes *working with* rather than *controlling* or subjugating nature" (Acquaah 2002, 288). The integrity of nature is a factor that needs to be respected. Value is added through the production of food, but only when a more basic validity inherent to the cooperation within the natural ecosystem is acknowledged and held in high regard.

Even those inclined to view agriculture as an industrial enterprise, in which farms are factories and fields the production plants, are beginning to understand the need for sustainability. As a result, the economic model has been augmented of late under the pressures of the ecological model; modified, particularly, in those places where the longevity of the productive process is advantageously extended or deferred production costs are reduced. I am not sure about the extent of agreement between ecologists and agriculturists, but many are beginning to find some common ground in their concern for "agro-ecosystems" and "sustainable agriculture."

Because ecological sensitivities have been the change-agent in this regard and make claim to being (more) holistic, I want to plumb a few of the depths and murky spots of the ecological pool.

Holism: Biblical or Otherwise

"Holistic" is an adjective with which few will take issue; after all, who would triumph the cause of a non-holistic pedagogy or non-holistic economics? A "holistic" approach clearly requires further definition. A holistic approach to whatever, says my dictionary, will be concerned "with wholes or with complete systems rather than with the analysis of, or treatment of, or dissection into parts": as in "holistic medicine attempts to treat both the mind and the body"—an attempt, of course, that assumes that mind and body constitute the whole—and "holistic ecology views man and the environment as a single system"—a view that assumes that man and nature constitute the whole. But where do these dictionary illustrations leave those who claim that body, soul, and spirit constitute the (whole) human being? So too: Is Marx's dialectical materialism any less holistic than the knowledge of some Christians that creation, fall, and redemption are cosmic in scope? And besides, if man and nature do constitute the whole, where does God fit in? What is a "holistic ecology"? Or is that a pleonasm?

Ecological Holism

The science of ecology arose as a 19th century Muirian awe of Nature was soon exchanged for a robust faith in science. The hope was that this science would allow people to continue to live and work (once again) in harmony with nature—giving humankind scientific confidence to manage the ecosystems of which we partake for maximum efficiency and mutual benefit. One of ecology's tasks, then, was to study the equilibrium with an eye to proving the unbalance humankind produces. But today the landscape is changing as science is coming to acknowledge the importance of disturbances and heterogeneity, of instability and perturbations, of "patch dynamics" and chaos theory. There is actually a plurality of holistic ecological models. These models are revealing in what each includes as constituting "the whole."

Frederic Clements, one of the grandfathers of modern ecology (1874–1945), anticipated the whole to be a relatively permanent ecological super-organism. The whole for Clements *is* an organism—one that lives in entire harmony with the climate. He was also convinced that after many generations of plants have grown in an area, a climax formation finally appears—a community of plants that is in dynamic adjustment with the habitat. He called this essential stabilization "the climax," convinced that this localized mature or adult stage of vegetation would persist until there would be a fundamental change in climate (*Plant Ecology*, 1938). But the interaction between the climate as cause and the climax as effect (which in turn, reacts upon the environment) proved to be more complex than Clement described.

Eugene Odum's view of nature, of "the whole," was shaped more by physics than by botany. What his precise measurements led him to believe in was a happy, homeostatic, thermo-dynamic system of ecological order, powered by a cybernetic flow of energy and trophic (nourishment) levels.

Ecosystems are capable of self-maintenance as are their component populations and organisms. Thus *cybernetics* has important application in ecology. *Homeostasis* is the term generally applied to the tendency for biological systems to resist change and to remain in a state of equilibrium. … The interplay of material cycles and energy flows in large ecosystems generates a self-correcting homeostasis with no outside control or set point required. (*Fundamentals of Ecology*, 1971)

For both Clements and Odum the whole is the sum of the parts plus the interaction between those parts, and for both it is the whole that remains central as system. The difference is that for Clements the whole is an organism; for Odum it is the self-correcting interplay of material cycles and energy flows. (And, yes, there is a fundamental difference between those two!)

Even the more recent "chaos theory" confesses the intimate relationship of everything to everything—although its message of unpredictability some do find disturbing. Edward Lorentz's (1958) chaos theory deals with simple, nonlinear, deterministic equations governing processes that pervade the domains, e.g., of physics, chemistry, and biology. The future states of these systems are per definition entirely determined by their present state and the forces acting on them, and are in this sense predictable. And yet, in many cases, the future states appear to be random—in part, because of our inability to specify their initial states with infinite precision. "Chaotic systems thus embody elements of both determinism, predictability, and unpredictability, even when they are treated entirely within the domain of classical physics" (Russell 1997).

Though different, the "ecosystems" of Clements and Odum were both described with deterministic equations common to the natural sciences in general and mathematical physics in particular. New discoveries of order in and through "chaos" have been confirmed as well, but I agree with Willem Drees's (1997) claim that "in relation to the science at hand: there is no new principle involved in chaotic systems."

I have two observations in that regard. If we can step back a moment, I would have you consider that, in general, the models people construct, however much they are intended to mirror or reflect the ways things really are or ought to be, are necessarily simplifications of reality. Even when they are intended as models of "the whole," they only map a part of the picture. When the natural sciences limit their focus and study of reality to logically independent variables that are causally connected—un-caused factors, miraculous or not, simply do not make the grade on scientifically respectable lab reports—then quite obviously the choice of the observation set will constrain the answers one can expect from natural scientific studies. But that truism certainly holds for the economic or production model of farming as well! In many ways the only difference between Odum's cybernetic interplay of cycles and flows and the industrial model of farming is that Odum's sees everything in terms of energy and the industrial model sees everything in terms of goods and services. In other words while both are "holistic" in their concern for "the whole," they both "flatten" reality by reducing everything that is worth talking about to either energy or economic inputs and outputs. Clements and chaos theory are on the same page as well. For one the whole is a super-organism, and for the other it is the conglomeration of processes governed by a complex set of simple, nonlinear, deterministic equations.

There are many reasons for an upswing in public concern about the environment, so too for the gradual move from "conventional" to sustainable agriculture. The one reason I want to mention here is the growing realization that the old Subject—Object model of bifurcation between Man and Nature is severely faulted. Bacon might have been right in claiming that knowledge is power, but there are limits too. We can condition the air in our classrooms, but not the air of our atmosphere; and where will we go to get new topsoil? Who will refill the aquifer? In terms of the old black box in the feedback loops of the input–output picture of how things work around here: the black box does not stand over against us such that we can explain, control, and manipulate functioning; we are now told that we ourselves are part of that "box" that makes all things work and function and hang together: planet Earth is a spaceship we are told—we have to make this work or the story will soon be over. (As though life and death on this planet is all there is!) Another way to talk about this change of mind is to point to the growing realization that we are part of the fields that we investigate and that we fool ourselves if we think that we (or some of us) can transcend it all and see it objectively: assuming that a transcendent view from "nowhere" is possible is as silly as thinking that when we throw our garbage "away" that it actually goes there.

If Christians will ever be able to decide which model—the super-organism, energy, or "chaos"—is best, then we have to ask: How are we to integrate noncausal factors like sin, human responsibility, or divine agency into this picture the sciences paint? On the other hand, to "integrate" these realities is probably wrongly put. To acknowledge that the models and knowledge we generate within a particular sphere of science is incomplete cannot mean that all we have to do is augment the model by integrating Christian assumptions about reality and the beginning and end of history (contra Norgaard 2002). For example, John Polkinghorne's attempt to find room for God in the unpredictables of chaotic dynamics—as indicating an ontological openness to the future, which in turn requires that God's knowledge of the world of becoming must be truly temporal in character—is clearly wrong-headed in refashioning God in the image of Lorentz's chaos theory.

Biblical Holism

Our conference planners clearly saw the need to articulate their sense of what constitutes "the whole." They described biblical holism as "directed toward the spiritual, physical, social, and emotional well-being of people, but also toward the non-human part of God's creation. Thus, when one speaks of Biblical Holism, one is referring to relationships between God and humans, humans with each other, and humans with non-human creation." Further reference to the biblical motif of creation, fall, and redemption through Jesus Christ makes it very clear that much more is at stake than immutable (or organic or energy-flow or simple, nonlinear, deterministic) relationships between Creator, human creatures, and non-human creatures. Although one might well wonder where the heavenly creatures fit into this scheme of things, the Creator/human creatures/nonhuman creatures triad is better than the traditional God/man/world framework which suggests that man (and actually God as well) is not part of the world.

That said, I am going to suggest a somewhat different description of "the whole" which I believe will serve us better, also when asking questions about the calling and task of agriculture today. It is a basic framework of "the whole" that I believe is in line with Scripture and in that sense may be called biblical. But before getting to that, a brief discussion of three senses of what is meant by one's "starting point."

Humankind's common *religious starting point* is God the Creator; all else is creature and as such subject to him and his laws and principles for creaturely beings. We are by our very (created) nature always related to God and required to love him above all.

The difference in religion is an antithetical duality in direction: since the Fall a person's heart is directed either to God or away from him, that is, either toward the Creator (true religion) or toward something within creation (false religion). And yet, the basics of true religion, as such, does not cut it when it comes to obedient responses to the challenges raised by agriculture, industry, ecology, and world hunger. The Christian has to do more than repent and believe, even though that is the place to start.

An actual, factual, or *existential starting point:* investigative (re)searches are most often prompted by a "problem," by a sense of wonder or deficiency that is always rooted in what one, at that time, knows to be the case. One leaves this "place to stand" unquestioned, at least for the moment; sometimes only to find that what one has learned along the way gives reason to ponder and possibly reassess what one had previously taken for granted. Topsoil loss or curiosity regarding the reasons for smog or deformities in an indigenous frog population can all be shared experience occasions (irregardless of one's religious orientation) for beginning a methodic analysis of a defined field of investigation.

Different fields will require different methods, but a *methodological* requirement holds for all: in order to investigate something one needs *to start with a sense of the whole*—of the field to be investigated—and to acknowledge both that one is related to or probably also a part of that field and that the most one will get of God within that field will be the results of his divine activity. It is impossible to investigate everything at once—once you have a positive sense of one's field of investigation, the laborious investigation of the synchronic (structural) and diachronic (genetic [as in "genesis"]) diversities within that field can begin. At the same time, it needs to be said that one is often busy scientifically for some time already before ever giving much thought to methodological questions.

My overview of "the whole" proceeds as follows (see figure following): Within the (cosmic) field, all of which is subject to God and his law, one can:

- distinguish between heaven and earth, that is, between heavenly (angelic) and earthly creatures; and further
- among earthly creatures distinguish between a number of different kinds or kingdoms; amongst which that of the

human race assumes the central place; distinguishing further among the nonhuman kingdoms, between living and nonliving, and among the former between animals and plants

- in the human race, distinguish between the religious office bearer and those who are "contained" in him, namely, the first Adam and Jesus Christ, the second Adam
- in every member of the human race, distinguish between prefunctional heart and mantle of functions; and more generally
- within this mantle of functions and the functioning of all earthly creatures, distinguish fifteen irreducible modes of earthly being; and
- within any one functional field, distinguish subjects and objects

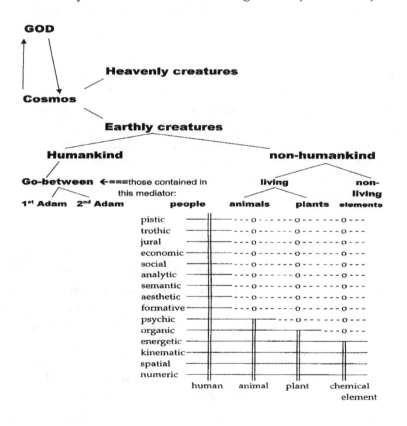

Some of the connections to be found in the ordered diversity of this cosmos:

- ❖ between things functioning as subjects and objects: subject/ subject as well as subject/object relationships

- ❖ within the functioning of any creature: modal anticipations and retrocipations

- ❖ between creatures: intra-individual and inter-individual relationships

- ❖ between the mediator and the human heart: how one stands religiously, with(in) creation, before the face of the creator God

- ❖ the connection between heaven and earth is found in the office of the mediator and is the most inclusive within created reality

Within this cosmic context all of God's creatures are dependent on and subject to the Creator. Although there is no genetic connection between plants, animals, and humankind, these realms do not exist completely separate from each other either. This is obvious from the many relationships between things belonging to the different kingdoms. These relationships are of two basic kinds. In one case, there is an *undeniable affinity* between subjects belonging to different realms. In the other case, the subject-object relationship predominates.

Affinity

As for the affinity between subjects from different realms, we can say that there are many kinds of inter-regnal connections (connections between realms). Involuntary cooperation is one kind: the sun generating warmth on the earth, the roots of plants preventing erosion, bees pollinating flowers while gathering honey. These can be said to all "work together," to the extent that this cooperation is in some ways like human activity. But one should be careful not to anthropomorphize or deify the activity of nonhuman things involved in this inter-regnal cooperation.

Inter-regnal connections of affinity are also evident when the relationship between subject functions of functors from different realms is paired with the correlation active-passive, as when the growth of plants and animals is intentionally promoted by human beings. A 4-H champion steer and its owner don't part ways easily. The affinity is even stronger when the interrelation shifts from an inter-individual to an intra-individual one. For example, inorganic salts are a basic requirement for plants and animals as well as human beings. These two are combined in other ways when we look at the biospheric environmental nexus of which all Earthlings are a part.

Inter-regnal connections are also very evident in subject-object relations. Here the activity of a member of the higher realm directs itself to or unfolds one or more things of another realm in their object functioning. This subject-object interrelation exists between all of the realms. A plant will use a stone to support or protect itself. Animals use plants for food and nests, but they also fertilize flowers, spread seeds, and provide manure. This connection plays an even more important role in the relationship of people to things in the nonhuman realms.

Dominion

Human knowing depends on much more than the subject-object relation. Think, for example, of one's understanding of one's self and others. Nonetheless, the subject-object relation plays a crucial role: if physical things, plants, and animals did not function as objects for analysis, even nonscientific knowledge about these realms would be out of the question.

Agriculture is a cultural (formation/unfolding focused) activity, and being an agriculturist is a vocation that comes in response to God's command to make something of creation—to have dominion. Both require knowing and controlling or mastering aspects of the creation with an eye to caring for creation as we serve our neighbor. Every cultural activity comes with a price—even the air we breathe is changed by our breathing and none of us can help but turn edibles into their opposite—but the change we bring to creation must be appropriate, fitting, and responsible, also over the long haul. For example, the predominance of technology too often tends to disconnect agriculture from its ecological context while at the same time contributing to overproduction

here and malnutrition there. When it becomes clear that the sim-
plification, homogenization, and manipulation of agroecosystems
is often ecologically unsound and unsustainable, then we have to
find alternatives.

The agriculturalist should not ask the philosopher which alternatives to pursue. Philosophers, as I said at the beginning, deal
with foundations and frameworks, not agricultural best practices.
But allow me to go back to Kelly and Brummer's recent article and
highlight a few of their challenges that certainly make sense to me:

✔ "agricultural science and practice must become context-
sensitive and holistic in methodology."

✔ "agricultural research and the activity of farming must be
gauged in terms of the unique ecological conditions of each locale.
Folk wisdom ... is revalidated when this approach is used. The
consequence of context-dependent agriculture is that universal
farming principles are not achievable."

✔ "methodological pluralism": the sociologist and chemist
cannot use the same methods of analysis and research because the
fields they investigate are different. The same holds for the different fields in agriculture.

✔ "farming as a multifaceted activity that, in addition to
mechanistic investigation and practice, involves the recognition of a
variety of noneconomic values in the land: ecological, aesthetic, historical, political, social, even spiritual. Our concept of agriculture is
that it is more than simply food production: It is the act of affirming
as many of these values a possible" (Keller and Brummer, 2002).

The Poverty of Our Day

I will conclude with a few words about both the broad Christian framework as well as the normative parameters for a biblical
ethics. The poverty of our day is not primarily a question of economics or information overload or monocultural farming. I suggest
that the unity of the ethical perspective that promises life and
peace in abundance needs to be rooted in the unity of life that can
only be found in the triune law of the Triune God.

There is no doubt about the God-given "norm" of self-sacrificial love that only Jesus met. Knowing what (the mind of) God requires is clear, as summarized by Christ in the double **Love command**. But what is our responsibility as God's co-workers with respect to "working" the garden and "caring for (guarding)" the earth—our home? Most Christians do not question that (the Creator) God has structured the cosmos and calls all his creatures into being and provides for them all: the good, the bad, and the ugly. But the love command holds primarily only for human life—which today is only more or less in line with this law. (It makes no sense to talk about Christian animals, plants, or stones and atoms.) Nevertheless, in our obedience, God's word revelation, including the norm to *shamar* the earth, can become a source of blessing (to the birds, and forests, and open ranges).

Structural lawfulness within the cosmos has to do with ascertainable regularities that are of different, irreducible—biotic, physical, or, e.g., aesthetic—kinds. Statistics can be collected with reliability regarding the likelihood of "natural laws" holding or predicted weather patterns happening, of increases in the number of murders committed or nitrates in the ground water, or of decreases in either the ozone layer or infant mortality. In other words, these regularities are affected both by what does and does not line up with the law in the earlier sense of "norm." But guilt and misplaced conviction do join indeterminate as well as predictable physical facts and causes in defining the subsequent course of creaturely affairs.

Lawmakers in government fill a delegated office as they seek to craft **positive laws** befitting the situation. Christian lawmakers will implore the Spirit's leading as they "build a bridge" between the state of affairs as upheld by God's structural law and the telos (goal/purpose) held up in God's law of love. The same is true, in a way, for the rules parents make for their children, the restrictions environmental protection agencies impose on the populace, the decisions farmers make about how to tend the land and what to produce, and, e.g., the guidelines resource management teams devise in industry.

The environmentally sound rules, restrictions, and guidelines we will then formulate and follow will be rooted with wisdom in the structure of creation, moved by a Christ-like loving sense of responsibility to the Creator, and yet always, through the leading of his Spirit, insightfully relative to our time and place.

References

Acquaah, George
>   2002   *Principles of Crop Production: Theory, Techniques, and Technology.* Upper Saddle River, NJ: Prentice Hall.

Fox, Stephen
>   1985   *The American Conservation Movement: John Muir and His Legacy.* Madison: University of Wisconsin Press.

Keller, D.R. and E.C. Brummer
>   2002   "Putting Food Production in Context: Toward a Postmechanistic Agricultural Ethic." *Bioscience*, Vol 52 No 3, March.

Kok, John H.
>   1998   *Patterns of the Western Mind.* Sioux Center, IA: Dordt College Press.

Norgaard, R.B.
>   2002   "Optimists, Pessimists, and Science." *Bioscience*, Vol 52 No 3, March.

The Agriculturalist
and Purpose

Agriculture
and the Kingdom of God

Darrow L. Miller

Introduction

Recently in Ethiopia, a Christian relief and development organization completed a "successful" agricultural project. The project, funded by USAID grants, had called for increased agricultural production to raise family income so that the children in families could have better nutrition, basic clothing, and pay school fees. At the end of the project, family income was up. Pictures were taken, reports written and the project was graded A+ by the USAID evaluators. Is this a success story for agricultural development? It is, only if you did not go back a few months later. Doing a post-project evaluation would have revealed that the farmers spent their increased income on alcohol, prostitutes, and gambling. When the farmers returned from their binge, their wives were furious that they had wasted resources intended to help their children. The "successful" projects actually left the families and community in greater poverty.

About twenty years ago, evangelical missionaries moved into the unreached agricultural communities of the poorest province of Guatemala. They journeyed there to evangelize and plant churches. The people they were working with, the Pokomchi, were the poorest people in the poorest province of one of the poorest countries in the Americas. Many people came to Christ. Churches were planted. By mission standards, the task was done. The missionaries moved on to other communities. But, in one sense, little had changed. The Pokomchi were living in as much poverty after the missionaries left as when they arrived. What was different? Now, the people were *waiting to die*! They had hope for heaven. Praise the Lord! But they had no hope for today! Is this a picture of "success"? Is this what the Great Commission all about?

These stories are replicated all over the world. Well-meaning Christians work in missions and private voluntary organizations to bring hope and help to poor agriculturists around the world. These farmers are usually physically and economically poor, and often socially outcast, with little hope in the world.

The missionaries, operating from the Evangelical Gnostic paradigm that separates the spiritual from the physical, have brought a "spiritual" solution, the "narrow Gospel of salvation." The Christ-motivated development workers, operating from the secular paradigm of the modern development industry have brought a "physical" solution, technical knowledge and outside financial resources, but little transformation of human life and communities. There can never be a comprehensive solution to a comprehensive problem based on inadequate paradigms and piecemeal methodologies.

If we want to see the lives of impoverished farmers not only improved, but also transformed, then missionaries and development NGO workers must connect their work in agriculture to the perspective and value-system of God's Kingdom provided in the Bible.

In this chapter, we will review the reason for this dilemma, build a more biblical understanding of *agriculture*, and challenge Christian agriculturists to be ambassadors for Christ and His Kingdom by connecting the Kingdom to agriculture and connecting agriculture to the Kingdom.

The Reason for the Dilemma

The reason for this dilemma cited above is a faulty worldview among both missionaries and Christian NGO workers. The biblical worldview—the Worldview of the Kingdom of God—was largely abandoned by the church about a hundred years ago. This has left much of the church functioning from a Gnostic paradigm in its religious life and the cultural paradigm (secularism or animism) in the rest of her life.

The worldview of the Bible is the objective worldview. The Bible describes reality the way God made it. All other worldviews are distortions of reality. Animism is the worldview of many of the impoverished communities around the world. Secularism is the worldview of modern, materialistic societies, and the paradigm of most of the relief and development industry. The Evangelical–Gnostic worldview has been the paradigm of much of the church since the beginning of the 20th century.

Each mindset answers man's basic questions differently. How we understand agriculture is dependent on how we answer the following questions: "What is real? What is man? What is nature?" and "What is man's relationship to nature?" Each worldview gives different answers to these fundamental questions. Thus, they each create a different framework for understanding agriculture.

Secularism leads to two distinct views of humanity in relationship to nature. In one view, man is the center of the universe in the sense that he is the highest evolved animal at the top of the food chain. He is, by nature, the highest consumer. Nature exists for man to harvest, exploit, use and consume. This often leads to a mechanistic view of agriculture, to the raping of the land and a lack of care for the soil.

Another view common to secularism is that humanity is merely another part of nature, of no greater or no lesser value than any other part. Everything ultimately is valueless matter. According to this view, man is often seen as a "cancer" in nature. He should live in harmony with nature or disappear. He should take only the food that nature freely gives. Man is to diminish in order to save nature.

In animism, nature is often seen as a god to be worshiped. The ecological system is "alive" with various spirits and deities, and is therefore often seen as more important than man.

In the biblical framework, God exists. He has made "creation" [note I have not said "nature"] good. He has made man in His image. Man is a creature, part of the rest of creation; and therefore he must show respect for creation. But man is also made in the image of God and has been placed on earth to steward creation and develop the earth. Creation belongs to God, not man. His stewardship is to be a reflection of his worship of God.

The Framework for the Agricultural Mission

The apostle Paul challenges us: "Do not conform any longer to the pattern of this world, but be transformed by the *renewing of your mind*" (Romans 12:2). The great need as we enter the 21st century is for the church to have a paradigm shift, to move from the mindset of our age and culture to having what the British apologist Harry Blamires calls a "Christian mind." We need to return to the worldview provided in the Bible. The biblical paradigm needs to become the integrating factor for our life and Mission. It needs to be the framework for the principles, policies and programs in the sphere of agriculture as well as those working among poor agriculturists in missions and relief and development programs.

What is the framework that establishes the Mission? What is the mindset that will help to transform the lives of agriculturists? What are some of the components of the biblical worldview that can help to lift poor farmers out of poverty?

God Is the First Farmer (Genesis 2:8)

"In the beginning God created the heavens and the earth." Genesis 1:1, the opening line of the biblical narrative reveals that God exists and that He made the universe. This is perhaps the most important sentence ever written. It informs us of the nature of ultimate reality. God existed before creation. He stands outside of creation. He is infinite! The fact that this is even recorded reveals that He communicates. God is *personal*! In addition, we can conclude that reality is both spiritual (God) and physical (the universe).

Genesis goes on to tell us that God planted the first garden. Genesis 2:8 reads, "Now the LORD God had planted a garden in the east, in Eden; and there he put the man he had formed." This has important significance for farmers.

A number of years ago, I was visiting the Alto Plano, the highlands of Bolivia at an elevation of 14,000 feet. The people living there are subsistence farmers whose staples are potatoes and the meat and milk products from their animals. As in many developing countries, in addition to the grinding poverty, they were the societal outcasts because they worked in the dirt.

I was blessed to be able to bring them a "word of encouragement." I opened the Bible to Genesis 2:8 and read these words: "Now the Lord God had planted a garden in the east of Eden; and there he put the man he had formed." I repeated it with emphasis: "Now *the Lord God* ... planted a garden;" And again: "Now **the Lord God** ... *planted a garden;*" I began to see a puzzling look in their eyes. They seemed to be asking, "Why is the speaker saying this again?" And I said it again: "... *the Lord God* ... *planted a garden!*" There was a dawning coming to their eyes. And a final time: "*GOD ... PLANTED A GARDEN!*" Their eyes were dancing. They understood. GOD WAS A FARMER! He was **THE FIRST FARMER!**

This was a new thought for them. No one—neither the missionaries nor the NGO development workers—had ever told them that. If God were the First Farmer and He put man in the garden, then farming must be a good thing. The dawning of their understanding of their dignity as human beings and the significance of farming was at hand.

Why had the missionaries or NGO development workers neglected such a powerful message? Largely because they did not think from the authoritative framework of the biblical worldview. Missionaries rightly wanted to see people saved for eternity. Development workers wanted to see technical improvements and outside funding brought in to help people develop. Neither understood the power of the biblical paradigm to lift people out of poverty.

Man, the *Imago Dei* (Genesis 1:26-27)

The next significant part of the revelation is found in Genesis 1:26,27: "Then God said, 'Let us make man in our image, in our likeness, and let them rule over the fish of the sea and the birds of the air, over the livestock, over all the earth, and over all the creatures that move along the ground.' So God created man in his own image, in the image of God he created him; male and female he created them." This passage reveals the wonder of what it means to be a human being. We are not merely animals to be fed as the Darwinists argue. We are not merely spirits inhabiting insignificant and burdensome bodies as animism holds.

Instead, the Bible asserts that man is made in God's image. He is the *imago Dei*. When God made the crown jewel of creation, He did not model it after dogs or monkeys; He modeled us after Himself. The poorest farmer is not to be seen as some impoverished wretch, but as nothing less than the *imago Dei*. Man, in fact, stands in the wonderful place of connecting heaven and earth. As one who is created, he is able to identify with the rest of creation. Yet because he alone is made in the image of God, this distinguishes him from creation and unites him with God.

The Creation Mandate (or the "Cultural Mandate") (Genesis 1:26, 28)

Second, since God is the Creator, to be made in His image is to be creative. Man was made to be an artist and a problem solver. Genesis 1:26 and 28 reveal the purpose for which man was made, 'Then God said, "Let us make man in our image, in our likeness, and let them rule over the fish of the sea and the birds of the air, over the livestock, over all the earth, and over all the creatures that move along the ground." … God blessed them and said to them, "Be fruitful and increase in number; fill the earth and subdue it. Rule over the fish of the sea and the birds of the air and over every living creature that moves on the ground."'

Here God revealed that He has a task for man. Some have called it the Creation Mandate, some the Cultural Mandate, and others the Development Mandate. Call it what you may, it's clear that man has a responsibility—to create culture and to develop the earth. We see that man is a co-developer with God. While creation is perfect, it is not *finished* yet. Just as the seed is perfect in itself, its purpose is not fulfilled until it is planted in the ground. Creation, like the seed, is filled with tremendous potential. It merely needs the touch of God's image bearer. There is still work to be done. God has made man to be the steward of His creation. God placed man in the garden and gave him the first "job description" as an agricultural worker. God is Creator of both man and creation. God owns creation, not man. Man has fellowship upwardly with God. Man relates to creation as its steward. There are two aspects of this stewardship, societal and developmental.

The *Societal Mandate* is established by the biblical statement, *"be fruitful, increase in number,* and *fill the earth."* To develop the earth there must be families, communities and societies. Adam and Eve were to have children and populate the earth. But fill the earth with what? It depends on your worldview. The filling of the earth is not with "consumers" as the materialist would say. Nor is it with "human spirits" that have no interest in the physical world. The mandate is to fill the earth with image bearers of God; it is to fill the earth with agriculturists and horticulturists, artists and painters, composers and poets, architects and craftsman. Fill the earth with families and communities of stewards.

The *Development Mandate* is established by the words *rule* and *subdue,* and later, in Genesis 2:15, with *work* and *care.* These words "rule" and "subdue" reflect that man is to have dominion over creation rather than the other way around as the animists and their New Age counterparts in the ecological movement would argue. The word "work" reflects that man is to *progress,* to expand and advance the garden, not to leave it as he found it. The word "care" reflects that man is to *conserve*—to protect and cherish the garden—to keep it healthy and thriving. This is in contrast with our consumer oriented materialistic culture that simply wants to harvest, deplete, use, and too often, rape creation.

The development mandate to progress and conserve is beautifully balanced. It stands in stark contrast to secularism's focus on "working but not caring" which can result in the abuse of creation. On the other hand it also contrasts New Age ecology movement that focuses on caring for, but not working the garden. This leads to underdevelopment. The development mandate celebrates *imago Dei,* calling man to expand the garden, create orchards, discover the wonders of creation through science, and to *fill the earth with the knowledge of God!* Worship leads to development.

History Is Going Somewhere

History began in a garden and will end in a *city*! The garden is the Garden of Eden (Genesis 2:8-10). The city is the City of God—the New Jerusalem (Revelation 21:2). In Revelation 22:1-4, the New Jerusalem appears as a city in a garden. There is wonderful symmetry in that the tree of life found in the Garden of Eden (Genesis 2:9) and is also found at the end of history in the garden of the City (Revelation 22:2). Agriculturists and horticulturists play a role from the beginning of the biblical narrative to the end.

From the vantage of the biblical worldview, the farmer is a maker of history. The Bible is clear that "history is something you make" (Jeremiah 5:1; Ecclesiastes 9:14-16). As farmers have introduced new crops, new agricultural technologies, and new methodologies, they have increased agricultural potential, feeding countless people. Contrary to this view, the fatalism of animistic cultures holds that "history is something that happens to you." In this mindset nothing ever changes. There is no reason to introduce new crops "because our fathers did not do it that way." In the purposeful view of history, the agriculturist has a significant role to play in the unfolding of the Kingdom.

Nature Is an Open System

God has created a universe that is both physical and spiritual. These two realms are distinct, but closely interrelated. There are natural laws that govern nature. But the system is not a "closed system" of cause and effect. There is a spiritual realm. Nature is open to the intervention of God, angels, demons and man. Animists understand the reality of the spirit realm far better than those of us raised in materialistic cultures.

The materialist, by nature, assumes that resources are physical things that "come from the ground." They are finite. Animists on the other hand, see resources as something spring mysteriously from the "outside." According to the biblical worldview, the physical proceeds from the spiritual. Creation proceeds from the mind of God. They also proceed from the mind of the *imago Dei*—they proceed from the mind of man. Resources are the product of human discovery, creativity and innovation; they are limited only by man's imagination.

An Israeli friend of mine was taking a group of Burundian pastors on a tour of Israel. As they passed by Nazareth, the pastors noticed a forest growing out of "the sand." They were amazed to see such a thing. They told my Israeli friend that in Burundi trees grow in dark soil. How could trees grow in sand? My friend responded, "God has given each people a land. He waits to see what they will do with it. To the Jews He gave a desert, and they transformed the desert into a garden. Today Israeli farmers send fruit, vegetables, flowers and arid land agricultural technology all over the world." Resources are a result of vision and human invention.

The Fall

The biblical narrative reveals that all of God's creation was very good (Genesis 1:31); all was in harmony with God and with itself. In Genesis 3:1-7 we read that sin entered the world through Adam and Eve's rebellion. Moral evil entered the world and so did *natural evil*; there is now pain in childbirth and weeds in the garden. There will be droughts and famines, earthquakes and floods. Man's relationship with God was broken and his role as steward of creation was distorted.

The good news is that hunger and famine are *abnormal*. God did not make this world to be a hungry world. In the "principle of the seed," we see that God intended the world to be bountiful. God's desire is to save man from sin and the ravages of sin, and toward that end, he is unfolding his history-encompassing redemptive plan. Because of this and because hunger and famine are abnormal, man is to fight against the weeds in the garden and the sweat of the brow. He is to use the principles of science to unlock the secret of the seed. He is to use technology, within the moral framework of the biblical worldview, to improve the land, to increase crops and to free man from drudgery and toil.

Redemption

God is a Missionary God. He has a Mission. The Mission is "to reconcile to himself **all things**, whether things on earth or things in heaven, by making peace through **[Christ's] blood, shed on the cross**" (Colossians 1:20). Why did Jesus die on the cross? To reconcile all things to Himself. The cross reaffirms the Cultural Mandate. This is God's BIG AGENDA!

The unfolding of the Mission begins with the Abrahamic Covenant in Genesis 12:1-3. Here God blessed Abraham because His plan was to bless **all nations** through him. We find God's big agenda emphasized again in the Great Commission. Here, the resurrected Christ called His disciples together and announced His reign: "All authority in heaven and on earth has been given to me" (Matthew 28:18). He then announced the task He had for the disciples: "Therefore go and make disciples of **all nations**, ... teaching them to obey all I have commanded" (Matthew 28:19,20). The Great Commission is nothing less than the **discipling of nations**.

Romans 8:18-23 reflects, again, the scope of God's big agenda. The **whole creation** is awaiting redemption. It is not merely the soul of man that is waiting for redemption. It is all of man and all of his relationships. But it is not just man that is broken. All of creation is groaning, awaiting redemption.

At the consummation of history, Jesus will return in glory to judge the living and the dead (1 Peter 4:5). He will come to marry His bride (Revelation 19: 6-8). One of the most glorious pictures at the completion of the Mission is provided in Revelation 21:23-26 where the kings of the earth bring the **glory of their nations** into the garden city—the New Jerusalem. Then the Cultural Mandate will be completed.

God is unfolding this magnificent story. It is the Transforming Story. It has the ability not only to save individual souls, but also to transform lives, lift communities out of poverty and build nations that are free, just and compassionate. The story creates the framework for the Mission. God calls the agriculturist into the story. This story can lift the poor farmer out of poverty. The task of the missionary, the development worker and the agriculturist is to tell the whole story.

Understanding Agriculture

The Cultural Mandate

The Creation Mandate of Genesis 1:26-28 and 2:15,19 is also known as the Cultural Mandate. This mandate has special significance for those working in agriculture, as we will see. But first, let's examine the word culture. What is culture? There is actually a family of words: *cult, culture,* and the agricultural term *cultivate.* The latter words are derived from the former word, *cult.*

The word "cult" means worship or reverential homage rendered to a divine being. "Culture" refers to the training, development, refinement of mind tastes and manners; the condition of being thus trained and refined; the intellectual side of civilization. The word culture is derived from the word "cultivate." "Cultivation" is used to speak of tilling or preparing for crops; to manure, plow, dress, sow and reap; to study; to labor to improve or advance; to cultivate the mind. These words have two senses: preparing the physical earth for planting and preparing the mind of the individual and society for growth and maturity.

The root of culture is worship. Culture is a reflection of the god that is worshipped. D. B. Hegman, writing in *Plowing in Hope* states, "The term [culture] could also be used in a religious context to mean *worship.* The idea here seems to be that in the same way the farmer actively fusses over his crops, so the worshiper gives rapt attention to the deity he serves. Thus the term is closely related to the Latin *cultus* meaning adoration or veneration. The English language retains this connection with such terms as *cult, cultic, occult,* etc."

Theologian Henry Van Til stated: "culture is religion externalized." In short, a people's culture is a reflection of the nation's deity. A culture is a manifestation of a people's cult.

In reviewing the Cultural Mandate, we see the twin aspects given to man, the *Culture Maker.* First, there is the *culti-*vation of the *soil,* using his **hands** to work and care for the garden (Genesis 2:15). Second, is *culti-*vating the *soul,* using the **mind** and **heart** in the naming of the animals (Genesis 2:19). Here man engages the mind in observation, reason, and categorization, and then inflames the heart in creativity and passion.

Indian scholar and development worker, Vishal Mangalwadi, summarized this when he said: "God speaks and creates the universe. Man speaks and creates culture that shapes the universe." Words are indeed powerful; the visible world comes from the invisible God through His spoken word. As God created by speaking, He then defined creation by using words as well: "God called the light day and the darkness He called night. ... God called the expanse sky. ... God called the dry ground land" (Genesis 1:5, 8, 10).

In Genesis 2:19 God established man's dominion over nature by making man a *word maker*, giving man the responsibility of naming the animals. As man mimics God by using language, he is separated from the rest of creation as the maker of culture. Thus in the Garden of Eden, the First Farmer created the first couple. In response to worship (cult), Adam and Eve are to create culture, by cultivating both soil and soul. The importance of man as culture maker is found in the language that we employ: *agri*-culture—cultivate the field, *horti*-culture—cultivate the garden, and *aqua*-culture—cultivate the water. Theologian Herman Bavinck wrote: "Culture in the broadest sense is the purpose for which God created man after His image...[which] includes not only the most ancient callings of ... hunting and fishing, agriculture and stock raising, but also trade and commerce and science and art."

Farmers are cultivators, not only of the soil, but also of culture. They have their role in the building of nations. As the societal mandate sends image bearers to the corners of the continents, the agriculturists precede them, finding innovative ways to nurture the "fruits of creation."

George Washington Carver conveyed the excitement of this: "When one fully realizes that every farm, garden and orchard product will yield new, strange and useful things to the thoroughly developed creative mind, an inexhaustible [sic] field of possibilities dawns upon us; a field in which all can work without clashing, indeed the greater number of workers, the more interesting their work becomes, and the more closely they are drawn together, as here we really walk and talk with the Great Creator; it is here that He shows His glory, majesty and power in such an understanding and unmistakable way."

God Has Created an Agricultural System

God created with a purpose; therefore there is a design. The design reflects the *beauty* and *order* of the mind of the Creator. In fact, in creation, science and art meet. We marvel as we see the beauty and science of a grand sunset or of a simple daisy. The First Farmer not only planted a garden, but He designed the system—one simple yet profound, beautiful yet rational. And this system is not a mere *mechanical* scheme, but a *lively* work of art, a *divine order*.

At the heart of the divine order is the simple seed. Genesis 1:11,12 records that on the third day of creation, 'God said, "Let the land produce vegetation: *seed-bearing plants and trees* on the land that bear fruit with *seed* in it, according to their various kinds." And it was so. The land produced vegetation: plants bearing seed according to their kinds and trees bearing fruit with seed in it according to their kinds. And God saw that it was good.' Seeds that reproduce life, a common miracle!

We find this divine order also reflected in Genesis 1:29–2:1.

> Then God said, "I give you every seed-bearing plant on the face of the whole earth and every tree that has fruit with seed in it. They will be yours for food. And to all the beasts of the earth and all the birds of the air and all the creatures that move on the ground—everything that has the breath of life in it—I give every green plant for food." And it was so. God saw all that he had made, and it was very good. And there was evening, and there was morning—the sixth day. Thus the heavens and the earth were completed in all their vast array. [Italics mine.]

Note the beauty of the passage and the power of the words. From the vast array of the heavens to the miracle of the seed, God created with patterns and textures. Order and beauty were spoken into this lively work of art. Plants and trees are seed bearing. They reproduce life after their design.

There is no place where we see this more profoundly expressed than in the seed. Seeds allow for reproduction, for the expansion of life, for the growing of the garden, for the sending out of culture makers to all the corners of the earth. Imagine if the system of the seed called for only a one for one exchange, one seed would reproduce just one seed. Death would have been built into the system. But the miracle of the seed produces a bountiful garden. From one seed comes a plant that produces many fruit, and within each fruit are many seeds. The agriculturist and horticulturist have the honor of participating in this miracle.

There is a wonderful Kenyan proverb that describes the glory of the seed: "You can count the number of seeds in a mango, but you cannot count the number of mangos in a seed." From one seed can come a virtually unlimited harvest. Is this not a common *miracle*? Or think of the DNA of a dog. The genetic code of one dog has the potential to produce all the wonderful varieties of dogs that we see in the world today—from one seed.

A Kenyan pastor named Joseph captured the wonder of the seed in this rather intriguing question: "What is more powerful, a seed or a bullet?" The profound answer: "A seed!" Why you ask? "Because, a bullet can kill *one* person. A single seed can produce food for a *million* people." Pastor Joseph concluded, "Man created the bullet. Who created the seed? God!" Ah! The wisdom of Africa!

T. D. Jakes, writing in his foreword to Dr. Mark Hanby's book *You Have Not Many Fathers*, describes the wonder of the divine order:

> "Our God is methodical. He is not chaotic. If we want to be prosperous both spiritually and naturally, then we must endeavor to know and function within His divine order. I am reminded of that truth whenever I read about the creation of our world as recorded in the Book of Genesis. It is there that God, through His eternal wisdom, whispers in the ear of His servant the unveiled blueprint of the creation of the universe.... It is here that God begins the order from which His methodical structure for all truth emanates and flourishes. For instance, He calls from the muddy montage of an uninhabited planet the herb, plants, and greenery. He brings forth these plants whose seed will reproduce and grow in the calm summer breezes of thousands of years.
>
> He will create only once the blade of grass which He expects to garnish His fields. His plan is so futuristic that it puts within each plant a seed of potential. The seed holds the key to reproduction and thereby eliminates the possibility of extinction. Each blade had a destiny created in its origin. Its future is perpetuated in the integrity of its seed. As long as there is a seed to germinate, the blade, through its progeny, will be represented. Its purpose cannot be aborted. It is this principle that governs all of God's creation".

Dr. Jacques Monod, a Nobel Laureate in biology, has also articulated this principle. In his book *Chance and Necessity*, Monod writes: "... one of the fundamental characteristics common to all-living beings without exception [is] that of being *objects endowed with a purpose or project*, which at the same time they exhibit in their structure and carry out through their performances. ..." While Monod is an atheist and materialist, as a scientist he was forced to acknowledge the design he observed while examining nature. All living things are endowed with a purpose. That purpose is expressed in both their design and function. For an atheist, this is a surprise. For someone operating from the biblical worldview, this is expected. There is a Designer. He has created with purpose. And man, in addition to appreciating beauty and design, can discover the purpose of the seed.

The Farmer Can Understand the Design

In Genesis 2:19, we find the most startling revelation: "Now the LORD God had formed out of the ground all the beasts of the field and all the birds of the air. He brought them to the man to see what he would name them; and whatever the man called each living creature, that was its name." God made the animals, but he left it to Adam, the farmer, horticulturist, and animal husbandry expert to name them. This reveals something very important about both man and creation. Creation reveals the divine order. Creation is not "disordered" or capricious, as animists believe. Man, being made in the image of God, is a reasonable, rational creature. As husbandman, Adam had the ability to observe the order that God had created and to use language to categorize creation. Not only does man have this ability, but also whatever Adam named the animals, *"that was its name!"* Let me say that a little differently. Whatever name Adam gave the animals, that was the name **that God would call them by**! The poorest farmer is not poor in endowment. The poorest farmer has the ability to *think about farming*! Speaking from their Central American experience, Flores and Sanchez state, "If the mind of a campesino (peasant) is a desert, his farm will look like a desert." Conversely, if the mind of the farmer is bountiful, his farm will produce bounty. Part of our task is to help the farmer to know the First Farmer, so that he may come to think about farming the right way.

What is the nature of God's revelation? God has revealed Himself in two major ways. In *General Revelation*, He has revealed Himself to all mankind, through "the book" of His *world*! In *Special Revelation*, He has revealed Himself to those who would be saved through the book of His *Word*!

Through General Revelation, God has revealed Himself to every human being in every generation, through the things He has made. Paul makes this point in Romans 1:19,20 (ASV): "because that which is known of God is manifest *in them* [italics mine]; for God manifested it unto them. For the invisible things of him since the creation of the world are clearly seen, being perceived *through the things that are made* [italics mine], even his everlasting power and divinity; that they may be without excuse:" Paul argues here that God has revealed Himself in two ways in His creation. First, He has revealed Himself "in them"—man the image of God. Second, He has revealed Himself "through the things that are made." This is why, even an atheistic scientist like Jacques Monod argues that all living things bear the imprint of design. The logical conclusion is that there must be a Designer.

Likewise, through Special Revelation, God has revealed Himself and His plan of salvation through His Word. First, He has revealed Himself in the *Living* Word, Jesus Christ (John 1:1,2,14). Second, He has revealed Himself through His *Written* Word, the Bible (Hebrews 4:12). God's General Revelation gives each man enough to know that God exists. In Special Revelation He discloses the plan of salvation and tells us how we might know God.

While we have discussed God's revelation in a "theological" framework, it is important to hear the wonder in our theology. The great American agriculturist and educator, Dr. George Washington Carver, understood the wonder of God's revelation. He called his research lab "God's Little Workshop." Carver was a Christian. As such, he understood that God spoke through both His creation and through His Word. He understood that each revelation shed light on the other.

Nature is a book to be read. It reveals the Designer and the design. As we study the form and structure of a thing, we can discover its purpose; we can "think God's thoughts after Him." The Scripture, on the other hand, helps us to interpret what we are seeing. It establishes principles and a framework for, in our case, agriculture. God's Word interprets and gives meaning to God's world. God's world reveals both the existence of God and something of His purpose.

George Washington Carver understood the wonder of God's revelation. When God's Word said in Genesis 1:29, "Behold, I have given you every herb yielding seed, which is on the face of all the earth, and every tree, in which is the fruit of a tree yielding seed; to you it shall be for food. ..." (KJV), Carver, in childlike wonder, commented, "'Behold' means to 'look,' 'search,' 'find out' ... That to me is the most wonderful thing in life." Carver took the Bible seriously. He understood that it informs us about our life and work.

Carver also understood that he was to "read" the book of God's world: "To me Nature in its varied forms is the little windows through which God permits me to commune with Him, and to see much of His glory, by simply lifting the curtain and looking in. I love to think of Nature as wireless telegraph stations through which God speaks to us every day, every hour, and every moment of our lives."

Carver came to creation to discover the purpose of a thing and then to put it to use to benefit man. When asked by agricultural journalist what prompted him to study the simple peanut, Carver responded:

> "Why, I just took a handful of peanuts and looked at them. 'Great Creator,' I said, 'why did you make the peanut? Why?' With such knowledge as I had of chemistry and physics I set to work to take the peanut apart. I separated the water, the fats, the oils, the gums, the resins, sugars, starches pectoses, pentoses, pentosans, legume, lysine, and the amino and amedo acids. There! I had the parts of the peanut all spread out before me. Then I merely went on to try different combinations of those parts, under different conditions of temperature, pressure, and so forth. The result was what you see—these 202 different products, all made from peanuts!"

George Washington Carver was born "the poorest of the poor." Both his parents were slaves in the state of Missouri during the Civil War. Carver was orphaned and thus never knew his parents. Yet he became one of America's greatest "farmers." He learned how to *think* about farming. God used this man of humble roots to impact a nation.

There is an old Chinese proverb that has helped to guide the development movement. It says: "Give a man a fish and he has food for a day. Teach a man to fish and he has food for a lifetime." "Giving a man a fish" is an act of charity during an emergency. This is called *relief*, and it can keep a man alive during a time of disaster. To "teach a man to fish" introduces the "how" skills and technology knowledge. This is called *development*, and it can help a man provide for his family in situations of chronic poverty and hunger. While these are good as far as they go, they leave the community in a static situation. The community is limited by the resources and knowledge that are "brought in" from the outside. Today, development is often thought of as outside help, outside money, and outside resources being brought to bear on a poor community. In cultures where fatalism shapes the mind, well meaning outside resources tend to reinforce the lie: "We are poor and there is nothing we can do about it!"

The proverb needs to be extended if people are going to be set free to dream and to reach their God-given potential. The proverb could read:

"Give a man a fish, he has food for a day!—*Relief*

Teach a man to fish; he has food for a lifetime!—*Development*

Teach a man to think about fishing and his life is changed forever!—*Transformation*"

In our context, the task of the Christian agriculturist, missionary, development worker or pastor is to teach farmers to "think about farming," to understand their life and work within the framework of the biblical worldview. It is to call poor farmers to live in the context of God's two forms of revelation. Through general revelation, the design reveals the glory of the First Farmer and the structure and functions of, among other things, the seed system. Special revelation allows us to have a relationship with the First Farmer, to understand biblical principles of agriculture and to have a dynamic framework for connecting agriculture to the Kingdom of God. It allows us to cultivate a Christian mind as it relates to agriculture.

We have seen this Christian mind in George Washington Carver. God's general revelation through creation and special revelation of the Bible were "the books" that he read to have his mind framed as an agriculturist and an educator. Another man who understood these things was "the father of modern missions," William Carey. In a profound little book, *The Legacy of William Carey: A Model for the Transformation of a Culture*, Ruth and Vishal Mangalwadi explore, not Carey's life, but his mindset. Carey was not only the father of modern missions; he was the pioneer of transformational (biblical) development. Carey was not a missionary in the 20th century sense of a "professional, cross-cultural religious worker." Bringing a Christian mind to the task of evangelism, church planting, cultural transformation and national development, Carey was, among other things, a botanist, agriculturist, and conservationist. Carey connected the Kingdom of God to these endeavors to see India transformed. Like Carver, William Carey was a remarkably gifted man. Both were born in poverty. Unlike Carver, who had a formal education past the doctoral level, Carey did not finish secondary school. Both men cultivated, not only the soil, but also a Christian mind.

Beyond Dualism

William Carey and George Washington Carver were men from a different era, a time when Christians functioned from the biblical worldview. Christ is the Lord of all of life, not just the spiritual part of life. In the biblical worldview, there is no sacred–secular dichotomy; there is no priest–laity hierarchy; there is no concept that doing religious or spiritual work is "full-time Christian service" and all non-spiritual vocations are somehow second-class. According to the biblical worldview, we live in one world, God's world. God is the Lord of the entire world, and as Christians, we are to live *coram Deo*—before the face of God. But today, many Christians live in two worlds—a spiritual world and a secular world. The spiritual world is the realm of church, Bible study and prayer meetings. The secular world is everything else, including, for many Christian agronomists, their work in agriculture.

The farmer and agriculturist have a different call than do the pastor or theologian. They have different skills and a different calling than the evangelist or church planter. The gifts and call are different, but one is not superior to the other. The issue is one of consecration, not one of higher and lower calling. A farmer may be leading a consecrated life and a pastor may not. In this case, the farmer is "more spiritual" than the pastor.

In an earlier generation, when the norm for Christians was to live *coram Deo*, a woman had a plaque made for her kitchen. It read, "Worship services held here three times a day!" What did she understand? She knew that she was a Christian, not only when she was in the church building, but also when she was in her kitchen. She understood that she was a Christian 24/7, not just on Sunday. She understood that the "horizontal" activity of preparing a meal for her family and friends was an act of worship. When her husband went out to his field to farm, he stood in the middle of the field and cried to the Lord, "Lord, this is your farm! I am your steward. How may I labor today so as to glorify you in my field?"

There is a great division among Christian ministries today because of the sacred–secular dichotomy. The "professional missionary," functioning as a dualist, wants to see souls saved for heaven and churches planted. When this occurs, the missionary's job is done. Some with a dualistic mind may use agriculture "to get a foot in the door" to do the "real work," of evangelism and church planting.

Conversely, Christian relief and development workers often see the needs of the poor, and are moved by God's mandate to help the poor, yet they often respond with materialistic patterns of solving the problems of poverty. Like their secular counterparts, they enter a country in response to a major disaster and set up a relief office, hire staff, buy vehicles and move commodities. As the crises subsides, they begin to receive training resources and funding from USAID or UN sponsored agricultural agencies which in many cases flow from a materialistic paradigm. They then proceed to implement essentially materialistic programs in the name of Christ. To make these programs "holistic" they may seek to add a "spiritual" component to their materialistic development efforts, like pastors' conferences or showing the Jesus Film.

Today, both Christian missionaries and relief and development workers tend to operate from a dualistic "two worlds" paradigm. What is necessary today for both is that they return to a biblical worldview driven perspective of their ministry. They need to answer the questions, What is the Mission? What is the role of the church in society? What does it mean to be a Christian? What is the responsibility of the church to the impoverished, from perspective of the biblical worldview?

Christians should not seek to start "Christian relief and development organizations," but relief and development organizations that are functioning from a biblical paradigm. To be motivated by Christ to do secular development is not enough. The motive, mindset and methodology should all reflect the biblical worldview. Missionary organizations need to learn from William Carey, and base their policies and programs on the biblical worldview as well.

My good friend and co-worker, Arturo Cuba, has a remarkable story that he tells from his experience in Guatemala. It illustrates a truly holistic approach to development, in contrast to the dichotomized ministries of missionaries and relief and development staff working among impoverished farmers in the mountains of Guatemala.

The Pokomchi Indians are among the poorest people in the poorest state of Guatemala. A generation ago, missionaries evangelized them and planted churches. Many Pokomchi accepted Christ, but their communities remained desperately poor. The young Christian converts gained hope for the future, but no hope for today. In fact, they were literally waiting to die, so they could leave their miserable existence on earth and go to be with Jesus in heaven. After awhile, several private voluntary organizations came to work with the Pokomchi, interested in helping them overcome their physical poverty. They brought in large amounts of outside money and completed many projects, labeling them successful. Now, there were pit latrines, but they were largely unused. There were school buildings, but very few children attended or graduated. Many of the projects that were carried out to improve the physical condition of the Pokomchi were completed, but there was no transformation in the lives and communities of the Pokomchi. The people remained desperately poor.

This began to change when Arturo, a young Peruvian pastor, began to work among the Pokomchi in the early 1990s. Unlike earlier missionaries and relief and development workers, Arturo understood the importance of the biblical worldview for individual and community transformation. Likewise, he understood that authentic Christian ministry is to be holistic—reaching out to every area of brokenness in the community. He began to work with illiterate Pokomchi pastors. He prayerfully took them through a comprehensive study of the Bible, in hopes of challenging their mindsets. Arturo understood that true repentance involves more than spiritual belief. It also requires a completely transformed frame of mind.

As Arturo taught them from the Bible, he used everyday illustrations to teach key biblical principles, such as God's intention that mankind exercise stewardship over creation. A common problem among the Pokomchi was the lack of proper storage facilities for harvested crops. Often, peasant farmers harvested a good crop, only to have rats eat it before their children could be fed. Arturo asked the farmers, "Who is smarter, you or the rats?" The farmers would laugh and say, "The rats." Arturo asked, "Do you have dominion over the rats, or do the rats have dominion over your lives?" The farmers reluctantly acknowledged that, in a real sense, the rats had dominion over them and their families. Then, Arturo introduced the farmers to the key biblical principle that men and women are uniquely created in God's image, and are given the mandate by God to exercise stewardship and dominion over the rest of His creation (Genesis 1:27,28; 2:15; 9:1,2; Psalm 8:3-9.) He pointed out that God had blessed them with creativity because they were made in His image. With their God-given creativity and a proper understanding of their role to subdue and care for creation, they could overcome this problem. The farmers later developed a plan for grain storage that involved the construction of simple, elevated corncribs. The food supply began to increase, as did the overall health of the children in the community.

Arturo continued to teach other biblical principles and their practical, everyday application, and gradually, the mindsets of these Pokomchi pastors were transformed. As their mindsets were transformed, the church was impacted. Through the church, the community began to be transformed.

Arturo taught the biblical principle that all human life is created by God, in His image (Genesis 1:26,27) and is therefore of incredible value. Community members came to realize that their children were a gift of the Lord (Psalm 127:3) and blessing of the Lord to the community. As a result, community members began to encourage their children to attend school. Children started to go to school because the people valued education, particularly education in God's Word.

Arturo taught the biblical principle that both men and women are of equal value and worth in God's eyes, and that husbands are to love their wives and treat them with respect and dignity (Ephesians 5:25-28; 1 Peter 3:7). As a result, husbands began to encourage their wives to learn to read because they came to realize that God cares equally for men and women.

In the Pokomchi community, it is traditional for wives to stay at home with the children during the day. These homes are typically small mud-brick huts, where the women prepare meals over open fires on the floors of the huts. A critical problem in the community was that the smoke from these fires caused health problems for wives and children living inside the huts, and often children would stumble into the open fires and be severely burned. The husbands, as they came to realize their biblical responsibility to love and care for their wives and children, began to apply these principles by building small mud stoves in their homes. The stoves were designed to channel the smoke outside, and to protect their children from getting burned. As a result, the health of both wives and children in the community improved.

A seminary professor from the United States visited Arturo recently. He witnessed how the lives of the Pokomchi had been transformed through holistic ministry, based on the power of biblical truth applied to all areas of life. Tears welled up in his eyes and he said, "This is the coming of the Kingdom of God to the Pokomchi!"

An Ambassador of the Kingdom

Most Christians separate agriculture from the Kingdom of God. Relief and development organizations traditionally connect agriculture to the materialistic paradigm. Many mission organizations, operating from a Gnostic paradigm, use agriculture (a "secular" activity) to create a platform for doing the higher activities of evangelism and church planting. We need to begin to repudiate these distorted models and replace them with a holistic model. We need to reconnect and integrate agriculture and the Kingdom of God.

Above all else, an agriculturalist or farmer is an ambassador of the Kingdom of God. We must encourage the continuation of the "great cloud" of pastoral and agricultural witnesses: Adam and Eve, Abraham, David, Amos, Peter, Carey and Carver to name a few.

Dr. Ted Yamamori, President Emeritus of Food for the Hungry International, has dedicated his life to calling the church to biblical holistic ministry. He talks frequently of the couplets "redemption that leads to development" and "development that leads to redemption."

In holism, cycles of interaction and understanding are created. In our context, redemption that leads to development may be identified as "connecting agriculture to the Kingdom," while development that leads to redemption may be identified as "connecting the Kingdom of God to agriculture." These are two sides of the same coin. In both expressions, the agriculturist who wants to function from the framework of the biblical worldview is the integration point of this holism. Let's look at these in turn.

Connecting Agriculture to the Kingdom

Responding to the Gospel proclamation should lead to Kingdom principled agricultural development. When a farmer becomes a Christian, his life is to be lived within the context of the Kingdom of God; his mind is to be transformed so that he begins to see agriculture within the framework of a biblical worldview. His purpose now is to be a steward of the land that God has given him.

How does one begin to think and function as a Christian in the domain of agriculture? First, Christians who are farmers can begin to develop a *Biblical Theology of Agriculture*. The Bible is God's "farmers' almanac," the owner's manual for agriculture. While it does not contain all there is to know about agriculture, it creates a framework for understanding agriculture and presents principles that relate to agriculture. The Bible is not only to be studied as a devotional book, but it is to inform the vocational life of the agriculturalist.

When the Scriptures inform a person's understanding of his vocation, it may be said that he is developing a biblical theology for vocation. This monograph can be used as a framework for that study. An agriculturist can keep a journal, and over a few years or the course of a lifetime, read the Bible from Genesis to Revelation to see what it reveals about agriculture. Other methods of study, such as "Scripture Search" and "word studies" may be used profitably to help develop a biblical theology of agriculture.

Second, as a farmer comes to Christ, he is to live *coram Deo*— "before the face of God." He is a Christian 24 hours a day, seven days a week. He is not merely a Christian when he is doing "spiritual things." His vocation is transformed and is to bring glory to God and hope to a broken world.

The Christian apologist and cultural critic Os Guinness shares a marvelous story from his own family in his book *The Call.* It is the story about the life of his great-great grandmother, Jane Lucretia D'Esterre. As an impoverished 18 year-old Irish orphan and widow with two children, D'Esterre sat on a riverbank in deep despair, contemplating suicide. While gazing "into the dark depths of the river … she looked up and saw a young plowman setting to work in a field on the other bank of the river. He was about her age but quite oblivious to her and to anything but his work. Meticulous, absorbed, skilled, he displayed such a pride in his work that the newly turned furrows looked as finely executed as the paint strokes on an artist's canvas."

Guinness continues that D'Esterre was "saved from suicide and reinvigorated for life by the sight of *work well done*." [italics mine] She returned to care for her children, came to faith in Christ and married Captain John Grattan Guinness, Os' great-great-grandfather. "Nothing is known of the Scottish farmer's son except what was seen in his plowing and could be guessed from his whistling hymns as he worked. But knowing the common motivation of that most Christian of centuries in Scotland, it is not too much to say that the incident underscores how *calling transforms life so that even the commonplace and menial are invested with the splendor of the ordinary.*" [italics mine]

A life lived *coram Deo* is a life that brings the simple things into the realm of worship. Dignity is given to the menial, the splendor of the ordinary is revealed to a watching world. Agriculture is transformed within the framework of stewardship, and God uses the simple and beautiful artistry of the farmer to speak life to the watching world. Farming is to be done to the glory of God and the advancement of His Kingdom. As the Christian agriculturist enters his field, he recognizes that "this land belongs to God;" the farmer in his field is a steward and has come to worship. The prayer he utters is, "Lord, how can I honor you today in this land? How can I make this land more bountiful? How can I enrich the land for a legacy for the next generation?" We saw this earlier illustrated in "Arturo's Story."

Third, the farmer, seeking to function from a biblical mind as it relates to agriculture is to apply biblical principles in his practice. In Genesis 1:26-28 and 2:15 we read that the farmer is to be a steward of the land. Instead of destroying the soil, he should work the farm in a way that leaves it more fertile for succeeding generations. This would speak against the slash and burn agriculture found in many developing nations and erosion of agricultural land found in others.

This is illustrated in George Washington Carver's call for the farmer to be "kind to the soil." He writes, "The farmer whose soil produces less every year, is unkind to it in some way; that is, he is not doing by it what he should; he is robbing it of some substance it must have, and he becomes, therefore, a soil robber rather than a progressive farmer." Carver continues, "We must enrich our soil every year instead of merely depleting it. It is fundamental that nature will drive away those who sin against it."

From Exodus 23:10-13 there is to be a Sabbath rest every seven years for the land. This was given to "rest the soil" and to remind the farmer that his dependence was on the Lord, not on his own initiative for prosperity. Carver comments on this and similar passages, "We take this very Book, here—go way back here, almost to the beginning of time and we find, way back in the time of the Pharaohs, the farmers were obliged to rest their lands and every fifty years was a jubilee year. This was picnic time for the soil."

From Deuteronomy 24:19-22 and Ruth 2:17 we read that the land is intended by the Land Owner for social good. The steward is to leave *gleanings* to meet the needs of the widow, stranger and foreigner. This is a reminder to the farmer that God cares for the poor and thus the Christian who is a farmer has a social responsibility to use a portion of his crop to meet the needs of the poor.

We know from Scripture, that we live in a moral universe and therefore farmers have a moral obligation to the community. Crops should be grown that edify and not destroy human potential. Two Christians working as agriculturists in the Mission in northern Thailand were confronted with a dilemma. The farmers they were working with were growing opium poppies for the drug trade. As farmers in these communities came to Christ, fruit orchards and vegetable gardens replaced poppy fields.

Fourth, the church is the body of Christ and is to be an incarnational community. Those gifted with equipping gifts, pastors, and teachers are to equip the saints for the work of service (Ephesians 4:11,12). Too often today, because God's people function from a Gnostic paradigm, we think that Christians are to be employed in "church jobs" like ushering, running programs, or being the church treasurer. While these may or may not be necessary, what is clear from the biblical paradigm is that the church is to be an incarnational community and her people are to be equipped when gathered on Sunday to be servant-leaders in the community when they are scattered the other six days a week. The church in agricultural communities is to equip the farmers to not only be servants to the community, but to be leaders in the agricultural sector. God's intention is that *nations* (not merely individuals) are to be discipled (Matthew 28:18-20). For this to occur all sectors of society need to be discipled—bringing a biblical worldview and biblical principles to that sector. Natural evil (weeds in the garden, drought, famine) is to be pushed back, farmers are to be equipped to provide leadership in their sphere of society to fight the ravages of the Fall and to make the land as bountiful as God intends.

The wealth of a nation is her people, being freed by the principles flowing from the biblical worldview to be all that God intends for them to be. It is the role of the church to create the conscience of the nation, to equip believers to be nation builders, including preparing simple farmers to become shapers of the agricultural sector.

Building on this, the fifth thing is to let Christians in the agricultural sector create or infiltrate existing institutions that train future farmers. Let them bring with them the biblical mind to shape those institutions. Let these institutions be places where the best research (reading the book of the world) is integrated with the reading of the book of the Word of God. Let them be places where the simple farmer is called into the Kingdom of God— where he is taught, not only the technical side of agricultural, but to also *think* about farming.

George Washington Carver articulated this spirit when he wrote, "Let farmers' institutes be organized, and all the methods of nature's study be brought down to the everyday life and language of the masses. Let us become familiar with the commonest things about us, of which two-thirds of the people are surprisingly ignorant. ... If every farmer could recognize that his plants were real, living things, and that sunshine, air, food, and drink were just as necessary for their lives as for that of the animal, the problem would become at once intellectual, enjoyable and practical."

Connecting the Kingdom to Agriculture

Now let's look at the other side of the issue, connecting the Kingdom to agriculture.

Agricultural development within the mental context of the Kingdom of God should lead to Gospel proclamation. As a natural part of the Christian farmer's life there is an opportunity to reveal the Kingdom of God in the agricultural sector. This is not to be a separation between the technical and the message. In some secular-founded Christian relief and development programs, the Christian technical people do the technical work and bring in the "spiritual people" to do the spiritual work (i.e., showing the Jesus Film, leading Bible studies, or holding pastors' conferences). Conversely, missionary organizations often leverage agriculture as a means to a "higher" objective—evangelism.

In the biblical paradigm of the Kingdom of God there is an integration of all of life. The Christian technical worker *is a Christian!* The world in which he works is God's world. Dr. Carver expressed this quite simply, "I know that my Redeemer liveth. I know the source from whence my help comes. Inspiration … means simply *God speaking to man through the things He has created* [italics mine]; permitting him to interpret correctly the purposes the Creator had in permitting them to come into existence. I am not interested in any science that leaves God out; in fact, I am not interested in anything that leaves out God."

The Good News of the Kingdom is both demonstrated and proclaimed in each sphere of society. The sphere of agriculture is a place *through which* "Thy kingdom come, Thy will be done, on earth as it is in heaven." The farm of the Christian agriculturist is the place where Christ wants to make Himself known. Within the normal everyday activities of farm life, the farmer will find opportunities for pre-evangelism or evangelism. He can utilize these opportunities in a number of ways.

First, the "Book of the World" can be used to reveal the Creator. These opportunities are called truth encounters. Christianity is objectively true because God exists and reality conforms to His existence. The book of the world is part of God's self-disclosure. Truth encounters reveal The First Farmer in everyday farm life. A report from a 1915 Farmers' Conference in Georgia reveals Dr. Carver's practice of truth encounters. "Prof. Carver is a genius. He not only knows his subjects but puts them in such simple form that a child can grasp them. His knowledge of the soil and plant life is simply wonderful. No one can spend any time with Prof. Carver in a grove or woods without getting some conception of nature and nature's God. He sees the good and beautiful in everything that God has made."

Truth encounters simply reveal the "fingerprints of God" all over creation. From His immensity seen in the vastness of the universe to His power seen in the pounding surf, to His artistry seen in the sunset, to His nurturing seen in the mother's breast, or to

His marvelous engineering seen in the miracle of the seed, God reveals Himself through the things He has made. It is the Christian agriculturist's grand journey to point to the First Farmer through the daily miracles on the farm or at the research institute. It was said of Dr. Carver's three-hour lecture to a group of orphan boys in 1939 in Michigan, "What began as a lecture on botany soon developed into a soul-stirring recital of how intimately all of the plants are related to one another, of how the plants and the animals—mankind included—are inextricably interdependent, and of how the whole of creation is related to its Creator."

Second, the Book of the Word can be used to establish practical principles of agricultural life. Bible studies can be developed from the farmer's journal used for tracing a biblical theology of agriculture. Studies on stewardship, the fallowing of the land, and gleaning for the poor can give guidance in improving the viability of the farm. Such studies can also show the veracity of God's word for other areas of life as well. These studies can be done informally, one on one, with individual farmers or can be part of the curriculum of the farmer's institute. When taught by the agricultural researcher or soil scientist, the seamless whole of God's creation is authoritatively revealed.

Third, the Book of the Word, can be used to teach timeless spiritual truths. The Old and New Testaments are filled with proverbs, sayings and stories from agrarian life in a poor Middle-Eastern setting. Jesus, Himself, was a master storyteller. In 30 places, He took common events from city and agrarian life to teach eternal principles. His simple agricultural parables acted as spiritual time bombs in the lives of those who heard them. Let's look at some examples. In Matthew 13:1-23, Jesus used the parable of the seed to illustrate that not all who hear the Gospel will respond in faith. In John, He used an illustration of the vine and the branches to reflect the need of the believer in Christ to abide in Christ. It also teaches the agricultural and spiritual principle of pruning. In Galatians 6:7-10, the Apostle Paul affirmed the principle that you reap what you sow! If you sow evil, you will reap destruction. If you sow charity, you will reap life.

Fourth, as mentioned in the previous section (Connecting Agriculture to the Kingdom), we can establish research and training institutes where the revelation of God's world and Word are integrated on the programmatic level.

Fifth, the local church can demonstrate the love of God through the use of "Seed Projects," simple projects using local resources to minister holistically to non-Christians in the community. This type of ministry has been articulated by the Harvest Foundation in their Leadership Development Training Program for pastors and church leaders. A story told by a Baptist pastor from Burma will help to illustrate how a group of Christian farmers in this predominately Buddhist country reached out to demonstrate God's love to an antagonistic Buddhist neighbor.

> "Following the conference I was visiting one of our churches in lower Burma. I taught them the lesson on Seed Projects. (This lesson emphasizes using local resources to demonstrate God's love.) While I was in the community I learned of a non-Christian man with five children that couldn't prepare his rice paddies in time for the rainy season planting because he only had one ox. I shared this situation with our church members who are from a different ethnic group than this man. Historically there has been fighting between the tribe to which the church members belong and the ethnic group to which this man belongs. In spite of the traditional inter-ethnic animosity, the church members responded and took six of their oxen to this man's rice paddies and helped him prepare his fields for planting. This action of kindness—especially across ethnic lines—had a great impact on the man and his family. I just returned from another visit on January 22nd and learned that the man's oldest daughter has become a believer and been baptized. The rest of the family is coming to church and learning about the Christian faith. However, the church speaks a different language than this man's family and he wants to learn about Christian faith in his own tongue. So he and some members from the church are building another building where they can hold services in this man's mother tongue. Another result of this demonstration of God's love by the Christians is a growing unity between the two ethnic groups in the village."

Conclusion

As I conclude this paper, I am reminded again, that the problems of hunger and poverty do not exist because of a shortage of resources. God has made a bountiful world. We have the technology to solve the problems of hunger and poverty. The root of the problem is faulty *thinking* about agriculture—the lack of the biblical worldview being applied in agriculture. We need to call farmers to have "bountiful minds" so their farms can begin to produce bounty. It is the task of God's people to bring the worldview of the Kingdom of God to those entrapped in poverty in agricultural communities around the world. May we call Christians working in agriculture to be ambassadors of the Kingdom on their farms and in their communities.

References

Bavinck, Herman

>   1999   Quoted in Charles Colson and Nancy Pearcey. *How Now Shall We Live?*, 293. Wheaton, IL: Tyndale House Publishers.

Carver, George Washington

>   1995   Quoted in John S. Ferrell. *Fruits of Creation*, 62, 72, 73. Shakopee, MN: Macalester Park Publishing Company.

Ferrell, John S.

>   1995   *Fruits of Creation*, 29, 36, 61. Shakopee, MN: Macalester Park Publishing Company.

Flores, M. and E. Sanchez

>   1992   "The Human Farm: People-based Approach to Food Production and Conservation." In *Growing our Future: Food Security and the Environment*, ed. K. Smith and T. Yamamori, 74-81. West Hartford, Connecticut: Kumarian Press.

Guinness, Os

>   1998   *The Call*. Nashville, TN: Word Publishing.

Hanby, Mark

>   2000   *You Have Not Many Fathers*. Shippensburg, PA: Destiny Image Publishers, Inc.

Hegeman, David Bruce

>   1999   *Plowing in Hope: Toward a Biblical Theology of Culture*. Moscow, ID: Canon Press.

McAlpine, Thomas H.

>   1995   *By Word, Work and Wonder*, Chapter 5. Monrovia, CA: MARC Publishers.

Monod, Jacques

>   1971   *Chance and Necessity*. New York: Alfred A. Knopf, Inc.

On Dams, Demons, Wells and Witches:

Managing the Message of Transformational Development

Bruce Bradshaw

*For God did not send his Son into the world to condemn the
kosmos,
but to save the kosmos through him.* John 3:17

Introduction

A Christian development agency built irrigation dams in a village in
a West African folk Islamic culture, expecting the villagers to become
more self-sufficient in food production. The village farmers had high
expectations for the project. However, they were disappointed before
the end of the first growing season; the rainfall was lower than
expected, and the dams were not collecting enough water to irrigate
the gardens adequately. The people who lived in the village knew the
harvests would be low; they feared a food shortage and possibly
death. The village elders asked the hydrologists what could be done
to improve the project. The hydrologists advised the elders that they
could not increase the amount of water the dams were collecting.
They believed the dams were as efficient as they could be, and they
determined that the shortage of rain, rather than dam design, was the
central problem.

The village elders met privately, and decided there was

another problem. They believed the water level was low because the Christians refused to make sacrifices to the local spirits before building the dams. The elders believed some local spirits controlled the rainfall in the region, and they thought the spirits were angry because the Christians built the dams without seeking their permission or making sacrifices to them. The hydrologists did not believe the demons damned the dams, and they told the village elders that the issue needed more consideration.

As we consider agriculture and purpose, the theme of my presentation, we have to ask how the hydrologists can respond to the dams and demons in some meaningful way. What should they do? Some people advocate some type of a "power encounter" with the demons, an effort to cause rain to fall by casting demons from the region. Other people, who don't even want to assume the existence of the demons, are not about to believe they control rainfall. We'll have to examine another story before deciding what to do about the demons and the rainfall.

A team of agricultural facilitators encouraged the farmers in an East African village to try some innovations that would increase their yields of sorghum and maize by 30 per cent. The farmers listened attentively as the agriculturalists told them about hybrid seeds and fertilizers. When the discussions were finished, the agriculturalists were disappointed that only one farmer accepted their invitation to use the innovations. However, they were content to begin their project with this farmer.

The farmer's name was Mdumbwa. The agriculturalists called Mdumbwa the "contact farmer." They believed he was the contact who would inspire the other farmers to follow him. The other farmers were called "follow farmers." The agriculturalists saw no reason why the other farmers in the village would not accept the innovations after they saw Mdumbwa's success.

Mdumbwa's harvest increased as the agriculturalists expected. He harvested six more bags of sorghum than he had harvested the previous year. The agriculturalists believed Mdumbwa's success was their success. They expected the other village farmers to follow Mdumbwa. However, the village farmers, including Mdumbwa, suspected that something was seriously wrong with the methods the agriculturalist introduced into the village. The people in Mdumbwa's village believed farmers could not harvest more than three bags of sorghum per acre unless they used witchcraft. The villagers suspected him of using witchcraft because they did not know another way to explain his success. When the farmers listened to the agriculturalists explain these innovations, they heard details about seeds, fertilizers, irrigation, soil conditions, etc. The agriculturalists spoke about what caused increased harvest, but they said nothing about who caused them. The agriculturalists said nothing about the spirituality of their innovations. The farmers wondered why the agriculturalists were silent about this issue. In a culture where the people assume that the unseen realm governs the seen realm, the agriculturalists neglected to address the spiritual issues of their innovations. The neglect convinced the farmers that the agriculturalists were propagating an expression of witchcraft. People who practice witchcraft are always silent about their craft.

Since witchcraft upsets the social harmony in any community, the villagers watched Mdumbwa and his family to learn whether he used witchcraft to increase his yields. They knew he would have to make a sacrifice if he used witchcraft, and they watched him to learn what he sacrificed. The villagers found the answer they were looking for when Mdumbwa's young son became sick. Mdumbwa brought the boy to the hospital, and the boy died a few days later. When news of the boy's death spread around the village, the villagers were convinced that Mdumbwa sacrificed his son to gain six bags of sorghum. Some people believed Mdumbwa was aware of what he did; others believed that he did not realize that the foreigners were using him to spread witchcraft. In either situation, Mdumbwa's son was dead, and the villagers decided that no amount of sorghum was equal to the lives of their children.

The villagers had nothing to say to the agricultural extensionists after the boy's funeral. They were sorry when they heard that Mdumbwa's son died, and they were perplexed to learn that the villagers made a relationship between the boy's death and their work. They believed their work was ameliorating the impoverished conditions of the village. The sanitation in the village was poor; food was scarce, and the infant mortality rate was as high as twenty percent. The agriculturalists believed they were making some progress toward improving these conditions. "How," they wondered, "could the villagers believe that their work was making a bad situation worse?"

The agriculturalists had to manage the message of their projects. The people were not wrong to interpret the meaning of the agriculturalists' work as they did. All people interpret new information and ideas according their assumptions of their particular worldviews. The farmers' worldview give them good reasons to believe the agriculturalists engaged in witchcraft, and they exposed the need for the agriculturalists to be more intentional about communicating the ultimate purposes of their work, challenging the agriculturalists to define the ultimate purpose of agricultural development.

In a third project, village farmers attempted to control the insects that were invading their gardens by hiring a sheikh, the spiritual leader of the village, to bury Qur'an verses along the boundaries of the gardens. The village sheikh and the farmers believed the Qur'an verses had the spiritual power, called baraka, to keep insects out of the gardens. The farmers resisted the encouragement to use insecticides instead of the Qur'an verses. They believed everything had a spiritual ethos, and they assumed, as a self-evident truth, that the spiritual realm controls all aspects of the physical environment, including insects that destroy gardens. The farmers did not believe a good wall between religion and science made good neighbors. They reasoned that if Allah had the power to create the world, the Qur'an must have the power to kill bugs since it embodies the power of Allah.

The clashes in each of these stories emerge from two different understandings of causation. These understandings, *agentive* and *empirical causation*, are major factors in many cultural conflicts, misunderstandings and collisions. They are particularly germane to agricultural development. Agentive causation is the belief that agents of change, such as spiritual beings or forces, govern the physical realm.

The nature of agentive causation is phenomenological; inquiries into it seek to answer questions concerning *who* caused something to happen. Empirical causation, the basis of science, is the systematic pursuit of knowledge by covering relationships between variety events, proposing explanations for these relationships, and testing the validity of the explanation by evaluating their ability to predict future events. While phenomenology is central to agentive causation, reliability is central to empirical causation. Managing the message of agricultural development in many traditional cultures requires the agriculturists to discern how they will address the worldview assumptions of the villages. How does agricultural development speak to cultures whose major worldview assumptions organized around agentive causation?

The Nature of the Kosmos

Any efforts to resolve the tension between agentive and empirical causation requires us to explore the nature of the *kosmos* (Sasse), that entity for which God did not send his Son into the world to condemn but to save through his Son. For our purposes, the *kosmos* is the matrix of human cultures that comprise the contexts in which people live. It includes the learned behaviors through which people provide themselves with the products, services and relationships they need to live in their physical environments and in community with each other. These products and services pervade every aspect of human life, such as government, economics, education, religious, health car, food production and preparation, social relationships, all types of tools, and science and technology. The kosmos, as a matrix of human cultures, is both socially inherited and socially constructed. People inherit their cultures from their parent, grandparents, and other ancestors. They also construct it by continuously modifying it to meeting the contemporary challenges of living in their physical environments. People construct and modify each element of their cultures, which contribute to the composition of the *kosmos* to fulfill particular purposes, presumably to enhance their welfare.

The *kosmos* embodies the collective values of humanity, and is good, bad and fallen. It is good to the extent that it meets human needs; yet, it is fallen, preventing it from fulfilling the purposes for which people created it. Throughout the biblical writings, the kosmos, in reflecting the fallen nature of the people who created it, invariably estranges people from God. The author of 1 John instructed his audience: "Do not love the world or the things in the kosmos. If anyone loves the kosmos, the love of the Father is not in him." (1 John 2:15). It is the kosmos, though, that "God so loved that he gave his only Son." (See John 3:16, 17).

The Good News concerning the kosmos, and all aspects of human cultures, is that the *kosmos* participates in redemption; the elements of the *kosmos* are among the elements that God reconciles to himself through Christ. (Col. 1:15-20). The Apostle Paul, in writing this passage, which serves as the fourth biblical account of creation, is intentional about affirming the supremacy of Christ. He is confident that seen and unseen elements of creation—which comprise the kosmos, are reconciled to God through the redemptive work of Christ, and the death of Christ brings peace to a fallen creation. This participation in redemption shifts the nature of the kosmos; it no longer estranges people from God, but fulfills its leading function (Clouser, 1991) of providing the context in which people live their lives in their fulfill the central purpose of humankind, which, according to the Westminster Confession, is to love God and to enjoy God forever. "When the *kosmos* is redeemed, it ceases to be the kosmos." The consummation of the redeemed *kosmos* is the full realization of the Kingdom of God, realized when the nations bring their splendor into the New Jerusalem. (see Rev. 21:26).

The Secular Nature of Redemption

The nature of redemption in contemporary Christian theology needs some attention. We are prone to equating redemption with salvation, and thinking of redemption in terms of what we consider spiritual; we believe people are redeemed when the receive salvation. Redemption, though, is different from salvation; it has more to do with restoration. When we consider the redemption of the kosmos, we get a sense of restoration. We become convicted that God, through the redemptive work of Christ, is restoring the elements of the *kosmos* to fulfill the purposes the purposes for which God brought this creation into being. The vision of Isaiah 65:17-25 offers vivid images of a redeemed creation, giving us the hope that infant mortality will be eradicated, and people will live long, productive lives. They will also live in the houses they build, and they will eat the fruits of the vineyards.

This depiction of redemption in terms of infant survival, productive lives, and social justice gives redemption a secular nature. Secular, in the context of redemption, refers to "a system of thought and practice which lies…outside of the direct responsibility of religion, but in which the will of God is to be done" (Hunsberger 1998, 143). The idea of secularization, which Lesslie Newbiggin featured in his writings, makes God's redemptive relationship with creation the central hope of the temporal realm. Newbiggin postulated, "the very idea of a secular order is a Christian idea." It is "rooted in the biblical faith which understands human history in terms of the mighty acts of God for the fulfillment of his purpose" (Hunsberger 1998, 143). While secularism denies that God has any relationships with the temporal realm, secularization features God, through Christ, as central to redeeming the temporal realm. Any expression of agricultural development requires us to grasp the secular nature of God's redemptive relationship with creation, bridging the gap between empirical and agentive causation.

The concept of leading function is also central to understanding the secular nature of redemption. A leading function is the central purpose for which people create various social institutions; it embodies the values of the people who created the social institutions. Cultures that place a high value on justice, create judicial systems who leading function is to render justice. A judicial system compromises its leading function when it fails to render justice.

Redemption is empowering people to organize the institutions of their cultures to fulfill their leading functions. Development facilitators participate in redemptive efforts by encouraging people in various cultures throughout the world to organize the elements of their cultures to fulfill their leading functions. Their efforts are often frustrated because leading functions clash. Science and religions, for example, have different leading function, but they often clash in agricultural development projects in traditional cultures. The leading function of science is to unfold the empirical nature of creation by observing relationship between varying natural events, proposing explanations for these relations, and testing the validity of these explanations by evaluating their ability to predict future events. Science is the vitality of empirical causation, making it central to agricultural development.

The leading function of religion, in contrast, is to empower people to live within the context of ultimate reality; religion is the vitality of agentive causation. Religion and science have two different leading functions, which contribute to the redemption of the kosmos. They are usually complimentary, but they are prone to conflicting. While people in Western cultures are prone to believing that science can disclose the nature of ultimate reality, people in traditional cultures are prone to using religion for scientific pursuits. The leading functions of science and religion clash when people attempt to use Qur'an verses as insecticides or attribute agricultural developments to witchcraft.

Some people claim that miracles happen when they use religious artifacts for empirical changes. They might be right, but we cannot base agricultural development on miracles; it happens when people respect the leading functions of various social institutions. Having said that, I feel vulnerable to removing any expression of spirituality from agricultural development. I want to address this vulnerability by proposing that the atonement is central to the redemption of the *kosmos* and to the spiritual ethos of all development efforts, whether agricultural or otherwise. The message of agricultural development is effectively managed when agriculturists can communicate the place of agricultural development in God's redemptive relationship with creation. The atonement is central to the message.

The Atonement Is Central to Redemption

One of my students protested in the middle of a lecture on the atonement. "Why do we need to know this?" he demanded. The atonement, our understanding of why God redeems creation through the life, death and resurrection of Christ, is the central event in Christian theology. Our understanding of the atonement governs the theology through which we interpret the purpose of agricultural development. The church has developed four views of the atonement throughout its history; they are ransom, substitution, moral influence and *Christus Victor*. I will define each view, and argue that they are not mutually exclusive; Christians can hold them together for a comprehensive understanding of Christian theology. My contention is that the *Christus Victor* view has to be included in any view of the atonement because it is most conducive to understanding how agricultural development has a purpose in Christian mission.

The idea of the atonement as ransom is based on several biblical passages, including Jesus' teaching in Matthew 20:28. This passage affirms "the Son of Man did not come to be served, but to serve, and to give his life as a ransom for many." The original intent of this passage is that Christ liberated people from the powers of the kosmos, delivering them from lives of meaninglessness. Unfortunately, this view became corrupted throughout the history of they church, depicting Satan as holding the creation, including people, hostage. The death of Christ is the "the price paid to Satan for freeing the sinners Satan held captive" (Weaver 1997, 34-35). While this view offers humankind the hope of living meaningful lives, its popular interpretation portrays the creation as the domain of evil, denying the creation any place in atoning death of Christ. It denies an intrinsically valid place in Christian mission to agricultural development.

The substitution theory is the inverse of the ransom theory. It portrays "Christ's death as an act performed on behalf of sinners to satisfy the honor of an offended God or as the payment of a penalty required of sinners by God's law." (Weaver 1997, 36). This view also has biblical support. However, like the ransom theory, it does not stand alone. It inspires people to consider their sinfulness in God's holy presence, but it does not give agricultural development a place in Christian mission.

The third view of the atonement, moral influence theory, focuses on inspiring humankind to live moral lives in response to the example of Christ, who died for his love of humankind. If Christ showed his love for us by dying on the Cross, how can we respond, except by living moral lives. Again, while this view influences our behavior, it does not stand alone; it might inspire us to eradicate global hunger, but it still makes agricultural development incidental to Christian mission.

The fourth view, *Christus Victor*, ironically, was the most prevalent view of the early church, but it is the least prevalent in contemporary theology. It portrays the work if Christ as defeating and redeeming God's enemies, which can be spiritual beings or social, economic and political structures. The early Christians felt powerless in relationship to the spiritual, economic, political and social powers that comprised the *kosmos* in which they lived. However, Christ, "having disarmed the powers and authorities ... make a public spectacle of them, triumphing over them by the cross (Colossians 2:15)"

Many theologians criticize this view as focusing on the non-personal nature of sin, a criticism that prevents it from standing alone. However, this view complements other views of the atonement by creating a place in Christian theology for the secular nature of redemption. It is necessarily concerned with redeeming the social and political structures of the *kosmos* because the redemption of these structures is necessary to empower people to exercise their freedom in Christ. People who live in many cultures of the world are powerless to overcome their fear of spiritual, social, economic and political structures, fearing the agents of causation who empower these structures. They need a view of the atonement that addresses these fears, and empowers them to bring redemption to their communities by empowering them to participate in God's redemptive relationship with creation. They need to see God, through Christ, as the ultimate agent of causation.

The *Christus Victor* view of the atonement has the potential to empower farmers to have power over spirits, witchcraft and any the social, economic, political or religious structures that prevent them from realizing the fullness of Isaiah's vision of shalom. This view of the atonement gives agricultural development a place in Christian ministry because agricultural development is necessary to empowering people to experience redemption. People need to eat, especially if the food is the product of their labor.

Agricultural development, as well as other expressions of development ministries, has lost its place in Christian mission, partially because Western cultures have lost their appreciation of agentive causation. Our worldview makes clear distinctions between the physical and spiritual realms of creation, influencing us to place God in the spiritual realm at the expense of assuming that God has no influence over the physical realm, apart from occasion miraculous interventions. This assumption, which emerges from our culture placing central value on empirical causation, prevents us from communicating the truth that our agricultural work has an intrinsically valid place in Christian mission, despite is central place in redemption.

Christians who are engaging in development ministries have the responsibility to manage the message of their work by depicting God as the agent of causation, the One who created a universe that is reliable to the extent that scientific research is possible. Cultures that are organized around agentive causation condemn people to the powerlessness of living in a phenomenological world; they believe their welfare depends on the capricious nature of the spirits, witches or other agents of causation. In contrast, cultures that are organization around empirical causation put people in the predicament of affirming the existence of God. However, they do not have a conceptual framework to understand how God expresses his redemptive relationship with through the ordinary activities of life.

We manage the message of development when we communicate the good news that God, through the atoning event of Jesus Christ, invites us to participate in his redemptive relationship with creation. This message empowers people to overcome their fears of various agents of causation. The development community is replete with stories of projects that have failed because the worldview assumptions of the development practitioners clashed with those of the project beneficiaries. People invariably attempt to resolve this clash of assumptions with more training. However, the central issue is not more knowledge, it is identifying the basic assumptions that govern our work. When the villagers who feared the spirits asked the Christians why Christians don't fear the spirits, the Christians answer confidently, "because of God's redemptive love." They managed to communicate the message of redemption, a message that brings hope to a fallen world. The Good News of the Gospel is that God did not condemn the kosmos, but saved it through the atoning death of his Son.

References

Clouser, Roy A.

1991   *The Myth of Religious Neutrality: An Essay on the Hidden Role of Religious Belief in Theories.* South Bend, IN: University of Notre Dame Press.

Hunsberger, George R.

1998   *Bearing the Witness of the Spirit: Lesslie Newbigin's Theology of Cultural Plurality.* Grand Rapids, MI: Eerdmans.

Sasse, Hermann

n.d.   "Kosmos." *Theological Dictionary of the New Testament*, p. 893. Gerhard Kittel, ed. Grand Rapids, MI: Eerdmans.

Weaver, J. Denny.

1997   *Keeping Salvation Ethical: Mennonite and Amish Theology in the Late Nineteenth Century.* Scottdale, PA: Herald Press.

The Agriculturalist
and Ethics

The Bible as Ethical Standard for Appraising Modern Agricultural Practices

Michael Oye

Introduction

Ethics is the study of concepts that we use to evaluate human activities, in particular the concepts of goodness and obligation. Although different from practical morals, it has some bearing on morality. Ethics is not concerned with descriptive accounts of what moral principles may happen to be generally accepted at a given place or time. However, for the purpose of this chapter, we will use the Bible as the primary foundation of ethics. That is, we will assume that the word of God, the Bible, is impartial and applicable to all men and women in the whole world and in all ages. God is no respecter of persons; He made people and, therefore, knows the ethical principles fit for their total well being (shalom). Hence we are going to take the biblical guidelines for wholesome agricultural practice as the norm for this chapter.

God says He has shown man what is good and what is required of him: Justice, Mercy, Humble Worship (Mic. 6:8). In Romans 1:19, 20, Paul states, "What can be known about God is plain to (men), because God has shown it to them. Ever since the creation of the world, his invisible nature, that is, his eternal power and deity, has been clearly perceived in the things that have been made. So they (all human beings) are without excuse. ..." The moral law handed down to Moses by God is binding on all men of all nations, eras and religions. Love, kindness, truth, hospitality, preservation of life, social justice, etc. are generally accepted as norms that should effect stability and progress among men. On the other hand, stealing, covetousness, murder, sexual immorality, lies etc. are condemned as anti-social traits among men everywhere. In this chapter, Jesus' New *Commandment*, which summarizes the moral laws of the Bible, is going to be used as the basis for discussing ethics in the Christian's practice of agriculture.

The New Commandment states, "LOVE one another as I have loved you. For by this shall all men know that you are my disciples, if you have love one for another" (John 13:34, 35). In practical terms, Jesus and some of the apostles explain this love. In the Sermon on the Mount, Jesus teaches us to feed our enemies and give them drink, so that we may be like our Father in heaven. (Matt. 5:44). He also enjoins us to do unto others as we will like them to do unto us (Matt. 7:12). Thus any agricultural practice that endangers human life should be considered unethical, while that which increases productivity and fair distribution of wholesome food should be viewed as ethically sound.

The apostle Paul says, "Love does no evil to a neighbor; therefore, love is the fulfillment of the law "(Rom. 3:10). Ethically sound agricultural practice should bring good and not evil to mankind.

The apostle John defines Love in a sacrificial way by explaining the concept of dying so that others may live (1 Jn. 3:16). It implies giving so that others may receive, losing so that others may gain, teaching so that others may learn. If love gives, then it must first of all have, before it can give. For what *have* we which we have not *received*? This brings into biblical ethics the concept of diligence. In Eph. 4:28, Paul says, "Let him who stole steal no more, but let him labor with his hands that which is honest, that he may have to give to the needy" He instructs the Christians in Thessalonica in the same way by saying, "study to be quiet, mind your own business and work with your hands, that you may control the respect of outsiders and be dependent on nobody"(1 Thess. 4:11, 12). Thus Christian ethics enjoins seriousness, concentration, purposefulness, diligence, professionalism, honest gain in knowledge wealth and property, and willingness to share what we have with those who need it. The implication of this concept in agriculture is an ever-increasing desire to gain more knowledge, technologies, expertise and good food for us and to extend the same to others far and near.

Biblical ethics of love demands that we should not share this "world's goods" with our Christian brothers and sisters only, but also with outsiders, unbelievers, (1 Thess. 3:12), enemies (Rom. 12:20), and strangers (Heb 13:2). By doing this, we bring the spiritual, social, economic and physical blessings of the kingdom to many peoples.

Direct preaching of repentance and teachings of obedience to God's moral law should be part of the package we seek to share with a world that needs to be developed. In an ungodly community, where drunkenness, drug addiction, sexual immorality, violence and intolerance are the order of the day, any major improvement in agricultural productivity and income is likely to lead to an upsurge in these life-destroying vices. The outcome is not DE-velopment (liberation) but EN-velopment (enslavement). It is like the thief coming to deceive, kill and destroy. But when Christ is preached to the people and their lives change, the Good Shepherd brings them abundant life (Jn. 10:10). Love thus constrains us to share the gospel with others by our words and our lives.

Ethics in Agricultural Production and Marketing

Five issues will be discussed in this chapter including soil fertility, pest and weed control, animal production, food processing/ storage and ethics in trade. These five areas have been chosen as a continuum highlighting the major processes in the farmer's occupational life cycle. Soil fertility has to do with land preparation for sowing, while weed and pest control has to do with tending crops from germination to fruiting in the field. Where mixed farming is practiced, animal husbandry goes on concomitantly with crop production. Most farm products need to be processed and stored in one form or another. The last stage is usually the consumption or sale of the products. We now want to discuss ethical issues involved in each of these farming operations and proffer some biblical working norms to Christian agriculturists and farmers. It is hoped that such norms or work ethics, if followed, will bring kingdom benefits to the church and beyond.

Soil Fertility

God commands the seventh year and the jubilee as Sabbaths for all agricultural lands. This is His method of rejuvenating the soil for continuous productivity (Lev. 25:4-12, 18-22) Age-long practices that enhance this norm include crop rotation, mixed farming, use of compost and manure, nitrogen fixation methods (such as inter-planting, alley cropping, cover, cropping). Moreover, the systems are simple to adopt and harmless to both man and animals.

Christian agriculturists should encourage the resting and rejuvenation of farm land by teaching farmers scientifically sound rotational systems that will enable the top layers of the soil to regain their productive vigor. It will also not be out-of-place for us to research into, and adopt, systems which will essentially promote the seventh-year sabbath for farmlands. For example, Christian farmers can begin to divide whatever piece of farmland they have into server portions, and in a system of rotation, leave one completely fallow for a whole year (verse 4). Whatever crops grow of themselves on such a land will not be harvested (verse 5), ensuring that nutrients from the subsoil are brought into fruits and leaves, which will later rot to fertilize the top soil. The Bible promises that land so treated will have miraculous harvests both in the 6th and 8th years of the cycle (verses 20-22).

Disregarding this Sabbath commandment of God has universal consequences. Unabated continuous use of farmland has resulted in land depletion and impoverishment. In many places, this has led to excessive use of artificial fertilizers to stimulate the land to produce good harvests. Unfortunately, in many developing countries the prices of artificial fertilizers are becoming prohibitive, and the majority poor who are the main food producers cannot afford to buy them.

For such poor farmers, the right application of well-prepared compost, Farm Yard Manure, alley cropping or interplanting will boost productivity. As Christian agriculturists extend such knowledge to farmers, food self-sufficiency is enhanced, hunger is reduced, and wealth increased.

For example, in 1990, I read of an experiment carried out in East

Africa in which a nitrogen-fixing *Crotolaria* species was planted along with maize. The results showed a three-fold increase in yield over the control experiment. I was motivated to replicate the treatment on my farm and found the results very encouraging. Since then, I have been using *Crotolaria* as one of my major sources of nitrogen and have introduced it to many farmers wherever I have been.

Again, in February 1999, as part of church-planting efforts in Igede land in Benue State (Nigeria), I introduced Christian converts to the use of *Gliricidia* branches for staking yam. *Gliricidia* sprouts easily and remains evergreen even in the dry season. Apart from exposing the yam leaves to sunshine, its roots fix nitrogen, which helps in the production of larger tubers. Many are now adopting the use of the stakes, since chemical fertilizers have become very costly for them.

The *Journal of Tropical Forest Resources* reports of a recent research work carried out by Adedire (1998) on the effect of mulching with *Leucaena leucocephala* prunings on maize yield in Egba North Local Government Area of Ogun State (Nigeria). *Leucaena* was used for alley cropping, while its leaves were used to mulch the soil of the experimental treatments. The study has shown that alley cropping in the study area offers a promising avenue for sustained crop production. This could be achieved by the continual addition of organic material, as pruning from selected trees and scrubs, which aid in the recycling of nutrients from deeper layers of the soil and improves the soil structure and moisture characteristics. Further, the work has revealed that maize grain yield can be sustained at more than 1.0t/ha with continuous application of Leucaena pruning alone. The study recommended that farmers should be encouraged to plant leguminous trees as hedgerows in their farms, and use the prunings of such trees to mulch their farms. "Such prunings," it says, "will improve their crop production, even without inorganic fertilizer, which is continuously becoming unavailable to the peasant farmers as a result of the increasing cost of procurement."

Soil Fertility, Food Surplus and the Needy

In the developed nations, where artificial fertilizers are relatively cheaper, its widespread use in combination with other agricultural technologies has brought bumper harvests over the years. In many cases, there has been so much food surplus that some is sold to other countries, while a portion is usually deliberately destroyed. One of the reasons usually given for destroying part of the surplus food is that the cost of exporting the food to some needy people overseas is more than the value of the products themselves. Yet the ethics of God's word says we must allow the poor to glean through our fields after harvest (Lev. 19:9, 10). If we equate the food surplus to the gleanings, it means the Christian farmer is ethically bound to find ways of reaching the poor of the world with the food surplus.

The Bible eschews laziness and commands diligence. Yet there are always many who are in genuine need, not because of laziness, but for many other reasons, including social injustice, sickness, natural disasters and man-made disasters such as wars and their attendant problems. It is here that we as Christian farmers should sacrificially work out relief strategies and send out 'gleanings' to the suffering until they are rehabilitated.

For instance, in recent times, for two consecutive years, heavy floods destroyed almost all the crops in Mozambique. The resulting famine brought untold hardship to the majority of the populace. Many nations and NGO's sent relief to the people. This act of compassion for the suffering is a basic commandment of God, and Christian farmers as co-creators with God, should endeavor to relieve and rehabilitate hungry people, starting with fellow Christians (1 Thess. 3:12; Gal. 6:2,9,10; Eph. 4:28).

All the same, God's concern for the poor is highlighted in the Bible. His legislation designed for their protection include: Daily payment of wages: Lev 19:13; Sharing of tithes Deut. 14 28,29; Lending without Interest: Lev. 25:35,37; Right to Glean: Lev. 19:9,10; Land Restoration In Jubilee: Lev. 25:25-30; Equal participation in feasts: Lev. 16:11,14. All this is designed to enable the poor to climb up the ladder of prosperity.

Although a lot has been done to solve the famine problem in Mozambique, it was sad news to see on the CNN screen a few months ago some very poor Mozambican women who had trekked over 50 km, to buy corn meal meant for cattle consumption but went back home weak and frustrated, because the corn was not available. It is this type of extremely helpless situations which the Christian farmer should know about and act swiftly. I suggest that there be an up-to-date information system that will let all Christian farmers around the globe know where their 'gleanings' should go to. I suggest that Christian bodies like FHI should intensify their challenge to Christian farmers to give of what they have received from God. Even poor Christian farmers should be taught the Kingdom culture of giving to the suffering (2 Cor. 8:1-5). Secondly, there must be trustworthy agents in each nation through whom relief should be channeled. Thirdly, a very effective way of getting relief to the very needy must be developed (2 Cor. 8:16-22; Acts 6:3)

Many times relief sent through government agencies has been hijacked by selfish nationals and sold for cash. Even Christians have on many occasions been found to be fraudulent. It is necessary, and possible, to identify men and women of integrity, who will carry out such work of stewardship. It is then that the Kingdom benefits will come to the poor.

The Principle of Reaping. Incidentally, our God, who is the author of sowing, is also the author of reaping. The command to give the tenth and offerings of our harvest to the Levite, the stranger, the widow and the orphan (Deut. 26:12-15) is a form of sowing and has multiple rewards.

According to Isaiah 58, if we give food to the hungry and the stranger (vs 6, 7, 9 and 10) it is a form of fasting or sowing (we lose part of what is legitimately ours), but the harvest outweighs the sowing.

This "harvest" includes (verses 8-12) :

• The breaking forth of light
• Improvement in health
• Righteousness (good works) being rewarded in some ways.
• Divine interaction in times of trouble. (vs 9)
• Prosperity where others are suffering. (vs 10)
• Divine guidance (research break-through) continually.
• Divine provision in adverse situations.

- The making of fat bones-rejuvenation of life.
- A watered garden: more fruitfulness.
- Continuous provision physically and spiritually so that one is always a blessing (vs. 11)
- Offspring shall be repairers and builders of good places to dwell in (vs.12)

I believe that the part of ethics that made Western Europe and the U.S.A. rise from poverty to prosperity was, and still is, the proper attitude of giving, rooted in the Christian faith of their fathers, a couple of centuries ago. If that spirit of giving stops, there will be a decline in development. Christian farmers in the developing nations have to learn to give. This will include readiness to network in appropriate indigenous knowledge and technologies that will enhance productivity.

A personal testimony here may help to prove Isaiah 58. On my 3-acre mixed farm, I have a piggery, which over the past seven years has grown from 3 to an average of 200 pigs. As a principle, I give some weaners free or sell them at reduced prices to the poor, and I have been able thus to help others develop their own farms. For the past three years, bovine fever has ravaged piggeries in Nigeria, including those in Osogbo, where I live on my farm. In a miraculous way, I have not lost a single pig through that epidemic. I believe this is God answering prayers and causing me to shine in obscurity. Christian farmers must expect divine intervention in their farming business, as they obey the Kingdom rules.

Controlling Weeds & Pests

The Lord who commanded us to multiply also gave us the mandate to have dominion over all that He had made for us in this world. (Gen. 1:21-30). At the beginning of man's existence, different plant and animal species grew together in the same environment. As human populations increased, however, there was the need to grow some crops as monocrops. Land clearance eliminated shade-loving plants and trees and encouraged the rapid multiplication of light-loving herbs, many of which are now weeds. In the same way, many otherwise harmless insects, worms and rodents in natural vegetations have now become pests because of monocropping.

Although growing different crops adjacent to each other or rotating crops makes it much more difficult for pests to spread, it is often necessary to treat crop plants with something the insects don't like. For example, some small-scale farmers prepare their own pesticides, using substances such as onions, garlic, peppers, pyrethrum, neem or other plants they know to be effective in controlling pests. Whatever measure of increase in food productivity that has resulted in the application of these technologies is as a result of men thinking, naming, identifying, analyzing and experimenting with different plants created by God in obedience to the mandate to subdue the earth.

With the rapid increase in human population, man's exploration into God's creation has made it possible for more powerful pesticides and herbicides to be manufactured to solve the problems of weed and pest control in large scale mono cropping.

The major moral issue involved in the use of farm chemicals is that, because most of the chemicals are very harmful, the Christian agriculturist should be his brother's keeper. Farmers and all others who handle agro-chemicals should be thoroughly instructed about how to use them, in order to avoid unnecessary human catastrophies. Also, as many spray chemicals are very expensive, I believe the Christian agriculturist has the moral obligation to encourage local research that will identify cheaper, (even if less effective) materials for weed and pest control among the many small-scale farmers. Most of the poorest farmers in the world are in developing countries of the tropics and sub-tropics, where the age-long broad-spectrum pesticide tree, the neem, grows easily. Motivating each farming family in those nations to plant at least a single neem tree and showing them how to use it could go a long way to increasing food production and reducing pesticide risks.

Raising Farm Animals

Livestock should not be allowed to graze in farms whose crops have not yet been harvested. If it is done, it is social and economic injustice; it causes constant clashes between herdsmen and peasant farmers. In Northern Nigeria, however, a form of mutualism exists whereby, after harvesting, crop farmers allow the livestock of Fulani herdsmen to browse through farmlands, leaving behind their droppings as fertilizer.

In modern animal husbandry, very useful vaccines and drugs have been produced to save the lives of many animals. If any animals happen to die during treatment or for any other unknown reason, such carcass may not be eaten or sold to the public, for conscience's sake. In the Lev. 11:39,40 and 17:15,16, Israelites and strangers who ate such meat were considered unclean, until they had washed their clothes, bathed themselves in water and remained separated the whole day. This implied that they were a health risk to the congregation. In Lev. 22:8, the priests are commanded not to eat such meat at all, since they were to set the highest example for God's people. If we apply the golden rule of loving our neighbor as ourselves, we Christian agriculturists will do well to make sure that the meat that goes to the market is of the highest quality. There is enough scientific information on the safe use of animal drugs and how long animals must be kept after treatment before they are safe for human consumption. Agriculturists should help to extend such knowledge to farmers to protect the public from diseases. Information on useful magazines should be made available.

It is also important for truthfulness and transparency to exist among Christian farmers engaged in animal production. The health of the public hangs on the trust they repose in those who produce the meat they consume. The consequences of betraying that trust can be grievous.

In Lev. 19:11 God says, "You shall not ... deal falsely, neither lie one to another." In discipling Christians, Paul taught the same Kingdom principle wherever he went. To the Ephesians he said "put on the new man, which is after God's creation in righteousness and true holiness. Therefore, putting away lying, speak every man truth with his neighbor; for we are members one of another" (Eph. 4:24.25). The recent episode of the Mad Cow Disease in the United Kingdom and a few other European countries is a good example of truthfulness. For conscience's sake and at a great loss to many farmers, thousands of cattle were deliberately slaughtered and burnt, instead of being sold to people. On the other hand, in a little town called Ofatedo, Osun state of Nigeria, an unsuspecting farmer bought about 1,000 growers (layers) from a breeder, who assured him all the necessary vaccines had been given. Within two days of the arrival of the fowls, there was an incidence of Gomboro which killed more than half of the birds. That was not all; the disease spread rapidly to many neighboring farms, killing hundreds of local chicks, which had not been vaccinated. For genuine progress to take place, truth and integrity must be the girdle of Christian farmers.

Processing and Storage of Farm Products

Joseph was able to store large quantities of grains for at least seven years without the use of modern pesticides (Gen. 41:46-57). Verse 48 says "the food of the field which was round about every city, laid he up in THE SAME (city)." This suggests a central storage facility in each city. Can co-operative storage and processing be part of the solution to the developing world's problem of massive post-harvest food spoilage? Poor people, when properly mobilized, can pool resources together to build cold rooms for the preservation of farm products. Christian agricultural scientists should endeavor to seek God's face for breakthroughs in community-based food processing and storage. Early in the last century, Le Tourneux, an American blacksmith who was a Baptist, sought God's face until He gave him the knowledge of how to construct the caterpillar earthmover and heavy-duty batteries. It was not so much through scientific knowledge but more by revelation. Our God is still in the business of answering the prayers of His saints.

"And Joseph opened all the storehouses, and SOLD unto the Egyptians" (verse 56). Any transfer of appropriate technologies that can help the developing nations, not only to process and store food for sustenance, but also for sale will be seen by God as a special act of Love (Matt. 25:34-36). Meanwhile, simple storage technologies like the use of ash, neem leaf powder, dry pepper and solar energy for cereals and pulses should be extended to farmers. Agriculturists should be acquainted with relevant publications on Appropriate

Technologies that will enable them to help farmers. "African Farmers," for example, usually publishes very good articles on new agricultural technologies.

As in the case of on-farm use of modern pesticide, wherever harvested crops are treated with chemicals for storage, instructions for use should be carefully explained to farmers to minimize the risk to human health.

An area of great loss in tropical countries is that of succulent fruits such as pineapples, pawpaw, citrus, guavas and mangoes. My visit to a Presbyterian women's Development Group in Douala, Cameroon, in the year 2000 exposed me to an effective fruit processing method. Women in the group have developed ovens whose temperatures are regulated to dry sliced fruits slowly until the moisture content is very low. Such slices are then sealed airtight in cellophane bags and sold locally or exported to European countries. They can be stored for over a year, and retain their tastes when eaten. Any method of preserving fruits enhances the health of people. It is a common sight to see thousands of mangoes and oranges rotting away in African villages, because there are no methods for preparing them.

Ethics in Trade

Contemporary local and global trade in agricultural products is viewed in the mirror of God's word. Godly King Solomon traded in an equitable way with Hiram of Tyre (1 Kgs. 5:6-9). In verse 6, Solomon recognized and valued the timber from Hiram and he was ready to pay for it. The terms of trade pleased Hiram (he rejoiced greatly) (verse 7), and he analyzed how timber would be supplied in exchange for an agreed-to quantity of food (verse 8 and 9). There was neither manipulation nor any intention to cheat. In fact, Hiram gave Solomon both cedar and fir trees according to all his desire (verse 10), while Solomon gave Hiram 20,000 measures (220,000 bushels) of wheat and 20 measures (1,700 gallons) pure oil year by year (verse 11). PURE OIL! No adulteration. Thus the whole trade transaction was built on trust and honesty, which are Kingdom principles for stability and progress.

The Christian should learn to distinguish between making fair profits and profiteering at the expense of others. Profiteering is built on lies and deliberate cheating, both punishable by God. In James 5:1-6, we find how God is totally against those who cheat the poor in their wages. Many Christian farmers hire labor on their farms. They should fear God and love the laborers by paying the correct wages to them, so that both parties may be blessed. Job, a wealthy farmer, says, "If I did despise the cause of my man-servant and my maidservant, when they contended with me, what then shall I do when God rises up? And when he visits what shall I answer him?" (Job 31:13,14).

In verse 15, Job gives the ethical reason why he would not cheat his employee: "Did not He (God) that made me in the womb make him? And did not one (God) fashion us in the womb?" What a godly conscience! Lev. 19:13 speaks strongly, "You shall not defraud your neighbor neither rob him: the wages of him that is hired shall not abide with you all night until the morning." God says in Malachi 3:5, "And I will come near to you and judge you; I will be a swift witness against ... those that oppress the hireling in his wages ... and fear not me."

Unfortunately, the human heart is so corrupt that we find the poor cheating the poor and the rich. The Bible says such people deceive and are themselves deceived. One implication of this discussion on trade is that Christian agriculturists should aim at producing high-quality products always. If some of our products are of lower grades than expected by our customers, we should make that known and price them accordingly. We should also pay our debts; the Bible says we should owe no one anything, except to love one another (Rom. 13:8). There are farmers who deliberately refuse to pay those from whom they have bought farm inputs, fraudulently using the money as additional capital for their business and causing untold harm to their benefactors. There are also those who take bank loans for their farm enterprises, but do not intend to pay back until the loans become 'bad debts'. The psalmist says, "The wicked borrows and pays not again: but the righteous shows mercy and gives" (Psalm 37:21).

The history of Trade Unions started in England in the 18th century from a Christian initiative. The ungodly ways in which employers were exploiting their workers called for social justice. If

Job listened to the complaints of his employees and saw to their welfare, we in the gospel dispensation ought to know and do better.

At the international level, the developed nations face the temptation of using their power to pressure other nations to purchase what they may not need. So far as agricultural products are concerned, Christian ethics will demand that Christian agriculturists of such developed nations should sensitize their governments or private companies implementing such policies.

In Nigeria, for example, during President Babangida's era in the eighties, two local research breakthroughs affected the bread-eating populace of the country. The Obafemi Awolowo University successfully produced high-quality bread from cassava, which is a staple food crop in the nation. Secondly, a number of states were found to be capable of producing wheat at least for local consumption. The Nigerian government then took a decision to ban the importation of foreign wheat, promote locally grown wheat and encourage the consumption of cassava bread. The U.S. government protested, and was ready to give Nigeria a loan of many million dollars to buy U.S. wheat. The tussle went on, until finally Nigeria gave in. Now we are almost completely dependent on foreign wheat. The economic stranglehold on many developing nations is such that most of our tastes have been completely replaced with Euro-American ones. It is a colonial legacy difficult to shed off. Yet for any tangible growth to take place, we must return to some of our original cultural tastes that can be met through locally produced agricultural products. For example, instead of eating wheat bread for breakfast many in the tropics can eat other energy foods such as yam, plantain, cocoyam and porridge (from maize, guinea corn, millet or cow peas) all of which are easy to produce locally.

It is understandable that every nation should protect her own interests in world trade, but from the Christian's point of view, there must be checks and balances. If there are nations that may never be able to produce cars, planes and computers, at least they should be allowed/positively encouraged to produce the natural resources that will empower them to purchase other basic necessities of life. Through stage-wise or incremental development, they may reach the level of food self-sufficiency.

This is a very delicate and sensitive area of discussion yet it must be grappled with. What type of pressure groups can Christian agriculturists form? Only one small suggestion comes to mind now, and it is because I practice it. For the past twenty years, I have lived on a three-acre mixed farm, where almost all I need to feed upon is produced. As an agriculturist, I have also gone to others parts of Africa to help others to do the same with as little a land as half-an-acre. The Church, parachurch groups and NGOs should be mobilized to teach diligence and good self-sufficiency at the micro level. One day the planted mustard seed will grow big and have branches.

One good news about world trade is that, as a result of many developing nations crying out under the yoke of the conditionalities of WTO's Trade Liberalization and IMF/World Bank Loans, Third World countries now have some say in international trading terms. At the recently concluded world Trade Organization (WTO) ministerial conference in Qatar, trade ministers from more than 140 countries agreed to launch the Doha Development Agenda. The agenda includes the following statements:

- For the WTO to be effective, all members must be involved in the decision-making process.
- If we are to have a successful round of global trade talks, developing countries must play a central role in the process.
- The needs and interests of developing countries must be at the heart of the future WTO work program.

According to Grant Aldonas, U.S. Undersecretary of Commerce for International Trade, a study by Joseph Francois of Erasmus University projects that new global trade negotiations would generate $90,000 million to $190,000 million a year in higher incomes for developing nations. The WTO operates by consensus, which should give developing countries a strong role in the negotiations themselves and, even more importantly, in the results of the new round of talks. Christian from all nations should be God's watchmen and, like the minor prophets, should advocate for social justice in trade at all levels.

Conclusion

This paper has tried to show how Christian work ethics should be the guiding principle in all aspects of Christian farming occupation. An all-round well-being (Shalom) can begin to develop in individuals, communities and societies, when they begin to be influenced by the holy, diligent and loving lives of Christians in their midst. The Christian agriculturist stands out as a strategic development agent in the farming community. His holy life gives him authority to preach repentance and faith in Christ to the lost. Through diligence, he brings knowledge and physical abundance to others. Because he loves, he aims only at excellence and pursues justice and honesty in all things. He is generous to the needy and practices equity in trade. He relates to God, men and the environment out of love and obedience to God's word. He serves as a faithful steward who is accountable to God. He is a builder with God.

His relief for the Afghanistan refugee makes the latter to say, "I am happy to be back; I am ready to plant; This is our home; We shall rebuild. You have given us food; You have given us water; You have given us shelter; You have preserved our lives. God bless you."

These were the very words I heard from an Afghanistan returnee interviewed on CNN on 27 April 2002. How similar to Jesus' words to the righteous in Matthew 25:34-36. Who knows? Because this man's physical life is preserved, he may have the chance one day to be given the spiritual food and water that will bring him new life in Christ.

May the Christian agriculturist be able to say with Christ, "The Spirit of the Lord is upon me, because he has anointed me to preach the gospel to the poor; he has sent me to heal the brokenhearted, to preach deliverance to the captives, and recovering of sight to the blind, to set at liberty them that are bruised, to preach the acceptable year of the Lord" (Lk. 4:18-19).

Reference

Adesire, M. O.
   1998   "Maize Yield as Affected by Lencaena Leucocephala Prunings and NPK Fertilizer in an Alley Farm." *Journal of Tropical Forest Resources*, Vol. 14.1, pp. 9-18.

Integration towards Ethical Agriculture:

Challenges, Principles and Practice in International Perspective

E. John Wibberley

Introduction

The Gospel of the Lord Jesus Christ as recorded in the Bible is holistic. Yet a false trichotomy has arisen between the spiritual (God-ward, theological), the social (human-ward, anthropological) and the rest of creation (earthward, ecological). There is a consequent crisis of faith, of society and of the environment. However, Christian hope lies in the concept and implementation of an Integrated Gospel which reaffirms original Biblical holism. Recommendations are made for practical action to encourage an integrated approach to agriculture based upon the ethical principles elicited.

Creation Theology

There has been an ongoing struggle to articulate a faithfully useful creation theology, colored in the West by Greek thought and logic. Some wish to place science or philosophy against theology rather than as co-travelers in seeking genuine understanding. For this writer, theology underpins these disciplines. The present ecological crisis is not a new phenomenon, though its scale may well be. Isaiah (24:4-11) catalogues calamity and gives reasons as covenant-breaking disobedience. Rae (2000) connects this passage with the structure of John's gospel, in particular the seven miraculous signs. He notes the Biblical usage of seven to signify perfection, as in the seven days of creation and the pairing of the first and seventh of John's signs—the first being the turning of water into wine at Cana (reversing the Isa. 24 loss of wine) and the seventh being the resurrection leading to re-creation; obedient stewardship was needed from those around Jesus in order for the water to be brought for transformation.

The enormous scope of God's redeeming grace for creation is encapsulated in Col. 1:21-23. The pre-eminence of Christ as Creator, Co-Equal in the Trinity has been rehearsed in verses 15-19, and His Supreme act of reconciliation through the blood of His Cross has been announced in verse 20. It is this theme which Paul expounds in verses 21 to 23 describing a sequence from alienation, through atonement to apocalypse. Commenting on Paul's Christology, Sanders (1991, 78-80) notes, "the very earliest Christians interpreted Jesus' death as atoning, and Paul accepted this understanding" (p.78) … "What matters is belonging to Christ, and His death makes this possible" (p.79) … For Paul, "Christ was completely human and completely Divine" (p.80). Paul argues that so great a salvation was necessary to remedy so great a fall. Paul reminded the Roman Christians that the whole creation was affected (Rom. 8:22). To re-create the new creation required an act of supreme scope by God Himself—to literally "buy it all back"—redemption (as if from a pawn-brokers, since He owned it in the first place). It required a supreme act of grace to create anything or any creature in the first place because the first thing God did (Gen.1:1) was to make room for creation (Moltmann 1985) to admit the constraints of space and of time into His eternal I AM THAT I AM (Exod. 3:14). In order to redeem creation, God was willing to suffer the pain of alienation within the Godhead (Psalm 22:1; Mark 15:34)—a kind of voluntary Divine Personality-Split or disintegration when His design in creation reflects an intentional integration based on integrity (for which the psalmist prays in Psa. 86:11, indicating the combined activity of mind, will and heart required to cooperate with God towards re-integration). The ultimate intimacy of relationship is found within the Trinity between Father, Son and Holy Spirit (Gunton 1992). The voluntary jeopardy of that on the Cross shows the extremity of God's love for His creation and His ongoing involvement in it, then, now and forever (Rev. 1:8; Heb. 13:8). God is not an Absentee Land-lord—deliberately grand, remote and demanding, but rather He is humble, close and giving in Christ (Phil. 2:5-8) despite the scale of the universe. God delights in repentance (Ezek. 18:23,32; Matt. 23:37—the "hen gathering her chickens," a maternal metaphor) leading by means of reconciliation to restored relationships, which are constantly being renewed (re-created) by the activity of the Spirit of God until the restoration of all things to Himself culminates in rest for all who receive His salvation (Col. 1:22). The pinnacle of the old creation was the sabbath but the start of the new creation is the resurrection through which supreme act of Christ reconciliation is achieved. The Gospel (Good News) is that this salvation is great and available to all who will receive Christ (John 1:11-14). It is a complete reconciliation i.e. a revolutionary change for the better (true development). The word Paul uses in Col. 1:21 is *apokatallasso*, meaning complete and utter change to be conformed to the mind of God; harmony replaces disharmony. From redeemed mankind will flow a restoration of creation (Isa. 11:6-8).

This is a transformational, integrated gospel indeed, of which humans are privileged to be stewards, fellow-laborers with God Himself (1 Cor. 3:9) enabled by His Spirit to operate as co-servant-leaders with Christ (fellow "foot-washers" as in John 13:14, not domineering overlords) careful to "work out our salvation with fear and trembling" (Phil. 2:12). In all of this Deane-Drummond (1997, 154-155) advocates "a re-rootedness of the individual in the community and in the cosmic." She asserts, "an environmental ethic grounded in wisdom is both personal, yet organic, generating hope in the future"… and "ability to see the big picture, to look at the whole story, is the capacity which springs from wisdom." Only God-given wisdom will suffice for current agricultural, ecological and cosmic challenges.

As Atkinson & Field (1995, 268) remark, "The doctrine of creation is one of the major theological themes that informs a Christian ethic. That God repeatedly declared His creation to be good, that it is purposely ordered to attest the perfections of its Maker and to contribute to the development of faith and righteousness in human beings made in His Image, and that they are entrusted with responsibilities in and for the creation—all of this has far-reaching ethical implications." They note that "the good which God purposed is … for all, and appeal can accordingly be made to universal moral law evidenced in universal human needs and potentials, despite cultural and religious pluralism." Furthermore, "a creation ethic stands against any ethical subjectivism that reduces moral beliefs to subjective feelings or attitudes devoid of objective basis … a Christian ethic finds its source of obligation in God, and it conceives what is good in terms of God's perfect will" (p.269) … However, "duties are not the whole story. If redemption's purpose is to bring about God's purpose for creation, then it means an ethic of virtues, character and social justice amid a creation blossoming in every way that glorifies its Maker" … bearing in mind that "creation, sin, grace and kingdom are inseparably joined in God's purposes" (p.270). Houston (1980) comments appropriately, "I need the belief in the personal reality of the Creator to help me distinguish idolatry from the real world, to understand the interconnectedness of life more than even ecologists can recognize and to know how I fit into place, at home in the world. … I believe in the Creator for by His Word all things were made, all things hold together and all things have meaning and purpose" (p.256). A central concept then is mutuality—inter-relationship (Welker, 1999) or ecological interdependence (triadic, God-humans-other creatures) based on the following three Rs as guiding principles:

Relationship—as exemplified most perfectly in the Trinity (Gunton 1992), but reflected in the whole web of creation, in the possibility of companionship, and creation of the "possibility of possibilities" (Page 1996); this has entailed the creation of both infinity (Fergusson 1998) and boundaries, transcendence and immanence as demonstrated within the Godhead. There is always the possibility of the management of balance; to care as God cares, that is the quest.

Respect—as reiterated in Genesis, "God saw that it was good" and brought out in the case of livestock as the crucial principle underpinning stockmanship by Gatward (2001). Respect includes a respect for boundaries of species and behaviors; boundaries are for the mutual blessing of creation, not its arbitrary or vindictive limitation; this is especially relevant to the genetic modification debate (Deane-Drummond 1997; Bruce & Bruce 1998; Runge 1998; Anderson 1999; Bruce & Horrocks 2001 and Appendix 1).

Responsibility—which is enjoined in the creation mandate to "Be fruitful and multiply and have dominion" a paternal/ maternal and priestly role, neither patronizing nor domineering.

The appropriate Biblical motif to select for agriculture and rural development may seem to be simply "stewardship" with delegated "complete authority" (dominion) under God to manage His creation as He (God) likes. However, the model for human behavior in agriculture does not have to be selected in a mutually exclusive way from those expressed in the Bible but rather this writer has proposed (Wibberley 2001) a corrective, "ecological" (mutually interdependent) synthesis of the material and the spiritual in dominion (Gen. 1:28), priesthood (Psa. 150:6), companionship (Prov. 12:10), stewardship (Luke 16:2) and teamwork (1 Cor. 3:9). Such a synthesis of the Biblical paradigms for our roles towards creation can be corrective for us in a number of ways.

Inclusion of dominion carries the risk of misinterpretation as "domination" (see White 1967 for a classical charge along these lines) while its omission would dilute the notion of "complete authority," a responsibility entrusted to humans by God and not to be shelved but rather to be interpreted as "complete authority to do as God likes" with His Creation. Inclusion of priesthood carries the risk of lapse into a superior sacramentalism whereas its omission would miss the goal to offer harmonized creation in praise to God, to let it be what He designed it to be to His praise and glory. Inclusion of companionship carries the risk of creature-worship but its omission would deny the respect for creation God Himself exhibits and reduce motivation for protective management. Inclusion of stewardship carries the risk of arrogated human power marginalizing God Who sustains all continuously, while its omission would remove the principle motif for practical caring management in agriculture, with accountability (as in Luke 16:2). Inclusion of teamwork carries the risk of relativism to accommodate different team members but its omission would neglect the vital co-workership with God, in His team which the whole tenor of the New Testament suggests through the disciples and the explicit words of 1 Cor. 3:9, "fellow-laborers together with Christ" in obedient team-based mutual servanthood as shown by Christ (but, notably, first needing to receive His husbandry of our lives to enable us to be His stewards in co-operation). This sequence has the strength of going beyond dominion into priesthood, contains companionship as the central relational linkage of these concepts to stewardship, but goes beyond stewardship into teamwork—not only between humans but crucially also in co-operation with the supremely integrated Trinity.

The outworking of a creation theology cannot (and must not in thinking) be separated from salvation. Jesus means "God saves"—sustainability depends upon the maximum mutual aggregate well being of soil-plant-animal-human-microbial systems. The concern is to undertake Kingdom-building work now, to perceive eternity as the cumulative "nows" of shalom (God's conquering peace), to address ecological threats now, to "occupy now until He comes" with an eye to the horizon but with feet firmly on the ground!

The State of Agriculture

The term "agriculture" is of seventeenth-century origin (Latin agricultura) a derivation which combines ager (land, field) with cultura (culture); the word "culture" itself is interesting, deriving from cultus (cultivation) and colere (to till, to cultivate, to "worship"—as in "cult"). Thus the word "agriculture" is intrinsically holistic as to physical land, land as a total context for human activity and being, and land as spiritually significant.

Internationally, post-1950 agricultural development was driven by the quest for higher yields to satisfy the ever-expanding populations, especially of so-called "developing" countries (actually, all countries are developing—none have "arrived"!). There have been many successes.

The "Green Revolution" was the name given to "the dramatic increase in production of rice and wheat [based on new HYVs—high-yielding, shorter-stalk varieties] that occurred mainly in the sub-tropical regions of the developing countries, especially during the decade 1965–75" (Arnon 1987, 322). This has proved controversial, requiring higher inputs of fertilizer, agrochemicals and irrigation yet allowing countries to maintain lower prices for their staple cereals; this has meant smaller farmers have been unable to stay in business while larger ones have had the imperative to expand [and mechanize to do so] in order to allow for lower financial returns per hectare. Furthermore, there have been ecological consequences of using a narrowing genetic base of new varieties, social consequences of reduced farmer independence, greater inequity and loss of dietarily preferred varieties. By the early 1980s, concern over negative trends in conventional American agriculture (decreasing energy-efficiency, increasing pollution, burgeoning farmer indebtedness and business failure) led to the commissioning of a review of alternative agriculture (Pesek 1989). This defined "Alternative Agriculture" (Pesek 1989, 27) as "any system of food or fiber production that systematically pursues the following goals:

- more thorough incorporation of natural processes such as nutrient cycles, nitrogen fixation, and pest-predator relationships into the agricultural production process;

- reduction in the use of off-farm inputs with the greatest potential to harm the environment or the health of farmers and consumers;

- greater productive use of the biological and genetic potential of plant and animal species;

- improvement of the match between cropping patterns and the productive potential and physical limitations of agricultural lands to ensure long-term sustainability of current production levels; and

- profitable and efficient production with emphasis on improved farm management and conservation of soil, water, energy, and biological resources."

Conford (2001) reviews the history of the organic agriculture movement, a key part of the quest for alternatives.

In the livestock sphere, huge increases in productivity have been accomplished by better nutrition, health and husbandry systems; better breeding from superior genotypes together with greater reproductive success through such techniques as AI (artificial insemination); better preservation and processing of animal products for improved food security worldwide. Manipulation of the male-female ratio is of great interest to maximize the productive female outputs in all livestock. Relatively new options are already in use, such as recovery of ova from abattoir material, embryo transplantation and various in vitro fertilization and culture techniques. Genetic engineering offers undoubted utilitarian possibilities such as accelerated breeding (including for conservation of rare breeds), uniformity through cloning for desirable carcass quality and high growth rates in beef cattle, incorporation of novel and useful characteristics such as disease resistance and adaptability to harsh environments. However, it raises the specter of many ethical dilemmas: genetic diversity may be neglected, the essential nature of a creature may be altered, unpredictable knock-on system effects may occur, and power over the whole food system may be further concentrated according to who owns the patents to the techniques involved; furthermore, structural changes in the farming sector associated with rapid novel technology adoption can have far-reaching and often dire consequences for rural communities worldwide.

The present trends faced by farmers internationally are:

1. Many farmers have left for various reasons, and many more are set to go, worldwide;

2. There is a huge differential between farm incomes in richest and poorest countries;

3. Farmer numbers go up in developing countries, though their % of population/"voice" is decreasing;

4. National governments have pursued cheap food; WTO encourages least-cost production;

5. WTO (World Trade Organization) key policy is non-discrimination against imports;

6. World prices for farm products would kill off UK Agriculture—and in other richer countries;

7. Real costs far exceed ex-farm food prices; these include environmental and social costs;

8. Farming families have delivered the landscapes and countryside care we have inherited;

9. Conserving farmers is a key issue; they perform multiple functions—production, care, hosting visitors, stewarding inputs, passing on skills/rural knowledge, conserving landscapes, nature and communities;

10. Integration is needed; farm/food systems can simultaneously yield many benefits sustainably;

11. Local relationships between producer and consumer do matter—and save transport costs;

12. There needs to be a re-valuation of natural "services" and products (including food).

Two things are crucial in the ethical pursuit of sustainable livelihoods in God's economy:

a) Achieving a fairer world, such as attempted by "Jubilee" to cancel debts for poorer nations;

b) Harnessing true free enterprise—to produce as well as to consume—for the maximum number of farmers which paradoxically can only be attained within responsible resource management limits and with minimal bureaucracy.

If so-called "free trade" is carried out to world prices, the USA, UK and other richer country farmers will disappear; some say "so what?"—poorest countries could provide food (probably commodified, GM via TNCs) much more cheaply than e.g. UK; UK can become a park/wilderness, they say. Alternatively, this could be allowed to happen within countries—with wilderness in one region and intensive food-factory commodity production elsewhere. Is this what we want? More importantly, is this what God wants? As the UK Women's Institute poster states "Farming is Everyone's Business" … so are its ethics.

Ethics for Agriculture

Relativism provides no coherent starting point for the development of ethics, though it has been increasingly preferred by many. The model for agricultural ethics considered here arises from absolutism, as represented by a straightforward reading of John 1:1-14. The starting point for ethical standards is the absolute of God as revealed through the Bible but applying these ethics, as in their original context, to relationships, including the wider environmental and social setting, and not simply to personal morality.

Christian ethics are well defined by Murray (1962, 397) as ethics where "faith in God is the fountain, love to God the impelling motive, the law of God the directing principle, and the glory of God the governing aim." They thus concern relationships to God as creatures, to neighbors as fellow humans and to the earth as stewards based upon the creation mandate or dominion covenant of Genesis 1:26-28. Some writers, such as White (1967) and McHarg (1969), have criticized the apparent interpretation of "dominion" too often as a license to exploit creation any way man likes. Though "benevolent rule as regents with complete authority under God" is actually intended by the use of the word "dominion" in the Genesis context.

It is apparent, based on widespread environmental concerns recorded internationally in opinion surveys, that the following basis at least is increasingly universally accepted for any consideration of ethics now, viz.:

1. We are all world citizens, each with a conscience potentially sensitive to ethical issues. We all have a place and a responsibility.

2. We live in what Marshall McLuhan (1964) called a "global village" of a common earth. We all need to share and care.

3. "Charity begins at home"—a proverb which dates from the fourteenth century, to which must be added "but it doesn't end there." We are to work lovingly and share the wealth created. "Home" implies "manageable place" and "rooted base" giving us a sense of proportion (scale), of accountability

and of belonging. The proverb, "there's no place like home" was first recorded in a Farm-Household context in Thomas Tusser's 1573 book, Five Hundred Points of Good Husbandry.

Higginson (1988) reviews the two main approaches to moral decision-making:

1. The consequential approach, dominant in Western culture, based largely on utilitarianism as developed by Bentham (1789) in his theory that pleasure rather than pain is sought by mankind and should thus be the experience provided for the greatest number of people possible. Bentham even devised a pleasure-calculator which he called a "hedonic calculus"! His individualistic ideas were developed by John Stuart Mill and are exemplified nowadays by cost/benefit analysis and its analogues. Taken to its logical conclusion, this approach alone leads to "valid ends justifying any means."

2. The deontological approach, dominant in considerations of human rights, is based on duty i.e. rules which pre-scribe what ought to happen in a given case. Springing from the consideration of love and justice as being abso-lutes, the interpretation is far from straightforward since some will base the rules upon their understanding of the will of God, others on personal intuition and yet others on reason,- with Kant (1724–1804) who aimed for a uni-versal set of moral imperatives. It is a common feature of human cultures to hold to certain core values such as: to abhor and to impose sanctions against murder, adultery, rape, theft and treachery, but to value and idealize free-dom. However, there will be dilemmas when rigid rules conflict such that to satisfy one involves diminishing or even denying another; thus hierarchies of principles and priorities will be needed. Logical support for the deon-tology view also requires resort to consequences argu-ments. Thus, in practice an integrated situational blend of both approaches is needed, as Higginson (1988) con-cludes, in order to cope with real world issues with some ethical consistency.

Ethical Objectives

The desired outcomes—objectives—of ethics are to answer the following great questions and sub-sets of them:

- What is good?
- What is right?
- What is fair?

These questions presuppose the moral excellence or virtue of, respectively, beauty, truth and justice, for the individual and for society. The enduring aim of ethics thus becomes the maximization of virtue, while that of economics has been secularly defined as "the maximization of satisfaction."

Furthermore, while ethics has developed as a discipline concerned largely with direct human welfare, it patently extends to the whole of creation—plant, animal and environment—which ultimately affects human welfare also, apart from its own intrinsic worth. In the case of sheep, the late Godfrey Bowen of New Zealand became concerned that as sheep mob size increased, his sheep were cut during shearing and the wool clip ended in pieces with excessive waste. After prayer about these welfare and quality concerns, he developed a shearing method which happens to be the fastest in the world and is now used by most shearers from Russia to South Africa! (Bowen, 1982).

An anonymous writer has elicited seven principles of Christian liberty—a liberty in which, paradoxically, we are urged "to stand fast" (Gal. 5:l). These principles are here proposed to be as relevant to agricultural activities as elsewhere:

(1) Does it violate any part of Scripture? (1 Thess. 5:21, 22)

(2) Does it weaken my testimony as a Christian? (Eph. 4:l).

(3) Can I ask God's blessing on it? (1 Cor. 10:31).

(4) Is it a stumbling block for someone else? (Rom. 14:21; 1 Cor. 8:2).

(5) Does it harm others or myself physically or mentally? (1 Cor. 6:19,20).

(6) Does it edify others and myself spiritually? (Rom. 15:2).

(7) How does it advance the cause of Christ?—the telos towards shalom—(Col. 1:10).

Agricultural Objectives

The scope of agriculture ranges from the sub-molecular, through biochemical processes, cells, organisms, populations of plants and animals, enterprises, farms, farm-households, rural communities, estates, farming systems and techniques, marketing, national policies to world trade. For all of these, underpinning ethics and ethical guidelines need to be established.

Agriculture exists to provide:

- Food

- Non-food renewable resources

- Creative employment

- Care for the soil, landscape, living things

- Maintenance of biodiversity and responsible environmental management

- Social and community needs for the Farm-Household (whether of owner, tenant, manager or employee) within the wider rural economy

- Reasonable profit, without which the capacity to act generously is diminished.

- Strategic/Political role—to supply adequate grain and other renewable resource reserves, together with reasonable access to a managed countryside.

Principles of Agricultural Ethics

The achievement of all of the above objectives requires the exercise of a comprehensive ethic, not simply one which focuses on humans only (anthropocentrism) but on the wider environment and creatures involved and which is integrated within the social responsibilities of science (Mellanby 1974). It "must argue from the natural to the moral"... "a comprehensive ethic will find values in and duties to the natural world. An ecological conscience requires an unprecedented mix of science and conscience, of biology and ethics" (Rolston 1992). Concluding his land ethic, Leopold (1949, 262) asserted that "a thing is right when it tends to preserve stability and integrity of the biotic community; it is wrong when it tends otherwise"—though naturalistic, this principle should contribute to a holistic theology. According to Cooper and Palmer (1992), concern and planning for future generations is part of what makes us human and "conservation" represents a "voluntary agreement with future generations"; though anthropocentric, this principle too should inform a holistic theology. Schumacher (1997, 172-181) develops the argument that land is what he calls a "meta-economic" factor along with the other three elements of the ancients (air, water and fire); "we want clean air as a value in itself" (p.173) in that "ends, as distinct from means are not matters of economic calculation", though he notes the lack of consensus of opinion on this point in present day society. "Does goodness pay? Is it worthwhile? Is it good business to behave decently?" all these Schumacher rightly calls "illegitimate, degraded questions." He argues that the use, maintenance, health and future of land is a similar value, noting also that "throughout the world, rural life is breaking down" (p.178) such that reconciliation of humankind with the natural world is not only desirable but imperative. While agrarian society is governed by the cycles of nature, industrial society dethrones nature and degrades it "to the rank of a reservoir of materials and resources to be exploited at man's behest for his own advantage by scientific technology" (Hendry 1980, 13).

Brueggemann (1982, 30-37) affirms that Gen. 1:3-25 "protests against an exclusively anthropocentric view of the world. The Creator God is not totally preoccupied with human creatures. God has His own relation with the rest of creation"—and repeats the verdict "good" upon it. However, God speaks directly only to humans indicating "a peculiarly intense commitment (by speaking) and to whom marvelous freedom has been granted (in responding). The human creature attests to the goodness of God by exercising freedom with and authority over all the other creatures entrusted to its care. The image of God in the human person is a mandate of power and responsibility, but it is power exercised as God exercises power … It has to do with securing the well-being of every other creature and bringing the promise of each to full fruition." Jesus (Mark 10:43,44) points the way of servant leadership to accomplish that; "the striking feature of Jesus (Phil. 2:1-11) is that He did not look after His own interests but always after the interests of others … Creation is God's decision not to look after Himself but to focus His energies and purposes on the creation" (p.34). Gen. 1:26-29 is "an explicit call to form a new kind of human community" to cooperate with God in that focus.

Brueggemann (1978) also provides a seminal theology for land ethics. He begins his case by noting that Yahweh and Land are inseparable (Psa. 24:1). To humankind, land is gift, covenanted, watered from heaven; it is not intended to be chartered for technological management for production. It provides humans with both promise and problem, task and temptation; it matters how we relate to land. Brueggemann (pp.15-27) identifies two histories: in Genesis 1-11 there is presumption in relation to secured land and being expelled from it, while in Gen.12-50 there is trusting toward a land not yet possessed and empowerment by anticipation of it. We too stand between being dislocated because of impertinence and being relocated in trust. Abraham travels by faith from his land to another (Gen. 15:18) while Joseph becomes a model manager in another land (Gen. 41:57; 42:6; 47:20,27).

The Exodus experience of being landless in a lifeless but surprising wilderness (Exod. 16:4,8,12) teaches people to trust in God rather than in land, while Numbers (14:1-21) charts the testings of landlessness. Deuteronomy records the blessings of God in the wilderness (2:7) and the provision of land as gift (Deut. 6:10-18). It warns that security is only to be sought in God and that land is not to be coveted for self-possession (Deut. 8:11-17).

Land involves task of responsible usage (Luke 12:48; Gen. 2:15, 3:17-19) yet this carries with it temptation. Land is covenanted place, not contextless space to fill as man chooses. The Sabbath is an affirmation that neither land nor people can be finally owned or managed (Amos 8:4-6). Land is not for casual trade as a commodity. While Ahab perceived land as an easily transferable, covetable commodity, Naboth considered himself to belong to the land rather than the land belonging to him (1 Kings 21)—for him land was "not a tradable commodity but an inalienable inheritance from God" (Brueggemann,1978, 93).

Land disputes and greed are recorded elsewhere (e.g. Prov. 22:28; 23:10-11; 15:25; Isa. 5:8; Micah 2:1-3). The history of Israel in its classical period is a tension between royally-secured land and covenanted, precarious land (Hos. 9:17; Zeph. 1:12; Jer. 1:10; 2:6,7, 27; 4:3). Jeremiah deals with land restoration (24:4-7; 29:4-14) and the connection between land and obedience (32:6,7,15,44). Ezekiel records land crisis (7:2-7; 33:28,29) but shows land gift again to be God's initiative (36:21-38; 47:13 ff., especially vv.21-23). Malachi (3:10-12) explains the conditionality of land blessing.

In the NT, Jesus, though landless Himself (Luke 9:58) accepted the principles of the OT land mandates (e.g. Luke 7:36-50; 12:16-34). The epistles express the importance of living as a pilgrim people (e.g. Rom. 4:13,14; 1 Cor. 4:7; Gal. 3:18; 4:28; Heb. 11:13-16).

Land must be managed as a gift of communal concern, requiring sustained care by humankind as Regent not King (Pawson 1974). The paradox is that we are to relate to land as settled carers—albeit temporary ones—yet remain "on the move" as pilgrims; for this Kneen (1989, p.75) proposes the Biblical word "sojourner." The further paradox is that God wishes us sojourners to cooperate with him in this task while we are equipped to do so as He wishes only by allowing Him to cultivate us as His "field," His "husbandry" (1 Cor. 3:9).

Agriculture as an occupation has long been perceived as desirable even though modern pressures of scale and of socio-cultural emphasis on maximizing gain may have diminished this. This writer has observed that contact with living creatures and requirement to care for them can be reformatory to delinquent children, therapeutic to the lonely and exciting to the uninitiated. Ethics applied to agriculture should provide guidelines for an ethical agriculture from this two-way traffic.

Many presuppose that economics is the antithesis of ethics in relation to agriculture. What is actually needed is ethics with economics, but that is not all. I have argued elsewhere that these are but two of many factors to be considered together in respect of agricultural systems, though it is apparent that economics has tended to become dominant and ethics sometimes seems absent, or at best marginalized. Indeed, hedonistic economics—by contrast with Prov. 16:8—is the foundation philosophy underpinning the increasingly dominant philosophy of secular materialism with its consequent moral vacuum and dangerously growing global inequities. However, it must be emphasized that economics is far from being an intrinsically unethical discipline; it only shows a tendency to become so when it is applied normatively rather than descriptively. Properly, like ecology, it is concerned with descriptions of "home" (Greek *oikos*), specifically linked with "laws" (Greek nomos, a word closely linked also to nemo which means "to arrange"): thus, "home laws/arrangements"—the means to "manage" or "steward." Within this etymological perspective, a reconciliation of ethics with economics is prescribed.

Attainment of sustainability is vital internationally in order to maintain and deliver:

a. conserved biodiverse (species-rich) landscapes—[already done by best farmers]

b. "commonwealth" integrated economies—maximizing local interdependence

c. networks of relational communities i.e. where good relationships are strengthened

Sustainability is a comprehensive concept. For the Christian, it is not only "for the grandchildren" but also "for creation's well-being for the Creator' s glory and satisfaction." It must simultaneously satisfy essential criteria:

a. ECONOMY (oikos = home; nomos = law/"management rules")—long-term earnings balance

b. ECOLOGY—balanced care of the environment and its associated flora, fauna and people.

c. EQUITY—pursuit of justice for all in a shared earth of shared wealth NOT shared poverty

d. ENERGY-EFFICIENCY—wasting much less energy in farming & food delivery systems

e. EMPLOYMENT—promoting creative employment to secure local farm product supply

f. ETHICS—doing what is good, fair & right in relation to Higher Authority (God's perspective).

All these require the practical promoters of education, enterprise, enthusiasm, effort-effectiveness with expectancy of some reward/success leading to enjoyment of living on a worldwide basis. Central to the Torah is a moral mandate towards creation. According to Sacks (1995, 208) "once we lose the idea of limits and focus instead on short-term enjoyment, we set in motion long-term disharmonies which have devastating effects on the human situation. Man must not abuse nature for he is part of nature." However, "Genesis sets forth a view of nature which is not man-centered but God-centered." Judaism highlights the significance of Shabbat when "we are commanded to renounce our manipulation of the world. It is a day that sets a limit to our intervention in nature and the pursuit of economic growth. The earth is not ours but God's. For six days it is handed over to our management. On the seventh day we symbolically abdicate that power. We may perform no "work" ... What Shabbat does for man and the animals, the sabbatical and jubilee years do for the land. We owe earth its periodic rest" (Sacks,1995, 209). Key principles of Biblical origin in relation to farming the land are explored by Brueggemann (1978) and by Schluter and Ashcroft (1990) as well as by Wibberley (1975, 1996). From them, several crucial factors emerge:

IDENTITY—the very essence of species, breed, variety/cultivar is important. Biotechnology raises huge questions of increasingly greater complexity and dilemma. However, the overriding thought is repeated in Genesis that God created everything "after its kind."

PLACE—is important for rooted identity of families and land care; yet, land is not intended to be a source of eternal security as a substitute for trust in God, so a tension exists between settled access to land and the concept of man as caring tenant (even if in

Roman law one is the legal owner), and the further concept of pilgrimage through this lifetime (as characteristic of nomadic pastoralism and the imagery of Psalm 23). The old farming adage reconciles well these paradoxical concepts of pilgrimage and comparative settlement, viz.: "live as if you will die tomorrow, farm as if you will farm for ever."

WORK—tending the fields and livestock combines physical and spiritual dimensions; this is expressed in the old anonymous saw *"orare est laborare, laborare est orare"* ("to pray is to work, to work is to pray").

SHARING THE PRODUCE—this includes the poor and the stranger, as in the case of Ruth gleaning in the fields of Boaz (Ruth 2:16). It also includes the provision of capital and the remission of debt every fifty years (Leviticus 25:10) with land rest and redistribution of land-use rights to re-establish equity (Numbers 33:54).

HUSBANDRY—the righteous man "regards"—considers seriously with loving concern and thus cares for—the life of his beast (Proverbs 12:10; 27:23) and his crops (Proverbs 24:30-34). Massingham (1945) called for a "return to husbandry" and Pawson (1973) deplored the use of "production" rather than "husbandry" of animals and crops.

SCALE—excessive expansion is condemned in both Old and New Testaments e.g. by the prophet Isaiah (5:8) who also points out the consequent isolation, both physical and social and by Jesus (Luke 12:15-21) Who stressed eternal investment.

Genetic Engineering & Biotechnology

Heap (1995, 2, 3) argues that medical and agricultural advances in biotechnology have "rejuvenated the moribund discipline of ethics" by the problems that they pose. Biotechnology attracts special attention because it directs … to key questions about who owns science and to ethics—how is common good best served, environments conserved, food safety and security ensured, and animal welfare protected?"

Some people would argue that we have been altering plants and animals for centuries by the usual techniques of selection and

breeding. Yet the situation is different and newly modified creatures are being created, frequently with DNA from totally different organisms, such as crops to match a package of chemical treatments which are liable to cross with wild species, so bringing
about a contamination of the natural gene pool. Not all this need
be detrimental but the point is that the ecological consequences
are unpredictable and irreversible.

While chemical pollution has become a great concern in recent
decades, in some cases this is reversible by a rigorous clean-up
operation. Such retrieval of the status quo will not be possible
after large-scale commercial release of genetically modified crops.
The large companies promoting this work argue that it is going to
be impossible to feed the growing world population without
recourse to such genetic engineering. As Madeley (2000, 116)
writes, "GM crops are not relevant to the main reason why people
go hungry, namely lack of the money to buy food or the land on
which to grow it"; he cites Ethiopia as a case in point. Many studies have shown that the highest yields per hectare, with least
dependence on chemical and other external inputs, come from
integrated, labor-intensive, tropical farming systems which recycle
nutrients adequately and manage weeds effectively by cultural
means. Such systems are sustainable by the most relevant technical criterion of sustainability, i.e. energy-efficiency. These systems are also replicable among the vast majority of the world's
farmers who are smallholders. Local efforts of this kind over the
centuries have conserved the genetic diversity on which the new
generation of plant engineers is drawing to produce their GM
crops (see Appendix 1). The acquisition and attempted patenting
by Trans-National Corporations (TNCs) of farmers' long-bred
plants has caused much consternation among organized farmers
groups world-wide, such as those half-a-million Indian farmers
who protested vigorously in 1993 against the TRIPS (Trade-
Related Intellectual Property rights agreement of the World Trade
Organization (WTO). There is a serious ethical issue here in that
multi-national corporations should not be able to legitimize biopiracy (as Shiva 2000 calls it) and to cash in on material bred carefully for centuries without passing some of the benefits back to the
communities who have so conserved these plants. GM crops will

also render farmers more dependent on the supplying companies not only for seeds but also for the herbicides and other inputs for which the GM crops have been engineered.

Genetic engineering of animals is most sharply challenging ethically when it involves reproductive cloning, as in the famous case of "Dolly" the sheep, produced after 277 "failures." Fox (1992) catalogues very high deformity and suffering rates in pigs modified with human genetic material while, in China, fish with growth rates dramatically increased after modification with human genetic material are already on sale.

A Christian approach needs consideration of the following:

1. God created everything after its kind—what right have we irrevocably to cross boundaries?

2. Transnational Corporations and the World Trade Organization (WTO) are bypassing the authority of national governments in their accumulation of economic and therefore political power. In this farmers are largely voiceless. The Bible has much to say about justice and the poor as a key issue.

3. We are stewards of creation. Earth is God's farm and we are to do what He likes with it, not what we like! We are to protect the vulnerable, to avoid harm and pursue sustained benefits for creation.

4. While it seems unreasonable and probably unnecessary to rule out everything which is described as "genetic engineering," we are clearly on the threshold of something which demands extreme caution in view of the unprecedented biological, ecological and rural community consequential effects, many of which appear irreversible, or at least reversible with great difficulty, once embarked upon.

Globalization & Trade

In 1788, the ex-British colonies of North America abolished all commercial barriers and laid the foundations of the present-day USA, by far the largest economy in the world. The USA has a GDP of more than double its nearest rival, Japan, and over six times that of the UK which ranks fourth in the world after Germany in third place. The deduction has been "trade freely to grow." Yet a debate over free trade versus protectionism has raged worldwide, and in Britain for well over 150 years with the notable repeal of the Corn Laws in 1846 leading to entry of cheaper colonial grain imports. However, never before the present has the context of the debate involved such instant international communication, so much speculative electronic money transfer and "globalization" in general. "Globalization" is not intrinsically negative—there are positives in shared innovations, regional products (e.g. tea) and greater intercultural understanding, but it has huge dangers. The World Trade Organization (WTO) succeeded GATT (General Agreement on Tariffs & Trade, operative from 1947) and began operating on January 1st, 1995. There is, of course, an ethical case for international trade but also a strong one against excessive trade (Appendix 2). Excessive trade is proving contrary to the signals to protect the environment to ensure sustainable livelihoods for future generations sent to all Environment Departments by the 1992 Rio Summit and its successors (including Johannesburg 2002). In practice, the WTO central policy of non-discrimination against imports is threatening all farmers (and other businesses—including the US steel industry!) worldwide since it is leading inevitably to:

1. Pressure to adopt least-cost production methods

2. "Grab markets" behavior [no matter how distant nor who's there already]

3. Destruction of farming, rural communities and businesses worldwide

4. Air pollution from "freight miles"—[greater oil dependence is getting riskier too ...]

5. Rapidly decreasing energy-efficiency of food systems; increasing political vulnerability

6. Loss of "food cultures" and community identity with land

7. Loss of equitable free enterprise (Loss of equitable free enterprise anywhere threatens true free enterprise everywhere).

The scourge of communism with its management failure was

overthrown from 1989 onwards by prayer and the collective common sense of people as witnessed by this writer in Eastern Europe and the former Soviet Union. The injustice of apartheid was defeated by prayer and the collective will of people not only in South Africa but internationally (Cassidy 1995 records how "God did it"—Isa. 30:8). Extreme greed corporate behavior is a serious issue to be firmly but constructively addressed in the context of a consideration of rival development models—the technocratic which assumes technology can triumph over all problems and the ecocratic ("inter-relationships rule") approach, not excluding modern technology (since a Living God reveals new songs, new ways to each generation) but with appropriate technology as the servant rather than the Master of the agri-rural system. The argument is that there is a Divinely intended connection between people and place, people and land and food. The increasing distancing of them proceeds apace.

Hope in Africa

The majority of African farmers are female and they are increasingly marginalized (Mazrui 1998). Kinoti (1994, 88) states, "What we need is a holistic theology, a theology that is God-centered and that treats man and the creation in the integrative manner that scripture does." Thankfully, there exist examples where this is being adopted.

In Uganda, the Kulika Trust operates effective extension of sustainable agriculture through farmer practitioners, led by Co-ordinator Elijah Kyamuwendo (himself a Christian farmer whose small farm incorporates voluntarily protected undisturbed woodland). There are associated Farmers' Study Groups who meet in their own districts, compare practices and co-operate in various ways. Some, such as Richard Tumushabe, function as farmer-evangelists sharing their integrated faith and farming lifestyle within their farming communities. On their 3.7 acres, farmers John & Josephine Kizza run some 16 commercial projects from a small-scale dairy, to poultry, bees, vegetables, rabbit-keeping and so on. The secret is composting with recycling of wastes, companion cropping, natural pesticides, biogas production and integrated management of trees, shorter-term crops and livestock. They do not keep this information to themselves and their visitors' book shows that they have entertained over 20,000 farmers per year in recent years. They can go away and benefit from what they have seen because the scale and resource management practices can be emulated simply with minimal external inputs but with the application of intelligence and hard work.

"Hard Work and Holy Living" is the watchword of IcFEM (InterChristian Fellowships Evangelical Mission) at Kimilili in Kenya. This interdenominational work is led by Solomon Nabie and his wife, Ruth. Solomon left his government job to adopt a "tent-making" approach to earning (cf. Paul in Acts 18:3) i.e. he freed up time to serve his community through the new work of IcFEM. This work is holistic, encouraging people by demonstration, advice and training how to make the most of their own resources in order to obtain sustainable livelihoods, giving glory to God and releasing their tithes from this work for the extension of God's Kingdom—bringing relief and the message of salvation to those who have yet to hear and receive it. Kenya has many such grassroots initiatives; another is Genesis operating in Kitui District and started by Robert & Beatrice Mutemi Mutua. Biblical holism in their case starts with medical help coupled with gospel preaching and sustained by agricultural self-help groups with shared appropriate technologies. Local people are enabled to be God's local stewards of all that they have and are.

In Tanzania, RURCON Facilitator Godwin Chetti who farms 10 acres himself has led his community in prayerful seeking of God about their regular drought problems and mobilized them to construct their own dam. He has catalyzed the formation of some 7 Farmers' Study Groups (of around 12 or so members each) which meet approximately monthly on each other's farms to discuss and compare management practices. As trust develops, such groups can come to support one another in various ways and they may begin to co-operate in sharing equipment, in buying inputs together, in selling produce together. The names of groups include *Pamoja Tujaribu* ("Together, Let's Try") and *Seje-Seje* ("Little by little"); these express a certain humility in acknowledging dependence on teamwork and on God's Providence. Group meetings are for all who have similar farming and interest; Christian members operate within them as "salt and light" (Matt. 5:13-16).

RURCON stands for "Rural & Urban Resources, Counseling, Outreach & Networking"—Service for holistic development through Christian Churches of Africa. It is a team of African Christian leaders started by Barnaba Dusu and Peter Batchelor in Nigeria in 1971 and serving interdenominationally and in community development in sub-Saharan Africa since then. Pre-dating RURCON was Faith & Farm which was begun by Peter Batchelor in 1958 and is still operating. The background is instructive in relation to an integrated gospel. The vast majority of missionaries at the time saw little point in agriculture as part of missionary work; the gospel was to be preached and people taught to read the Bible. Essential medical attention and relief of starvation was legitimate alongside the urgent preaching but many appeared unready to perceive the wholeness of the gospel to be proclaimed. Yet the emergent Church saw the point because people who followed animism had a worldview, which totally involved their faith (in the ancestors as "living dead") and their everyday lives. To be told to burn fetishes, stop praying to rocks and ancestors and to attend Christian services and prayer meetings at narrowly proscribed times was no substitute for such holistic religion. It invited syncretism whereby new converts might pray earnestly in church and then consult the witchdoctor for medical and other material answers to their problems. In the West today, when the Church fails to provide an integrated gospel which promotes a whole Christian approach to the environment, people are similarly tempted to syncretism in New Age Beliefs. Faith & Farm proved so effective that many other churches of different denominations and in different countries—starting in neighboring Chad—asked the Nigerian team to "come over to Macedonia and help us" (Acts 16:9); thus, RURCON was born—but not until the work of Faith & Farm had been taken over by a Nigerian Christian, the late Joseph Jibi. God has indeed called local people to be His stewards right where we are (see Appendix 5 and Batchelor, 1993). RURCON has been instrumental in the formation of CRUDAN (Christian Rural & Urban Development Association of Nigeria) which works nationwide in that country to train and otherwise encourage for Biblical holism in development. Similar Associations are being catalyzed by RURCON in other African countries— including Liberia and Sierra Leone. In the latter country, a recent workshop sought to encourage Christians to understand and engage with governance and globalization issues, to start groups for weaving and recovery of cottage industry in that needed sector of the economy.

In Nigeria, Eunice & Dung Pwol in their Loving Care Center are encouraging linkage between food grown and its proper preparation in balanced nutrition for needy nursing mothers; child mortality reduction is linked with clear Bible teaching and commitment with practical skills for constructive living. Hosts of other examples abound in Africa where people are thinking and living Biblical holism in an agricultural context (see for instance Case Study 8).

In Ghana, Tom and Agnes Ahima run the Ofuman Agricultural Project—their own farming business but also providing an agricultural extension service, support on rural banking, rural supplies, seed outgrowers (over 200 providing a significant proportion of that country's maize seed) and a training scheme for young graduate farmers. The key into Ofuman's work was the small thing of Agnes bringing a few seeds of eggplant in 1978 from their former workplace in northern Ghana when they moved to the mid-west region. These grow well and the farm now produces three crops per year but they shared this with many local small-scale farmers and now some 800 of them have formed a co-operative to supply the city of Kumasi, to gain good nutrition in the dry season, to gain dignity and to support the local church much more effectively than before with their tithes. When I was last there, the sermon was on Nehemiah 10:38—tithing on the tithe! As one approaches Ofuman, there is a noticeable increase in the frequency of smiles on people's faces, hardworking and relatively poor as they are; it reminds me of the Indian friend's description of the purpose of his development project, "It is to increase the joy!" Biblical holism is about increasing the joy of the Lord as we seek to build His Kingdom.

Afrikaaner Christian businessmen were distressed by apartheid so in 1979 they began the Africa Co-operative Action Trust (ACAT) modeled on a Savings Club scheme instigated by a missionary brother Waddilove in Zimbabwe (when still Rhodesia in the 1960s). ACAT is an interdenominational Christian Mission Agency which offers training to farmers and a private extension service to advise and encourage them. Farmers meet in local groups of some 12-25. Each group has its own farmer chairman, vice-chairman, secretary, assistant secretary and treasurer—all of whom receive training to build their own capacities to do the job well. Members compare each other's practice in farm visits, make savings together so that they can buy in supplies collectively and as trust develops they begin to do other things together according to their local decisions. Some market produce together, others process it together first; some engage in community water schemes and the like. Bible study is applied to these daily farming activities. Several thousand of such groups now exist in southern Africa, headquartered in Pietermaritzburg, Natal, RSA but spread into Swaziland and elsewhere. With original founders motivated by Christ's compassion and concern for justice, these groups receive God's blessings and pass them on.

Farmers Together

Jesus and the 12 disciples inspired this writer's international work over the past three decades with what I have called the Farmer-Dominant Study Group (FDSG). It is instructive that Jesus:

1. Chose a manageable group size of 12;

2. Chose ordinary people to be group members, not those of special aptitude;

3. Took a multidisciplinary approach;

4. Related study to practice continually;

5. Used demonstration and practice throughout;

6. Trained them to work itinerantly as "catalyst/lubricant extensionists";

7. Taught them to identify, encourage and enable local leadership;

8. Taught them to focus on permanent change for the better;

9. Constantly emphasized achievement of group mutuality (teamwork).

Local initiatives among farmers enable mutual trust and understanding to develop, together with cross-fertilization of ideas among practitioners. Farmer-back-to-farmer (Rhoades & Booth 1982) needs small groups. To achieve this, a Farmer-Dominant Study Group (FDSG) can be the "vehicle" worldwide (Wibberley 1978; 1991; 1992; 1993; 1995;1999; Kyamuwendo 1999). Such a group is characterized by the following:

- Chaired by a farmer with most (but not all) members being farmers to ensure that farm practice and reality remains the central focus.

- Meets on-farms with each member's farm providing a proportion of Group data

- Compares farm assets (thus requires farms of reasonably similar size and soil type)

- Focuses on Study together with no other hidden agenda by advisers, commerce etc

- practices Methodical Monitoring Management of both technical & financial performance.

- Considers the wider context of farming and its implications for farming communities.

Charles Dickens, in 1868 after visiting his son "Plorn"—then a student at the Royal Agricultural College, Cirencester, UK—wrote "That part of the Estate of a farmer or landowner which pays best for cultivation is the small estate within the ring fence of his skull. Let him attend to his brains and it shall be well with his grains!"

Past groups (1970s/1980s) may have been enterprise-specific e.g. livestock, cereals; then came a shift to look at integrated farming systems (1990s, especially gearing to reduced inputs and more environmentally-friendly farming). Now, it is clear that we need to consider together whole farm assets with a view to achieving sustainable rural livelihoods (survival!) not only from traditional farm outputs but also from whatever other opportunities present themselves in the SWOT (strengths, weaknesses, opportunities, threats) analysis of a particular farm—from its land, location, buildings and any special features or interests/skills of the owner. Post-trauma (e.g. Rwanda, Sierra Leone, UK after FMD in 2001 when some 6 million livestock were slaughtered on some 10,000 farms) recovery self-help groups may be needed for ex-farmers and re-starters.

Towards Ethical Agriculture

It is essentially one in which God, people and non-human creatures matter; where human relationships to God, neighbors, living creatures and land are harmonious, and where the conditions of their work are creative. The relevant unit for this is a tripartite Farm-Household (FAO, 1989):

FARM—provides employment, food and income;

HOUSEHOLD—takes decisions, sets goals, controls and works land;

OFF-FARM—provides inputs, competition, employment and alternative income opportunities.

The objectives of the Farm-Household are considered five-fold: Supplying basic needs; Performing social duties; Providing security; Obtaining a better lifestyle; Sustaining the ecosystem.

The 12Es criteria for evaluating and planning for the sustainability of Farm-Household systems are shown above (Fig.2). Farm-Households are perceived as complex, dynamic systems which have taken time to develop up to present. They are seen as rich in traditional wisdom and know-how possessed by rational, receptive rural people. Wisdom suggests their development rather than their demise but this requires a concerted "Farming Systems Development" approach (Fig. 3).

Fig. 3

Essentials of a Farming Systems Development Approach

It Is Not:	It Is:
Sector-confined	Whole system based
Farm only	Farm-Household based
Linear process emphasis	Cyclical process based
"Blueprint" approach	Location-specific
1st Capital-intensive	1st Management-intensive
External input oriented	Local resource based
Subsidy dependent	Effort dependent
Finite and exhaustive	Sustainable
Outsider-led (only outsider-served)	Farmer-dominant
Market first	Family 1st; animals 2nd; market 3rd

Farmers' options include leaving farming altogether, "tightening belts (already done by many), improving gross margins, reducing fixed costs (e.g. by co-operating in various ways), increasing the balance of more profitable enterprises (some have nothing in profit!) diversifying to incorporate new enterprises (needs drive and capital—both often at a low ebb), adding value to ex-farm produce (huge scope to capture more of the Food Chain etc. end-prices) or going for part-time farming (it is still a large psychological barrier for some to accept that this is not failed full-time farming nor its poor relation). Thus, Policy options include encouraging Farmers to:

1. Get Together—to study, to share, to buy, to sell, to lobby, to think ahead

2. Join FARMS Groups = Farm Asset Resource Management Study Groups (Appendix 6)

3. Form Farmer-Controlled Businesses (FCBs) to combat big business power

4. Support Farmers' Markets to rebuild communities, cut out middlemen, save energy

5. Add value to ex-farm raw products, move further down Food Chain, sell locally

6. Pursue agro-ecotourism for greater public access and countryside awareness

7. Explore Community Service Agriculture & small box schemes as in Japan, USA, EU

8. Accept agri-environment (land-care) payments and provide some more public access

9. Convert to Organic and more environmentally friendly, integrated farming systems

10. Part-time farm (mix other income sources with traditional food production)

11. Explore all survival options, with advice to facilitate them doing so

12. Leave farming where inevitable by providing an "outgoers package" deal.

Conclusions

The following agritheology principles were compiled by the present writer at an international gathering on agritheology held in Wurttemberg, Germany in July 1998 and have been shared widely since for thought, modification and application as underpinning for an ethical agriculture:

1. God is Creator and Sustainer of the Universe

2. Human Beings are created in God's Image.

3. All creation is fallen through sin.

4. Creation shares in Christ's salvation.

5. Agriculture is stewardship of creation for food and primary products.

6. Dominion means authority to manage creation as God desires.

7. The Kingdom of God is both now and future—creatio continua

8. The Kingdom of God is global and beyond.

9. Perfect relationship is exemplified in the Triune God.

10. People are designed for right relationships—UP (God), OUT (neighbors) DOWN (earth)

11. Only an integrated person can answer for this (Psalm 86:11)

12. Agri-rural Systems need a (w)holistic approach

13. Farmers are human stewards intended to be in tripartite relationship

14. Viable rural communities are desirable objectives

15. Farmers need to be—sensitive to nature; related to land; decisive operators; well-integrated realists; co-operators with God

16. Rural development needs to provide capacity to:

    CARE for creation e.g. Prov. 12:10—know one's beasts

    SHARE with those who do not have enough

    WORK in harmony with God (1 Cor. 3:9)

    BE IN PLACE—relate locally to land and community

    ACCESS ENOUGH—avoid excessive scale (Isa. 5:8)

17. Greed can apply equally to production as to consumption

18. Christian Ethics are required in agriculture simultaneously to reconcile Economy, Ecology, Energy-efficiency, Equity and Employment

19. Agriculture needs linkage with Christian Spirituality

20. Agriculture is a vocation; Earth is God's farm.

> "If these [agritheology] principles are conceded then we can be in a land of plenty both naturally and spiritually"—2001 quote from a Christian leader in Sierra Leone—the world's poorest country, yet diamond and soil-rich ...

Psalm 8:3-9 expresses the cosmic and creaturely comprehensive setting for human life. Man was created to communicate with God, with delegated responsibility for other creatures and with other special characteristics which defy easy measurement by the established methods of science. We have been given the dignity of responsibility and the privilege of companionship not only with creation but with the Creator. We need to link Biblical principles with agricultural realities and relational aspirations in a holistic vision as we work towards the shalom of the Kingdom of God.

Comprehensive criteria and promoters of sustainability for the international development of sustainable livelihoods have been proposed (12Es) as being designed to build practically towards the goal of shalom—Kingdom peace under God's rule—which is only made possible through the Cross.

I conclude with a poem, BOUNDARIES FOR BLESSING.

> O God of all our boundaries, of landmarks tried and true,
> We bow in humble access through Christ Our Lord to You.
> When we transgress those boundaries, grow consequential
>   "weeds."
> And many are the sufferers of such ill-placed misdeeds.
>
> We ask Your blessing, King of Kings—our sovereign Nation
>   bleeds
> As we behold sad outcomes of materialistic creeds.
> Help us recover Your good sense to mend each broken
>   bound'ry fence—
> The fence round species, farm and life, our nationhood's
>   defence …
>
> From BSE to FMD, far distant errors strike
> The heart of rural livelihoods, on vale and hill and dyke.
> Eternal values beckon yet and hope's clear beacon seals our
>   debt
> To you, Our Father, please forgive when we ourselves forget.
>
> When we forget You own each cow on thousand hills around,
> Where You, Great Shepherd, tread and love each spot of sacred
>   ground
> And You each seed make to abound, give ev'ry animal its
>   sound …
> We offer You time, talents, skills; our hearts, our minds and
>   stubborn wills
> Great Mender of earth's many spills, grant us a blessing that
>   fulfills.

References

Adeyemo, T. et al
1991 *The Church as an Agent of Change in Africa.* Nairobi, Kenya: AEAM

Akehurst, P.R.
1974 *Liturgy & Creation: A Reappraisal of Rogationtide & Harvest Festivals.* Grove: Nottm.

Alexander, D.R.
2001 "Cloning Humans—Distorting the Image of God?" *Cambridge Papers* 10 (2).

Anderson, L.
1999 *Genetic Engineering, Food and Our Environment.* Devon: Green Books.

Arnon, I.
1987 Modernisation of Agriculture in Developing Countries, 2nd ed. New York: Wiley.

Athananasius
c 298-373 *De Incarnatione* ("On the Incarnation"), 1982 edition. London: Mowbray.

Attfield, R.
1999 *The Ethics of the Global Environment.* Edinburgh: Edinburgh University Press.

Batchelor, P.G. and H.R. Boer,
1966 *Theology and Rural Development in Africa.* Grand Rapics: Eerdmans.

Batchelor, P.G.
1969 "Christians & Rural Development." TEAR Fund.

Batchelor, P.G.
1993 *People in Rural Development,* 2nd ed. Carlisle, UK: Paternoster Press.

Bediako, K.
1993 "Jesus in African Culture." *Evangelical Review of Theology* 17(1) 54-64.

Bennett, R.
1995 "The Value of Farm Animal Welfare." *J. Agric. Econ.* 46 (1) 46-60.

Bentham, J.
1789 *An Introduction to the Principles of Morals and Legislation.* Republished 1982. London: Methuen.

Berry, R.J.
1999 "Christian Approach to the Environment." *Transformation,* 16(3) 73-74.

Berry, R.J., ed.
  2000   *The Care of Creation*. Leicester: IVP.

Bosch, D.
  1984   "Missionary Theology in Africa." *Journal of Theology for Southern Africa* 49, 15.

Boutflour, M.
  1965   *Bobby Boutflour*. London: Crosby Lockwood.

Bowen, E.
  1987   "Ethics: Looking to Its Roots." *Time* (May 25, p.26).

Bowen, W.G.
  1982   *The Ringer's Stand*. Levin NZ: Kerslake.

Bruce, D. & A. Bruce
  1998   *Engineering Genesis: The Ethics of Genetic Engineering in Non-human Species*. London: Earthscan.

Bruce, D. & D. Horrocks,
  2001   *Modifying Creation?* Carlisle, UK: Paternoster.

Brueggemann, W.
  1978   *The Land*. London: SPCK.

Brueggemann, W.
  1982   *Genesis: Interpretation*. Atlanta: John Knox Press.

Brundtland, G.H.
  1987   "Our Common Future." Report of World Comission on Environment & Development, OUP, Oxford & NY, USA.

Calvin, J.
  1554   *A Commentary on Genesis*, 1965 ed. London: Banner of Truth.

Carney, D., ed.
  1998   Sustainable Rural Livelihoods: What Contributions Can We Make? UK: NRI/DFID .

Carruthers, S.P. & F.A. Miller
  1996   "Crisis on the Family Farm: Ethics or Economics?" CAS Paper 28, University of Reading.

Cassidy, M.
  1995   *A Witness for Ever: the Dawning of Democracy in S Africa*. UK: Hodder & Stoughton.

Chambers, R.
  1997   *Whose Reality Counts?: Putting the First Last*. London: IT Publications.

Chandler, R.

  1988   *Understanding the New Age.* Waco: Word.

Cochran, G.

  1995   *Shaping Our Environmental Conscience: The Caring Christian's Environmental Guide.* GA : Old Rugged Cross Pr.

Coffman, M.S.

  1994   *Saviors of the Earth?: The Politics and Religion of the Environmental Movement.* Chicago: Northfield.

Colman, D.

  1994   "Ethics & Externalities: Agric. Stewardship & Other Behaviour." *J. Agric. Econ.* 45(3) 299-311.

Commoner, B.

  1971   The Closing Circle: Nature, Man & Technology. New York: Bantam Books.

Conford, P.

  2001   *The Origins of the Organic Movement.* Edinburgh: Floris.

Cooper, D.e. & J.A Palmer, eds.

  1992   *The Environment in Question: Ethics and Global Issues.* London: Routledge.

Cromartie, M., ed.

  1995   *Creation at Risk?: Religion, Science and Environmentalism.* Grand Rapids: Eerdmans.

Dasgupta, B.

  1977   *Agrarian Change & the New Technology in India.* Geneva: UNRISD.

Deane-Drummond, C.

  1997   *Theology & Biotechnology: Implications for a New Science.* London & Washington: Geoffrey Chapman.

Derrick, C.

  1972   *The Delicate Creation: Towards a Theology of the Environment.* London: Tom Stacey.

De Waal, E.

  1988   *The Celtic Vision.* Darton, Longman & Todd.

Donald, P.F., R.E. Green, & M.F. Heath

  2001   "Agricultural Intensification and the Collapse of Europe's Farmland Bird Populations." London: *Proc. Royal Society*, 268, 25-29.

Duckham, A.N. & G.B Masefield

  1970   *Farming Systems of the World.* London: Chatto & Windus.

Dyrness, W.
    1991   *Let the Earth Rejoice! A Biblical Theology of Holistic Mission.* Pasadena
            CA: Fuller.

Eliot, C.
    1983   "Learning to Receive from Africa." *Christian* 7(3) 34-41.

Elliston, E.J.
    1989   *Christian Relief & Development.* Waco: Word.

Elsdon, R.
    1992   *Greenhouse Theology: Biblical Perspectives on Caring for Creation.* Tun-
            bridge Wells, UK: Monarch.

English, P., G. Burgess, R. Segundo, & J. Dunne
    1992   *Stockmanship.* Ipswich: Farming Press.

Fao
        "Farming Systems Development." Rome: UN.

Fergusson, D.A.S.
    1998   *The Cosmos and the Creator.* London: SPCK.

Fisher, G.L.
    1978   *Farm Life and Its Changes.* USA: Pequea.

Fisher, M.
    1997   "The Role of Ethics in Agriculture." *Agric. Science* 10 (4) 28-31.

Fox, M.W.
    1992   *Superpigs and Wondercorn: The Brave New World of Biotechnology and
            Where It All May Lead.* New York: Lyons & Burford.

Gatward, G.J.
    2001   *Livestock Ethics.* Lincoln: Chalcombe.

Gunton, C.E.
    1992   *Christ and Creation. The Didsbury Lectures, 1990.* Carlisle: Paternoster
            Press.

Hareuveni, N.
    1980   *Nature in Our Biblical Heritage.* Israel: Neot Kedumim.

Harris, P.
    1993   *Under the Bright Wings.* London: Hodder & Stoughton.

Harrison, P.
    1987   *The Greening of Africa.* Paladin, lIED.

Harrison, R.
    1964   *Animal Machines.* London: Stuart.

Heap, R.B.
  1995   "Agriculture & Bioethics: Harmony or Discord?" London: RASE 5th Annl. Lecture.

Hendry, G.S.
  1980   *Theology of Nature*. Philadelphia: Westminster Press.

Higginson, R.
  1988   *Dilemmas*. London: Hodder & Stoughton.

Hines, C.
  2000   *Localisation: a Global Manifesto*. London: Earthscan.

Houston, J.M.
  1979   *I Believe in the Creator*. London: Hodder & Stoughton.

Humphrys, J.
  2001   *The Great Food Gamble*. London: Hodder & Stoughton.

Imasogie, O.
  1993   *Guidelines for Christian Theology in Africa*, 2nd ed. Ghana: Africa Christian Press.

Jacoby, E.H.
  1971   *Man & Land*. London: Andre Deutsch.

Jakonda, S.Z.
  1998   *Thy Kingdom Come: A RURCON Manual on Wholistic Development*. Jos, Nigeria: RURCON.

Johnson, W.A., V. Stolzfus, and P. Cranmer
  1977   "Energy Conservation in Amish Agriculture." *Science* 198, 1-6.

Johnstone, P.J.S. & J. Mandryk
  2001   *Operation World*. Carlisle: OM.

Jones, C.
  1991   "Biblical Signposts for Agricultural Policy." ACF.

Jones, C. & I. JONES
  1996   "Winner Takes All & Families Lose All: A Nightmare for Farming in the US." Leicester: ACF/UCCF.

Kato, B.H.
  1975   *Theological Pitfalls in Africa*. Kisumu, Kenya: Evangel.

Keller, P.
  1970   *A Shepherd Looks at Psalm 23*. UK: Pickering & Inglis.

  1979   *A Gardener Looks at the Fruit of the Spirit*. UK: Marshall Pickering.

  1984   *Lessons from a Sheepdog*. London: Hodder & Stoughton.

King, F.H.

 1910   *Farmers of Forty Centuries,* reprinted 1977. Rodale Press.

Kinoti, G.

 1994   Hope for Africa and What the Christian Can Do. Nairobi, Kenya: AISRED.

Kivengere, F.

 1980   "Hope for Uganda and the World." CA, USA: AEE.

Kneen, B.

 1989   *From Land to Mouth: Understanding the Food System.* Toronto, Canada: NC Press.

Korten, D.C.

 1995   *When Corporations Rule the World.* Connecticut: Kumarian Press.

Krauthammer, C. et al

 1997   "A Special Report on Cloning." *Time* 149 (10) 42-55 [March 10th].

Leach, G.

 1976   *Energy & Food Production.* Guildford: IPC.

Leckie, R.

 1981   "Arvorum Cultus Pecorumque." *RAC Journal* LXIX, 36-37.

Leopold, A.

 1949   A Sand County Almanac reprint, 1970. New York: Ballantine Books.

Lewis, C.S.

 1943   *The Abolition of Man.* London: OUP.

Lilley, M. & L. Butler

 2001   "A Fair Deal for Rural England: Church Action." *Country Way* 27, 4-20.

Linzey, A.

 1995   *Animal Theology.* Univ. of Illinois Press.

Madeley, J.

 2000   *Hungry for Trade.* London: Zed Books.

Maff

 2000   "England Rural Development Plan (ERDP) 2000-2006." London: MAFF.

Massingham, H.J.

 1945   *The Natural Order: Essays in the Return to Husbandry.* London: Dent.

Mazrui, A.A. & A.M. Mazrui

 1998   *The Power of Babel: Language and Governance in the African Experience.* Oxford: James Currey.

McGrath, G.

1991   "The Significance of the New Age Movement." *Churchman*, 105 (1) 30-40.

McGregor, M., J. Willock, & I. Deary,

1995   "Farmer Stress." *Farm Management* 9 (2) 57-65.

McHarg, I.L.

1969   *Design with Nature*. New York: Doubleday.

McKeown, J.

2000   "Creation's Destiny in Jesus Christ." Cheltenham, UK: RI Briefing Paper No.3.

Mellanby, K.

1974   "The Social Responsibility of the Biologist." *Biologist* 21, 7-13.

Mepham, B., ed.

1996   *Food Ethics*. London: Routledge.

Miller, E.

1989   *A Crash Course on the New Age Movement*. Grand Rapids: Baker.

Moberg, D.O.

1985)   *Wholistic Christianity: An Appeal for a Dynamic, Balanced Faith*. Elgin, Illinois: Brethren Press.

Moltmann, J.

1985   *God in Creation: An Ecological Doctrine of Creation*. Transl. by M.Kohl. Minneapolis: Fortress Press.

Moomaw, I.W.

1966   *Crusade against Hunger*. New York: Harper & Row.

Morel, E.D.

1911   *Nigeria: Its Peoples and Its Problems*. London: Smith, Elder & Co.

Mosher, A.T. & C. Hallock, eds.

1949   *The Christian Mission among Rural People*. New York: Agric. Missions Inc..

Murray, J.

1962   "Biblical Ethics." *In* F.F. Bruce, et al, eds. *The New Bible Dictionary*. London: IVF.

Musasiwa, R.B.

1993   "The Finality of Jesus in Africa." *Evangelical Review of Theology*, 17(1) 65-69.

Museveni, Y.K.

1997   Sowing the Mustard Seed: The Struggle for Freedom and Democracy in Uganda. London: MacMillan.

Newby, H.
   1974   "The Changing Sociological Environment of the Farm." *Farm Management* 2 (9), 474-487.

Northcott, M.S.
   1996   *The Environment & Christian Ethics*. London: Cambridge University Press.

O'Donovan, W., with K. Maiyo (Kenya) & J. Gado (Nigeria)
   1992   *Introduction to Biblical Christianity from an African Perspective*. Nigeria: Nigeria Evangelical Fellowship.

Odum, E.P.
   1963   *Ecology*. New York: Holt, Rinehart & Winston.

Oduyoye, A.
   1973   *Flight from the Farms*. Ibadan, Nigeria: Daystar Press.

Oruka, H.O.
   1990   *Ethics*. Kenya: Nairobi University Press.

Osborn, L.
   1993   *Guardians of Creation: Nature in Theology & the Christian Life*. Leicester: Apollos.

Osei-Bensah, G.
   1990   *Wanted: Servant Leaders*. Ghana: ACP.

Page, R.
   1996   *God and the Web of Creation*. London: SCM.

Park, C.
   1992   *Caring for Creation*. London: Marshall Pickering.

Pawson, H.C.
   1973   *Hand to the Plough*. UK: Denholm House Press.

Pawson, J.D.
   1974   "The Responsibility of Christians in Agriculture" (Proc. of Agric. Christian Fellowship, 2nd Conf., UCCF, Condensed in *Christian Graduate* 28, No.2).

Pesek, J., ed.
   1989   *Alternative Agriculture*. Washington D.C.: Nat Acad. Press.

Polkinghorne, J.C.
   1986   *One World: The Interaction of Science and Theology*. London: SPCK.

Ponting, C.
   1991   *A Green History of the World*. London: Penguin.

Prance, G.
  1996   *The Earth under Threat: A Christian Perspective*. Glasgow: Wild Goose.

Pretty, J.N.
  1995   *Regenerating Agriculture*. London: Earthscan.

Pullan, R, ed.
  1990   *Caring for God's World*. A Rocha Occasional Publication No.2, 94 pp.

Rae, M.
  2000   "To Render Praise: Humanity in God's World." *In* Consultation on Environmental Stewardship. Windsor Castle, Sept.

Rappaport, R.A.
  1971   "The Flow of Energy in an Agricultural Society." *Scientific American*, 224 (3), 116-132.

Reader, J.
  1997   *Africa: A Biography of the Continent*. London: Hamish Hamilton.

Runge, C., ed.
  1998   "Old Crops in New Bottles?" RASE.

Ruthenberg, H.
  1980   *Farming Systems in the Tropics*, 3rd ed. Oxford: Clarendon Press.

Sacks, J.
  1995   *Faith in the Future*. London: DLT.

Sanders, E.P.
  1991   *Paul*. Oxford: OUP.

Sandoe, P., N. Holtug, & H. Simonsen
  1996   "Ethical Limits to Domestication." *Journal of Agricultural & Environmental Ethics*. 9(2) 114-122.

Schaeffer, F.A.
  1970   *Pollution & the Death of Man: A Christian View of Ecology*. London: Hodder & Stoughton.

Schluter, M. & J. Ashcroft
  1990   *Christian Principles for the Ownership of Land*. Cambridge: Jubilee Center.

Schluter, P.M. and D. Lee
  1993   *The R Factor*. London: Hodder & Stoughton.

Schumacher, E.F.
  1974   *Small Is Beautiful*. London: Abacus.

Schumacher, E.F.
   1980   *Good Work*. London: Abacus.

Schumacher, V.
   1997   *"This I Believe" and Other Essays by E.F.Schumacher*. Resurgence, Devon: Green Books.

Seaton, C.
   1992   *Whose Earth?* London: Crossway Books.

Seaton, C. & G. Dale
   1994   "Creation Care." Evangelical Alliance.

Shiva, V.
   2000   *Stolen Harvest: The Hijacking of the Global Food Supply*. Cambridge, MA: S. End Press.

Sider, R.J.
   1993   *Evangelism & Social Action*. London: Hodder & Stoughton.

Sine, T.
   1981   *The Mustard Seed Conspiracy*. Waco: Word Books.

Sire, J.W.
   1987   *The Universe Next Door*. Downers Grove: IVP.

Smith, A.
   1776   *The Wealth of Nations* Books I-III, reprinted 1997. London: Penguin Classics.

Stott, J.R.W.
   1982   "Evangelism & Social Responsibility." The Grand Rapids Report, Lausanne Committee for World Evangelization/World Evangelical Fellowship. Paternoster Press.

   1992   *The Contemporary Christian*. Leicester: IVP.

   1999   *The Birds Our Teachers: Essays in Orni-Theology*. Carlisle: Candle Books.

Sugden, C.
   1993   "Evangelicals and Environment in Process." *Evangelical Review of Theology*, 17, 119-121.

Taylor, J.V.
   1963   *The Primal Vision: Christian Presence amid African Religion*. London: SCM.

   1975   *Enough Is Enough*. London: SCM Press.

Thirsk, J., ed.
  2000   *The English Rural Landscape*. Oxford & NY: OUP.

Tiénou, T.
  1990   *The Theological Task of the Church in Africa,* 2nd ed. Ghana: Africa Christian Press.

Tucker, R.A.
  1983   *From Jerusalem to Irian Jaya: A Biographical History of Christian Missions*. Zondervan: Academic Books.

Tusser, T.
  1557   *Five Hundred Points of Good Husbandry,* reprinted 1984. Oxford: OUP.

Van Dyke, F., D.C.A. Mahan, J.K. Sheldon, & R.H. Brand
  1996   *Redeeming Creation: The Biblical Basis for Environmental Stewardship.* Downers Grove: IVP.

Watts, E.R.
  1969   *New Hope for Rural Africa*. Uganda: East Africa Publishing House & Makerere Univ.

Webster, J.
  1991   "Farm Animal Welfare, Science and Humanity." *Biologist* 38 (5) 160-162.

Webster, J.
  1995   *Animal Welfare: A Cool Eye towards Eden*. Oxford: Blackwell.

Welker, M.
  1999   *Creation & Reality*. Minneapolis: Fortress Press.

Westermann, C.
  1974   *Creation*. London: SPCK.

White, L.
  1967   "The Historical Roots of Our Ecologic Crisis." *Science* 155, 1203-1207 (March 10).

Wibberley, E.J
  1975   "God's Husbandry: Towards a Christian Approach to Agriculture." Nigeria: Gindiri.

  1980   "Rural Development: Short Course Manual for Christian Leadership. "

  1984   "Farmer Groups and Agricultural Development." *Agric. Progress* 59, 35-44.

1984b "Land Tenure Options with Reference to a Developing Africa." *Rural Life*, 29 (2) 25-37.

1984c "Agriculture, Education and Rural Well-being: Lessons from Africa." In *Learning from the South: What, Why and How?* ed. T. Mebrahtu, pp. 117-133. Bristol: Classical Press.

1987 "Microbiology and Soil Management." In *Rushall: The Story of an Organic Farm* by C.B. Wookey, pp 191-196. Basil: Blackwell.

1989 *Cereal Husbandry*. Ipswich, UK: Farming Press Books.

1991 "The Survival of the Family Farm: Family-worked Dairy Farms and the Viability of Rural Communities." Report for Nuffield Farming Scholarships Trust and Trehane Trust.

1991b "Agricultural Ethics—the Neglected Dimension?" *Agric. Progress* 66, 76-79.

1992 "The Farmer-Dominant Study Group: A Practical Paradigm in International Extension Strategy." PhD Thesis, Agricultural Extension and Rural Development Department. University of Reading.

1992a "Farmer Conservation: Survival of the Family-worked Farm." *Journal of the Royal Agricultural Society of England*, 153, 54-66.

1993 "Farmer-Dominant Study Groups (FDSGs) in International Extension Strategy & Management." Proc. Australia-Pacific Extension Conference, Vol.2 (QC93012) 599-604. Brisbane (DPI, Queensland Government).

1995 "Farmer-Dominant Study Groups for Farming Systems Development Under Stress Conditions in Africa." In *Environment & Development in Africa: Challenging the Orthodoxies*. Proc. Conf. University of Leeds, African Studies Unit (on CD-ROM '96).

1996 "Agricultural Ethics & Ethical Agriculture." In *Crisis on the Family Farm—Ethics or Economics?* CAS Paper No.28, eds. S.P. Carruthers & F.A. Miller, pp 48-65. Center for Agricultural Strategy, University of Reading.

1997 "The Role of Farmer Groups and Farmers' Knowledge in Optimising Cereal Growing Systems. *In* "Optimising Cereal Inputs: Its Scientific Basis." *Aspects of Applied Biology* 50, 471-480.

1999 "Farmers Together." *Journal of the Royal Agricultural Society of England* 160, 106-112.

2000 "Rural Stress & Future Farming." *Rural Theology Journal* 52, 20-25.

2000a "Agricultural Missions." In *Evangelical Dictionary of World Mission*. Grand Rapids: Baker.

Wibberley, E.J and D.C. Joy
1979   *A Tropical Agriculture Handbook.* Cassell.

Wibberley, E.J. and Rachel Thomas
2001   "Integrated Rural Development: Agriculture & Rural Development Forestry." *Journal of the Royal Agricultural Society of England* 162 , 89-96.

Wilkinson, L.
1991   *Earth-keeping: Christian Stewardship of Natural Resources,* rev. ed. Grand Rapids: Eerdmans.

Wright, C.J.H.
1995   *Walking in the Ways of the Lord: The Ethical Authority of the Old Testament.* Leicester: Apollos.

Wright, N.T.
1996   *Jesus & the Victory of God.*London: SPCK.

The Agriculturalist
and Economics

Is Our Agricultural House Built on Sand?

Biblical Holism in Agriculture and the Assumption of Monotonicity in the Utility Function

Kara Unger Ball

Introduction

"Why do you call me, 'Lord, Lord,' and do not do what I say? I will show you what he is like who comes to me and hears my words and puts them into practice. He is like a man building a house, who dug down deep and laid the foundation on rock. When a flood came, the torrent struck that house but could not shake it, because it was well built. But the one who hears my words and does not put them into practice is like a man who built a house on the ground without a foundation. The moment the torrent struck that house, it collapsed and its destruction was complete." (Luke 6:46-49, NIV)

Traditional economics makes several starting assumptions about the nature of people. It assumes that people are rational (act in their own best interests), insatiable (more is always better), and indifferent to others (are neither envious nor compassionate). These assumptions are foundational to the theory of consumer demand, and extremely important to modern economics. Without these assumptions, and attendant models of consumer demand and production, our economic systems come in to question. How true are these assumptions? What are the implications if they are not true?

251

The focus points of this paper are the second assumption, that of insatiability (more is always better), and the third assumption, that individuals are indifferent to others. From a Christian perspective, these assumptions are erroneous and incomplete descriptions of human nature. Further, they are contrary to the Great Commandments and the golden rule to love your neighbor as yourself. It is certainly acknowledged that human beings are sinners. Accordingly, each of us does have a tendency toward seeking our own interest above others and to seek our own good first. However, as Christians, we contrast this with Christ's teaching of seeking God's kingdom first (Matt. 6:33) and loving our neighbor as ourselves (Matt. 22:39). We know that, in contrast to the current economic characterization of human nature, humans are defined in large part by their relationship to others and God, and so what gives satisfaction is the nature of these relationships, not what we consume. These are two judgments about the facts of human nature in which there are large differences.

Do these differences matter? This paper will argue that these differences are critical, and that we are building our economic and agricultural houses on sand to the extent we build on these assumptions. It explores whether more really is better, for individuals, for society, and for the rest of God's creation and concludes that the assumption that more is always better is a fatal flaw. Further, by establishing economic and agricultural systems that have this flaw, we are setting up systems that have within them the ultimate cause of their own destruction because they are not built on Christ's way and they are not capable of being supported by the physical limitations of the planet. We know from the passage quoted above that everything—including human economic institutions—not built on Christ's teaching is destined not to succeed. From a Christian perspective, it can be concluded that our current economic system, which is built on an incomplete view of human nature, will ultimately fail. We can also see that Christ points toward sustainable economic and agricultural systems that will endure. These are systems built on Christ's teaching of love for neighbor and care for creation (Col. 1:15-20; Gen. 2:15; Rev. 11:18). This paper goes on to discuss a case study of action being taken in a rural farming community built on

Christ's foundation of love of neighbor expressed as caring for natural resources.

These findings directly relate to agriculture and economics because agricultural economics has been reduced to a subset of current microeconomics. Agricultural economics thus carries within the same fatal flaw and is thus destined to fail as well if built on the same foundation. A better, biblically holistic approach is thus desperately needed in agricultural economic models and systems.

Background

Traditional, neoclassical economics is driven by consumer preference, represented in economic models by what is termed "the utility function" (a graphical representation of consumer preferences). The assumption that people are insatiable (more is always better) is expressed through the monotonically increasing form of this function (that is, the utility function always increases as consumption increases, albeit at a decreasing rate). Rational individuals will always be happier with more. While it is acknowledged that an individual can be satiated with respect to a single good (one apple is good, but the tenth makes you sick), for all goods together, marginal utility (the utility derived from the last unit received) is always positive. Accordingly, utility always increases the more one consumes. The monotonically increasing form of the utility function thus both expresses and legitimizes no limit to self-gratification through consumption. The model goes further to define optimal social welfare as the aggregate of maximizing individual utility, which means (according to this model) that society is best off when everyone maximizes her utility through unsatiated consumption.

The danger of this assumption is that it has become no longer just an assumption. As economic growth becomes the desired model for economies worldwide, the "more is better" assumption becomes not just the assumption but also the goal. As economies worldwide are allocating resources according to this model, they look to this model of truth to find truth, and thus the model becomes true. Countries are thus actively building a world of individual and societal unsatiated consumption, in direct contrast to a world of sufficiency and sustainability. And as countries become more successful according to this definition, the resulting economic structures and pervasive cultural expectations built on this model carry within the seeds of their own destruction, since unsatiated global consumption is not physically sustainable. As Christians, we see that this foundational assumption is exactly where Christ teaches us not to build, and there is no solution for these destructive patterns except a biblical one.

Why is this issue important for biblically holistic agriculture and agricultural economics?

Biblical Holism is "... God's work, through Jesus Christ, to redeem and restore all things that were created good but became damaged and broken as a result of man's sin (Col. 1:20)" (Evans and Wright 2001). As further defined by Darrow Miller, this understanding is fundamentally relational, comprising our relationships with God, each other, ourselves, knowledge, and the rest of God's creation. The nature of these relationships is thus critical. As we establish our relationships with God, others, and the rest of creation through agriculture—through the provision of food and fiber for ourselves and our societies—whether we establish these relationships through agriculture in a way founded upon Christ's teaching or in some other way makes all the difference in whether these systems will endure.

Any agricultural system built on a foundation that does not establish right relationship of the individual to others, God, and the rest of creation is not biblically holistic. As Jesus teaches, such a system will not ultimately endure. If it can be shown that the dominant agricultural economic system currently in place is such a system, it can be concluded that this system will not endure and that another approach—one that is biblically holistic, is desperately needed.

If one assumes a physical world ultimately limited in its energy capacity by its ability to utilize solar energy and one that needs that maintenance of ecological and hydrogeologic systems to sustain life, reducing current consumption and production levels is necessary to maintain the long term viability of the earth's regenerative and productive capacities. A "steady-state" economy as described by Herman Daly is the desired goal—one that mini-mizes the physical flow of goods required to maintain a desired quality of life (for a certain number of people). By contrast, a suc-cessful economy in terms standards currently accepted globally as desirable is one that maximizes economic growth by maximizing production and consumption. Further, by the nature of decreasing marginal utility (utility increases with each unit of consumption, but at a decreasing rate), as a person consumes more, she requires relatively more consumption to obtain further units of "utility." Thus, consumption becomes exponentially greater, the wealthier one gets.

The question of whether more is always better cannot even be asked, much less answered, until there is agreement that people can be happy with, indeed may be better off with, "enough." From a spiritual perspective, setting up right relationships is the way we live out God's kingdom on earth. We cannot even begin to establish these right relationships if we assume that the self can never be satisfied with enough.

Is the assumption of a monotonically increasing individual utility function a true characterization and desirable goal?

We all need food, clothing, shelter, and other material posses-sions to survive and live a comfortable life. Once certain needs and wants are met, how much more is needed for happiness and self-fulfillment? That depends on human nature, and the purpose of human existence. The unrestrained consumption and attendant greed posited by monotonicity are a fundamental part of human nature, many would argue. However, this picture is incomplete and fundamentally erroneous from a Christian point of view. Caring and concern for others, desire for service, development of individual skills, are also part of the complexity of human nature. As well, for Christians, grace empowers us to fulfill our rela-tionships to God and others by empowering us to move beyond self-gratification to serve others. Many religions and cultures warn of the dangers of submitting to this form of selfishness, both for the harm it does to the individual and because it is not a "right" goal in life. Jesus often warns that riches (as opposed to sufficiency) hinder one from spiritual progress, and a relationship with others and God (Matt. 6:25, Matt. 6:32,33, Matt. 19:23,24).

Moderate wealth should be the goal. Unsatiated consumption, the assumption and goal of current economic models, is perverse in that it leads to self-absorption and estrangement from others and from God—the center and meaning of life.

The truth of the monotonically increasing utility function in accurately reflecting human nature further comes into question by observing that even the wealthiest do not appear much happier than the poor. We have misplaced the longing for loving relationships with the longing for material goods, and by so doing created a situation where we crave an infinite amount of material goods as a substitute for relationships with others and God. Thus, material goods will never completely satisfy in making one happy. Further, from a Christian perspective, our deepest fulfillment comes through attaining right relationship with God and others through Christ Jesus. Any system that seeks fulfillment through the accretion of material wealth is perverse from a Christian perspective.

The monotonicity assumption is harmful to the individual who pursues it as a goal, whether consciously or not, because it leads to perverse relationship between the individual, her community, and God. "... since consumption is merely a means to human well-being, the aim should be to obtain the maximum of well being with the minimum of consumption." This "Christian optimum consumption" is not based on a level of unsatiated consumption but is based on the level of consumption and resource use that brings about the best relationship with others, the rest of creation, and God. The assumption of monotonicity, by contrast, says that well being is only maximized when consumption is maximized. From a Christian perspective, this is fatally flawed.

Is optimal social welfare, as defined as the optimization of aggregated individual utility, good for society?

Current social welfare theory states that social welfare is maximized if the aggregate of individual utility is maximized. With the assumption of monotonicity, i.e., that individual utility is always increasing the more goods one has, maximum social welfare can only be reached if everyone consumes as much as possible subject to their budget constraints. In a world of limited resources, if everyone seeks to consume as much as possible, one person's gain becomes another's loss. The resulting world becomes one of unlimited competition with others for scarce resources. As the "haves" gain more economic power, they are better able to control their circumstances and thus consume even more. Stress, violence, and a world "where we are at each other's throats..." results. Additional distributive inequities arise as the decreasing marginal utility of each unit consumed accelerates distributive inequities, since increasing consumption is required for each additional "unit of happiness" for the relatively wealthy. This leads to a world of two extremes—great poverty and great affluence, "... neither of which is normal and healthy" nor biblical (Prov. 30:8; Lev. 25:13-17; Deut. 17:16-20). Evidence of this is seen in a comparison of the increasing relative magnitude of wealth between rich and poor countries: in 1960, the wealthiest country was 30 times wealthier than the poorest; in 1991, this had grown to 61 times wealthier (class 2/1/96). One in five globally do not have access to clean, safe drinking water, while the relatively wealthy buy frozen treats for their dogs. Distributive mechanisms may alleviate some of the discrepancy (e.g., taxes, welfare payments), to the extent that distributive equity is sought, but these structures currently only work in a national setting, and cannot address the global inequities that result when entire cultures consume insatiably. The distributive inequity extends to future generations as well, who are deprived of access to scarce resources, living space, and places to put their waste, as these resources are used up by the insatiable consumption and attendant waste of current generations.

Further as monotonicity becomes self-fulfilling, the living out of this assumption removes us from our true nature as "persons in community," and insidiously encourages the focus of time and energy on self-gratification versus devoting time and energy connecting with and serving others. By consuming insatiably, people become self absorbed and inwardly focused, their relationships with others are weakened, and they become disconnected from their communities. Further, "[t]here is no reason to suppose that the quality of relationships constituting the society has been improved by the increase of commodities. On the contrary, there is extensive evidence that the means used to increase production often lead to a decline in the quality of social relationships. Society becomes more like the aggregate of individuals that economics theory pictures it as being." In other words, the nature of unlimited consumption creates, ultimately, a non-Christian society and unsustainable society because it is built on the gratifications of self rather than right relation with God, neighbor, and community.

Monotonicity is also dramatically damaging to the environment. Massive species extinction, loss of wild areas, desertification, and global pollution problems are caused by current and increasing human consumption patterns and levels. Increasing resources are needed as inputs into increasing amounts of products fueled by consumption. Waste products and disposable goods are filling up land, air, and water. Unsustainable use of natural resources and places to put wastes are threatening the ability to sustain life in the future. Pursuing unsatiated consumption, as modeled—and required—by monotonicity of the utility function, precludes addressing these problems in the profound and fundamental way needed to establish an economic system that functions within the carrying capacity of God's creation. Until the assumption of monotonicity is replaced with the concepts of sufficiency and sustainability, resources will continue to be used up at an increasing rate, ultimately leading to the overloading of the earth's carrying capacity as well as distributive injustice of the fruits of natural capital.

A better, indeed the correct starting assumption for the economic model of individual utility and social welfare is one where the individual is viewed as a member of society, interconnected with others in a profound and fundamental way, whose members recognize this role and its attendant responsibilities. In a world of scarcity and individuals living in community, this would mean some limit to individual consumption as well as a change in production patterns. An individual's happiness derived from consumption would be based on the impact her consumption had on neighbors, other creatures, and the community. Accordingly, an individual's utility function would at some point become zero or negative with further consumption. This assumption is opposite the assumption of a monotonically increasing individual utility function and has a profound impact on what successful a successful economy would look like.

Have We Built Our Economic House on Sand?

It seems so. We have built an economic order, now being promulgated globally, that has at its root a view of human nature devoid of God's grace. As Christians, we see that we have built an economic system that turns people toward self and away from God, our neighbor, and the rest of creation. By Christian standards, any house so built will come down.

A change towards a system organized to promote "Christian optimum consumption and production" is needed to keep the house standing. This conclusion greatly impacts agricultural economics, which is a subset of microeconomics. It implies that Biblical holism in agriculture cannot be reached within the current institutional setting so long as the "more is better" model is used. It further implies that the current agricultural economic system, built on the same foundation as current neoclassical economics, will not last.

The need for another way could not be clearer. Christians, through the grace of God, are uniquely equipped to propose another way. By establishing agriculture and economics based on God's commandments to love God and to love what God loves, as opposed to agriculture and economics based on indifference to others and unlimited individual consumption, Christians can show the world agricultural and economic systems that will last, and that are equitable to others and the rest of God's creation. While such a profound shift is daunting, Christians operating in a way not grounded in the current model can reach it. This is our hope for agricultural and economic systems that provide sufficiency and sustainability.

A Christian approach to economics and agriculture would not posit an individual utility function that is ever increasing. Instead, individual utility would stop increasing and even become negative past the point where individual consumption began to break the bonds of community. As well, a view of social welfare would not be an aggregation of individual welfare, but would instead be defined in larger, macroeconomic terms not based on growth but based on indicators of sustainability of the ecological system of which the economic system is a part. Our neighbors, those we are to love, would be those who are our neighbors both now and in the future. Other aspects of creation would have intrinsic value, and there would be limits to consumption, both locally and globally.

Both the "… ancient preoccupation with production and the pervasive modern search for security…" have led to the justification of existing consumer theory. And as production keeps pace with consumption, global carrying capacity is threatened. As the concept of monotonicity is reconsidered on the demand side, it must also be reconsidered from the production side. Thus it makes sense to consider the effects of a change in the monotonicity assumption on the means of production, and in particular on the means of agricultural production. It can be argued that the means of production, including agricultural production, would take the forms of sufficiency and sustainability as monotonicity is reconsidered from a Christian perspective. Accordingly, the rest of this paper is spent considering a case study of Christian individuals in a rural community who are voluntarily choosing to reduce the impact of their agricultural practices on nearby streams. By so doing, these individuals are explicitly choosing to care for their neighbors downstream who depend on clean water for their livelihood as well as helping to maintain their local resources for future generations. They are thus practicing biblically holistic agriculture in a way contrary to the assumptions of traditional economics.

The Farmers of Sideling Hill Creek Watershed: A Case Study

Two groups, one fishermen and one farmers, both from Christian communities, have chosen to live, and make their livings, in a way that is centered on God and on loving their neighbor. These individuals in this case study have chosen a way of living that is contrary to the assumptions of current economics and agricultural systems, and is founded on Christian principles of biblical holism. Their explicit Christian actions in the caring of the resources under their responsibility and caring for their neighbors downstream illustrate acts of biblical reconciliation.

An important conclusion drawn from this study is that, in rural Christian communities, *caring for your neighbor* is a compelling force for changing behavior. It is already a part of the cultural value framework of rural communities. Also, ties of community are strengthened by the commandment to love your neighbor as yourself and a recognition that all others, but especially Christians, are our neighbors and how we act toward them is an expression of our God-commanded love for them. Caring for the resources under our responsibility is one way of showing our love for neighbor, because how we use these resources impacts others. As this case study illustrates, someone is always "downstream" from our choices of resource use.

The Story

Two groups comprised of landowner/farmers and fishermen in the Chesapeake Bay watershed have recently come to know and serve one another better as they have begun to explore a biblical approach to creation-care together. Members of both groups make their living off the land or water around them, and the church is the center of community life. The farmer/landowners in the Sideling Hill Creek watershed live in the rural mountains of south-central Pennsylvania. Their land is part of the Chesapeake Bay watershed; water from their creeks and streams ends up in the Chesapeake Bay. The fishermen of Tangier Island, Virginia are known as "watermen." They make their living by fishing crabs, oysters, eels, and other fish in the Chesapeake Bay. These two communities are thus physically connected by water. They are also connected because they are two groups of Christians seeking to work out God's commandments to care for the resources that God has entrusted to them.

The Sideling Hill Creek watershed is comprised of rural hills in south-central Pennsylvania and Maryland. Some residents do not explicitly consider themselves farmers, even if their land is in agriculture. This is usually because these residents also hold other jobs. For the purposes of this paper, all landowners with land in some form of agricultural production are referred to as farmers. The Sideling Hill Creek watershed is also an attractive location for foreign-owned "corporate" hog farmers because there are no zoning or land use ordinances. The watershed has a concentration of over 90 rare, threatened, and endangered species and is thus a top priority for state environmentalists. The region's residents generally mistrust environmentalists and government officials, with a history of animosity toward the former especially. Residents are generally indifferent to polluting their streams. This has begun to change, however.

The Tangier Island community is similar in many respects. This church-centered community also makes its living off its resources, is suspicious of outsiders, has a history of conflict with environmentalists, and is facing threats to its way of life as the fisheries are being depleted and increasingly regulated. The watermen also have a history of polluting the water by throwing their trash and motor oil overboard, as well as a history of overfishing their fisheries. In 1998, some of the Christian Tangier watermen became personally convicted that their actions were unbiblical and not in keeping with their Christian responsibility to care for their resources. They had a transformation of faith and in 1998 formed their own explicitly Christian stewardship group called Tangier Watermens' Stewardship for the Chesapeake (TaSC). Members of this group have taken a personal covenant to care for the resources God has entrusted to them by not overfishing and by not polluting their water with trash or oil. They took this covenant and formed this group because they became convinced, based on their Christian faith, that this was their responsibility. As part of their mission, the TaSC group has also committed to sharing their story with other communities in the Chesapeake Bay watershed, and encouraging resource-dependent communities to take similar action.

In March 2000, the TaSC group shared their story and video with the community in the Sideling Hill Creek watershed. The TaSC members literally live downstream from the Sideling Hill Creek community and depend on clean water for their livelihoods. The TaSC group generated so much interest that ten members from the Sideling Hill Creek community went down to Tangier Island to learn more about the watermen's way of life, see and experience the Chesapeake Bay firsthand, and share fellowship with other Christian believers on the island.

One notable and important similarity between the Sideling Hill Creek residents and Tangier Islanders is that each has a distinct sense of community, where neighbors share a sense of obligation to help one another. As the Sideling Hill Creek residents got to know the Tangier Islanders better through visiting the island and experiencing their way of life firsthand, their thinking about the islanders changed. The Sideling Hill Creek residents began to view the Tangier Islanders as their *neighbors*. Accordingly, they should be treated as neighbors—that is, the Sideling Hill Creek residents became aware of their obligation to help and not harm these neighbors downstream.

This new understanding of their relationship to the islanders was critical in motivating changed behavior. As they began to understand that the Tangier Islanders were in fact their neighbors downstream, the Sideling Hill Creek farmers transformed their thinking about polluting their streams. Just as they would not knowingly harm their neighbor's crops, so too they now saw that their decisions whether to pollute their local streams or not directly impacted the health of the fisheries that their watermen neighbors—and Christian brothers—depended upon. As the bonds of community were established in this new way, farmers began to see the need to ensure that their practices did not send dirty water downstream to their neighbors' crab pots and fishnets.

This was a profound change. The Sideling Hill Creek farmers returned to their farms desiring to live out lives that expressed their love for their neighbors downstream by not polluting the waters they send down to the Chesapeake Bay. They have examined their own practices on the land to make sure they do not allow sediment or pesticides to enter the water. They have joined a local volunteer water-monitoring group. Most importantly, they have decided to share this story with their own neighbors by producing a video to share with other landowners in the watershed. This video will feature these farmers sharing their reasons for caring for water quality—that this is a way of caring for the Tangier Island watermen and protecting the water quality of the Chesapeake Bay and expressing their love for God and neighbor.

Conclusion

The Sideling Hill Creek residents have shown that expanding the meaning of loving your neighbor to include those downstream can motivate change in rural Christian communities. This is an important finding for those working in rural communities to implement biblically holistic agriculture and encourage proper land use and stewardship. Those working in these contexts can build upon the existing cultural value framework of helping your neighbor that is present in rural communities, and on the Christian commandments to love your neighbor as yourself, by expanding the definition of neighbor to include all those currently impacted by their land use decisions as well as those in the future. This approach has a much greater chance of success than appealing to a general environmental stewardship ethic as usually conceived by secular environmentalists, which is usually not part of the existing value framework of these communities. This approach may also serve as a way to open the door for stewardship for the rest of God's creation.

Loving your neighbor through right action can also be a compelling theme in a development context. Even for those who do not have an opportunity to meet their neighbors downstream, everyone has inter-temporal neighbors downstream as well as others in this generation that are affected by our resource use decisions. The message of expressing love for others by showing that our resource use decisions either harm or help them, depending on what we choose, can be a powerful motivator for conscious stewardship in agricultural and resource dependent communities when expressed in terms that show that future generations are our neighbors through time and that we all have neighbors downstream. This message will thus work in the context of Christian relief and development efforts for Biblically holistic agriculture. If we believe that "through Him all things are created and in Him all things hold together," (Col. 1:16,17), making right choices becomes an expression of love for our neighbor and for God. These choices thus become part of our reconciliation with God, others, and the rest of creation.

The acts of reconciliation that resulted from the meeting of the Tangier Islanders and the Sideling Hill Creek residents reflect a reconciliation of man with others by man's reconciliation with the rest of God's creation through biblically holistic caring of the land. This shows the multi-dimensional nature of the relationships we have through God. Restoring one restores the other. The Sideling Hill Creek residents and Tangier Islanders have shown a biblically holistic form of agriculture that is in contrast to a traditional economic model of indifferently insatiable individuals acting solely in their own best interest. And in so doing, they are living out the Lord's Prayer and building their houses on stone.

References

Ball, Kara Unger

2000   "Fishing in Living Waters." *Creation Care* Number 11, p.14. Wynnewood, PA: Evangelical Environmental Network.

Daly, Herman E.

1996   *Beyond Growth: The Economics of Sustainable Development.* Boston: Beacon Press.

Daly, Herman E. and John B. Cobb, Jr.

1994   *For the Common Good: Redirecting the Economy toward Community, the Environment, and a Sustainable Future.* Boston: Beacon Press.

Daly, Herman E. and Kenneth N. Townsend, editors

1992   *Valuing the Earth: Economics, Ecology, Ethics.* Cambridge, MA: MIT Press.

Emmerich, Susan Drake.

2000   "Praxis of the Kingdom: Bible-Grounded Environmental Stewardship as a Ministry of Reconciliation." *Creation Care* Number 11, p. 4. Wynnewood, PA: Evangelical Environmental Network.

Evans, David and Keith Wright

2001   *Framework for a Conference on "Biblical Holism in Agriculture."* Unpublished paper. June 8.

Galbraith, John Kenneth

1969   *The Affluent Society,* 2nd ed., rev. New York: The New American.

Ruthorford, Thomas F.

1995   *Demand Theory and General Equilibrium: An Intermediate Level Introduction to MPSGE,* Section 2, "The Theory of Consumer Demand." Department of Economics, University of Colorado.

Schmookler, Andrew Bard

1991   "The Insatiable Society." *The Futurist.* July-August, pp 17-19.

Redeeming Agriculture and Economics through Worldview Transformation

Greg De Haan

Introduction

Agriculture and Economics both emerged from the desire to better meet human needs. The recent "marriage" of these two disciplines has created global agribusiness; a productive but still seriously flawed food production and distribution system that fails to adequately meet the needs of humanity and the broader created order.

The limiting anthropocentric foundation of both Agriculture and Economics needs to be recognized and challenged. A holistic Christian worldview starts and ends with God, not humanity. Simply recognizing God as "chief economist" can pave the way for powerful renewal and redemption.

Economics has recently emerged as a trusted value free foundation for life, but several true stories from the farm will highlight the urgent need for escape from the limiting mindset of standard human economic thought. Markets need full and true information to work efficiently. Markets must fail if shaped by selfish and broken worldviews. Rather, Biblical wisdom must provide a right foundation for understanding and action in the marketplace.

Christians must address the urgent need for building moral foundations upon which agriculture and economics can stand. Opportunities may exist for redemptive service at various levels, but in all cases God needs image bearers who testify with bold and prophetic lives.

Working Definitions and a Summary of the Agricultural Landscape

Agriculture Viewed from a Broader Perspective

The present day global agricultural system is a complex and diverse economic reality that defies simple description. Humanity made the transition from a hunter gatherer lifestyle to a more intentional and intensive system of food production many generations ago.

Given the above, agriculture can be broadly understood as various successful human efforts to increase the supply of vital food resources through intentionally selecting, cultivating and managing specific plants and animals. In addition, it should also include the necessary steps of harvest or slaughter, processing, storage, and distribution. This definition would rightly encompass the diverse agribusiness concerns that now supply various inputs like equipment, chemicals, seed, finance, transportation, marketing, sales, or other key services.

As such, the broad working definition for agriculture in this paper will include all the activities related to meeting human food needs. It would also be unwise to exclude any person who depends upon food for daily existence from an expanded definition. All people who enjoy the final products of the food production system are undeniably linked to agriculture, a key point to keep in mind for later consideration.

Economics Viewed from a Broader Perspective

Economics certainly shares important common ground with agriculture, as both areas of activity are rooted in the desire to more adequately address human needs. The underlying market dynamics that economics builds upon, like agriculture itself, are also thousands of years old. However, economics as a distinct field of human inquiry emerged more recently. Scottish philosopher and economist Adam Smith is widely believed to have launched the new science when he published *Inquiry into the Nature and Causes of the Wealth of Nations* in 1776.

The early economic thinkers followed the lead of Adam Smith in embracing private property, free markets, and individual self-interest as the path to wealth creation for the good of society at large. The influence of classical theory remains strong today, even if economists and society have now granted government an important role in setting appropriate macro-economic policy. Areas of specialization developed with time, and today economics is highly differentiated science.

Agricultural economics is one recognized and important niche in the present structure of the discipline, and it deals primarily with unique modern day agricultural trade structures, policies and market dynamics. Of particular importance is the impact of "perfect competition," a situation with many small producers who individually exert no influence over supply and prices.

However, for the purpose of this paper both agriculture and economics will be considered in very broad terms. For many people economics (quantifiable financial considerations in the mar-ketplace) has now become the unquestioned central organizing force guiding individuals and society. This alternative and more comprehensive understanding of economics will be developed more fully in section III below. As was already previously sug-gested, all people who eat food are connected in a meaningful way to agriculture. All those who purchase food in the mar-ketplace, or play some role between field and table, are likewise more actively involved in shaping economic "realities" than is often acknowledged

Biblical Holism and Christian Worldview Defined

All people, regardless of their faith commitment, have founda-tional assumptions and beliefs about life that provide a frame-work for interpreting their "reality" and respond accordingly. Missionary Anthropologist Paul Hiebert (1985) provides the fol-lowing definition:

> "Taken together, the basic assumptions about reality which lie between the beliefs and behavior of a culture are sometimes called a worldview. Because these assumptions are taken for granted,

they are generally unexamined and therefore largely implicit. But
they are reinforced by the deepest of feelings, and anyone who
challenges them becomes the object of vehement attack. People
believe that the world really is the way they see it. Rarely are they
aware of the fact that the way they see it is molded by their worldview."

A Christian worldview would then be shaped primarily by
Biblical assumptions (or truths) about what is in fact real. Including the concept of Biblical Holism seems to indicate that perhaps
some "Christian" worldviews need to be re-examined and challenged by the fuller light of scripture. This might well be the situation for many Christians in the North American context. Hiebert
(1985) also notes that, "During the past century North Americans
have placed a high value on technology and material goods, and
business is their central activity. Their status is determined largely
by their wealth, and their culture is focused on economic themes."

It is worth noting the key role that worldview plays in shaping
our lives, and this truth also helps underscore the broad scope of
Christian mission. Holistic efforts "... are concerned with all the
dimensions of the human race (spiritual, social, physical, psychological) and of the society in which humanity lives (economic,
social, political, legal and ideological)." (Yamamori, Myers, Bediako, Reed 1996)

Biblical Holism can provide a conceptual framework allowing
the agriculturist to transcend the present worldview so dominant
by the limited economic perspective of our age. Worldview is all
encompassing. Section V. below will highlight key themes of a
biblically informed holistic worldview.

Summarizing the Sweet and Bitter Fruits of Global Agribusiness

The recent productive marriage of agriculture and economics
has created a new global system of agribusiness. This complex
food production and distribution system responds remarkably
well to human needs and wants. However, the actual fruits of
global agribusiness remain both sweet and bitter.

The market driven agricultural system has worked very efficiently supplying wealthy people with an abundance of food. People
with money to vote are always well served. The market has been

far less kind to poor people with little voting power and the non-human (non-voting) dimension of creation. As such, the relative "success" or "failure" of global agribusiness will usually depend a great deal upon questions of perspective and worldview.

1. Modern agricultural systems have become astonishingly productive. The growth in food production has more than matched the recent dramatic rise in human population, and the horrific prophesies of famine and calamity on a global scale (a theme of some early economic thinkers) have so far failed to materialized. According to Kaleb Jansen (1989), the global production of cereal grains alone is over 1,000 pounds per person per year. It is impossible to dispute the fact that global agriculture produces tremendous abundance and choice. In fact, if Adam and Eve were given the opportunity to browse even the produce section of a modern supermarket they might well conclude Paradise was overrated.

2. Abundance and choice are certainly features of our global marketplace, but only for those who can afford it. Participation requires money, and all around the world poor people still struggle to find their daily bread. Millions of people suffer food shortages that prevent them from leading productive lives.

3. Low wages for farmers and agricultural workers are also a constant feature of the modern food production system. Food surpluses may certainly be viewed as a blessing for humanity at large. The rich and poor alike enjoy the benefits of a bountiful harvest. However, the individual small producers who have little control over total production or prices are constantly under pressure for their economic survival. The history of the past 100 years has been a dramatic exodus of farmers from the land. This transition has been largely viewed by economists as a healthy and necessary reduction of excess capacity in the sector. Even so, the historical trend continues unabated, and this raises some foundational questions regarding the relationship between worldview, agriculture and economics.

4. Environmental destruction and loss of bio-diversity are also notable sideaffects of present day agriculture. Obviously, creatures do not have money, and they fail to vote in the marketplace. Creatures (and the physical world of soil, water, rocks, etc) are valued only indirectly through human preferences and interest. The results are truly alarming. Three or more species may be driven to extinction daily. (DeWitt 1991) Soil loss each year from cropland in the Midwest farm belt still exceeds the production of grain in many places. Large areas of the globe remain under threat of desertification, deforestation, and salinization.

Modern agriculture is certainly "productive," but it is also very "destructive." Biblical Holism requires that we question some of the economic forces and market wisdom that have pushed us to this stage. The transformation of worldviews may be necessary, and this becomes the primary work of Christian disciples and prophets. Such vital issues will be considered more fully in future sections of this paper. However, attention must first be given to ground our discussion more firmly in present farming realities. Two short stories that include agricultural, economic, and worldview themes follow.

Contemporary Realities of Global Agriculture

Tropical Poultry Production

Farm fresh eggs and chickens are valued items in many markets around the world, and the small West African country of The Gambia is no exception. The Anglican Mission Farm, located on an 80 acre school campus near the regional trading center of Farafenni, helps meet this demand with a flock of 500 laying hens and periodic broiler production on a similar scale.

Day old chicks are not available from any hatchery within the country, and are purchased instead from Senegal or even Europe via airfreight. Locally available feed components (maize, millet, peanut cake, oyster shell, and dried fish) are ground with a small diesel powered hammer mill on the farm and mixed under the direction of the farm manager. Vaccinations and other antibiotics must also be purchased to maintain flock health.

Poultry business was good (profitable at a sustainable level) during much of the 1980s. This was due primarily to the absence of any strong external competition. However, during the last ten years the economics of the local poultry business have changed dramatically. The market is now periodically "flooded" with cheap eggs imported from Europe. Frozen whole chickens of mostly 2-pound size arrive from Brazil and other international sources. The quality of these products is usually questionable, and some crates of eggs are even marked as "fertilized eggs not intended for human consumption."

All production costs for the local poultry enterprise continue to rise. Items that are only available outside the country are more expensive due to steady devaluation of the local currency. The economics of local commercial poultry production in The Gambia are not promising. Determining the "right" proactive path will now largely depend upon how the present agricultural and economic context is informed by worldview.

The North American Family Farm

African farmers are not the only "people of the land" with economic survival now in question. The following is a paraphrase of what one Midwest farmer's wife wrote in a recent letter:

"My husband is a farmer. He also runs a lawn care business during the summer, does contract work for the local government agricultural office, and fills in as cook at a nearby restaurant. I work fulltime as a C.P.A for a local company and also manage a seasonal tax office out of our home."

The letter went on to explain various activities in church, school, and community life that were important to their family. Nothing more was said about the farm enterprise or their activities as farmers. The rather ominous silence regarding the farm and farming itself suggests a lifestyle that may no longer be sustainable. Will this family soon be another exodus statistic? The economics of farming in North American have been and remain uncertain. Determining the "right" proactive path will also largely depend upon how the present agricultural and economic context is informed by worldview.

The Emergence of Economics as Trusted Value Free Foundation for Life

At this juncture it is necessary to more fully establish the role and place of economics in our global society. Herman Daly and John Cobb (1994) believe economics has developed over time to achieve what they term "misplaced concreteness." Economics is now viewed by many as a hard science built upon proven theories and rigorous mathematical proofs. The economic view is widely believed to present the "true" picture of reality.

Daly and Cobb (1994) also remind us that "Economic theory builds on the propensity of individuals to act so as to optimize their own interests." Looking out for number one (self) is considered normal and rational. Concern for others and the common good is not part of the original economic equation. Humanity now largely chooses to trust "the invisible hand" of the market to transform the numerous desires of individuals into the common good

It seems reasonable to assert that agriculture (now emerging as global agribusiness) is also just a subset of the dominant overarching economy. The invisible hand of the marketplace makes religious and moral judgment unnecessary. The market will know best and serve best. Self -interest can be for the good of everyone. Economics is King.

Some Limitations of Economic or Market Forces:

The modern worldview may indeed be dominated by economic considerations, but the sum total of individuals in pursuit of self-interest has hardly proven a blessing for all. Several examples of "bitter agricultural fruit" were already mentioned earlier, but we do well to more fully acknowledge the shortcomings of Economics as Savior.

Markets Only Respond to Effective Demand

Markets "ignore" even the most basic needs of humans who lack the financial resources to "vote." The world is clearly blessed with huge stocks of food, but market forces alone cannot move it from warehouse or store to the human mouth without money to drive the system. Financial poverty equals no economic vote, even for the necessities of life. Many people in the world today are not well served by the market.

The size and purchasing power of certain markets also determines the scale of investment and attention that will be given by the market players. Industrialized North American agriculture offers an attractive market for numerous suppliers of seeds, fertilizer, pesticides, farm equipment, and a host of other products and services. The large agricultural market also draws considerable amounts of money for basic research and new product development. In contrast, the far more numerous but economically weak farmers of the third world often "go it alone" with limited support from business, research bodies, and various nongovernmental organizations. (NGOs)

The Gambian peanut industry provides one real life example of how effective demand in the market place can overlook the needs of smaller players. Peanuts are the primary Gambian crop, and one of the few sources of hard currency for the country. Purchasing, processing, and sales are all managed by a central marketing board. Oil extraction at the national level also yields peanut cake, an excellent source of protein for animals. Ironically, Gambian farmers have no opportunity to buy back this indirect product of their own labors to improve the health of their animals. All peanut cake is exported.

Global Markets Can Easily Disrupt Local Supply/Demand Equations

Prior to the recent emergence of global agriculture, a linkage could usually be established between the quantity of food produced and price in the marketplace. Farmers could expect higher prices for production in the event of a poor harvest. This certainly held true on a regional or national level, and in some cases even locally. This important linkage between production and price has now been largely lost in the global trade equation. A poor growing season and low yields may not have any significant impact on price, and farmers too often find themselves punished for the productivity of their global neighbors now turned competitors.

Economics Readily Acknowledges the Important Impact of Externalities

Externalities are usually negative consequences (or costs of production) that are not carried by the producer. The true "cost" of soil erosion, ground water contamination, environmental odors or other negatives may not be reflected in the price of farm produce. One partial economic solution is an attempt to "internalize" all costs related to a certain product. Farmers should in some way be required to compensate for unintended collateral damage tied to their production. The theory is promising, but the practical implementation is a virtual impossibility on the scale and scope required. As such, economic theory is left without any effective carrot or stick to encourage the efficiency desired. The difficulty in managing externalities points to the need for an alternative motivation for choosing the common good.

Markets Need Accurate Information to Work Efficiently

People like to assume that the combined wisdom of the market is correct, and that market valuations provide an accurate picture of reality. Such assumptions can prove to be a serious error. Market valuation is only as solid as the information available to the human players concerned.

The sudden financial collapse of the Enron Company provides just one telling example. (Booth Thomas, 2001) This large publicly held company was providing a regular flow of information to all stakeholders. The external auditor's reports were public knowledge. Yet, during the span of just a few short weeks, this large and "successful" company suddenly vanished from existence. The market was wrong because of some serious "misinformation." The market can often be wrong.

In fact, results in the market will never be right, because all markets are shaped by the values, beliefs, and limited information of people. Humanity is broken and sinful. The result cannot be perfect. How solid is some of the information that informs our view of the world, agriculture, and economics?

Clear Ownership Rights as Only a Partial Solution

The National Research Council (1993) published a substantial book devoted to sustainable agriculture in the humid tropics. The text's practical economic guidance can be reduced primarily to the importance of land tenure and ownership rights and dealing more effectively with externalities. Ownership can certainly provide advantages, but the actual outcome may only be as healthy as the worldview of the person or persons assuming clear responsibility.

Briefly consider the care and upkeep of a college campus. Is appropriate stewardship of school environment determined by members of the ground's crew? Perhaps we might envision some guidance role for the Ecology department. Maybe the theologians or philosophers on campus could provide Biblical perspectives on "caring for the garden." Still, the ultimate responsibility may well rest with the college president or advisory board. Clarifying responsibility cannot guarantee right outcomes. Many farmers have been watching "their soil" blow and wash away for years. It may be necessary to consider the importance of ownership rights but also place greater emphasis on God as the creator and sustainer of all.

A Holistic Christian Worldview with Roots for the "Redemption" of Agriculture and Economics.

A Biblically informed holistic worldview must necessarily contain a multitude of facets. In fact, the truth of God's Word and the scope of His Kingdom are far too beautiful and encompassing to be captured in this brief context. As such, only a few central themes with special relevance for agriculture and economics will be mentioned.

A. "In the beginning God created the heavens and the earth." (Genesis 1:1a) The Cosmos did not emerge by chance, but rather by God's grand design and plan. God created everything and declared it to be "good," and this goodness does not depend upon some derived value for human utility or aesthetic preference. Biological diversity is not important simply for what it provides (or may possibly provide) to humans. *The creation has inherent value ascribed by God.*

B. After creating a universe of goodness "The Lord God took the man and put him in the Garden of Eden to work it and take care of it." (Genesis 1:15) The original human job description was no small task, but one that we should continue to regard seriously today. Clearly it was not just corn, soybeans, cows, chickens, and hogs that man was to care for. *The Biblical mandate to care for the whole garden is clearly stated.*

C. *It is also God's desire that people, land, and animals all have a Sabbath rest.* "… but the seventh day is a Sabbath to the Lord your God. On it you shall not do any work, neither you, nor your son or daughter, nor your manservant or maidservant, nor your ox, your donkey or any of your animals …" (Deuteronomy 5:14) "For six years sow your fields, and for six years prune your vineyards and gather their crops. But in the seventh year the land is to have a Sabbath of rest, a Sabbath to the Lord." (Leviticus 25:3, 4) The continual push for greater efficiency and productivity can clearly threaten community well being. We need to question the assumptions of any system that wears down the land, people, or creatures by withholding the Sabbaths God intended.

D. *Bigger fields are not necessarily better.* "Woe to you who add house to house and join field to field till no space is left in the land." (Isaiah 5:8) One modern day parallel may be removal of the old property line fences and hedges now often unnecessary given continual consolidation of ownership. Soon no place is left for even a rabbit to hide. Soon the few small remaining sanctuaries of garden diversity can be swallowed up by "progress."

E. *Poor neighbors need special consideration.* "If one of your countrymen becomes poor and is unable to support himself among you, help him as you would an alien or a temporary resident, so he can continue to live among you. Do not take interest of any kind from him, but fear your God, so that your countryman may continue to live among you. You must not lend him money at interest or sell him food at a

profit." (Leviticus 25: 35-37) Our special market consideration for the poor today is often higher interest rates. The
poor often pay more for food because bulk purchases (rice
by the bag) are beyond their reach.

F. *The wealth that we do enjoy is a gracious gift from God* and
should be recognized as such. "When you have eaten and
are satisfied, praise the Lord your God for the good land he
has given you. Be careful that you do not forget the Lord
your God, failing to observe his commands... You may say
to yourself, 'My power and the strength of my hands have
produced this wealth for me.' But remember the Lord your
God, for it is he who gives you the ability to produce
wealth." (Deuteronomy 8:10,11a,17,18)

G. *Business and Economics is best understood as helping (serving)
others.* The core of economics should not be pursuit of self-
interest, but rather meeting the needs of humanity and
creation. From this perspective God can perhaps be understood as the "Chief Economist." God invites his household
to gather around the table to celebrate the Eucharist. Meeks
(1989) believes that in taking up the towel of service for his
disciples Jesus revealed the power of God's service to the
household. Christians are likewise called to diakonia, the
mutual self-giving in service for the household. "The
'household of God' exists as an agent of God's work to
make the world into a household in which all of God's
creatures will find access to life. The church's public acts of
evangelization and mission will have increasingly to focus
on God's economy in relation to the world's existing economies." (Meeks 1989)

A holistic Biblical worldview certainly provides a foundation
for the transformation of individuals, and by extension, the broader marketplace. The markets fail us because of sin and the distorted worldviews (bad information) that shape how we are willing to vote in the market place. In North America this applies to
the 3 % who supply from the farm and the 97 % who demand
with their votes in the marketplace.

Farm Stories Viewed from the Economics of Humankind or the Economics of God.

The section on modern economics noted just a few limitations of the conventional economic perspective, and the previous section followed with some Biblical foundations for a more holistic worldview. Determining the "right" proactive future for farming will largely depend upon how the present agricultural and economic context is informed by worldview.

Tropical Poultry Production

As was already noted, the future of the fledgling poultry industry in The Gambia is in question. Local production costs have continued to rise, and numerous global producers are now supplying a variety of poultry products at very competitive prices. What might be the "right" path forward? Much depends upon the perspective taken.

Conventional economic theory can certainly provide some helpful guidance. Small poultry producers may expand operations to achieve greater economies of scale, thus reducing production costs per bird. For example, a five hundred mile round trip by car to the hatchery in Senegal costs the same amount to collect fifty, five hundred, or one thousand chicks. A larger scale of operation also provides opportunities to purchase inputs like grain, premix, and medicines at a discounted bulk price. Higher production may even open the door to favorable sales opportunities with local hotels and other institutions. The best human wisdom seems to be "get bigger and manage carefully to remain globally competitive."

The economics of God might well move the poultry farmer in some alternative directions. For starters, God's "flock of birds" includes far more diversity than what we now know as the domestic chicken, a bird that may survive but rarely thrives in the often-punishing African heat. Why not consider instead the redemptive reintroduction of a perfectly adapted bird God originally placed in the garden but man eliminated? The Ostrich might be one such option. These native birds would not require long trips to the hatchery, special feeding, expensive vaccinations or direct price competition in the now international poultry markets. One local hotel has already expressed an interest in adding ostrich to their menu as a truly African entrée. God's economics (with a broader concern for his entire created order) may even prove more "profitable" for the farm/garden stewards.

The North American Family Farm

Small farmers in America are clearly in trouble, but why? One possible explanation is the strong emphasis placed on increasing output. Higher production is found through new technologies, improved genetics, or site-specific farming. Very high capital investment and financial risk also characterize the present system. Farms today are often producing not "food" but rather commodities for the well-supplied global markets.

The standard economic solution is for farmers to specialize, to get bigger and more competitive. The end result has some surprising similarities to the Fulani cattle curse. People are now often forcing the economics to work with a big infusion of outside money. The system is painful for farmers and their families. Even the land can suffer and cry out! All pay the price. How can this be? Perhaps farmers have come to understand themselves not primarily as obedient disciples stewarding the earth and providing food for humanity, but rather as masters of a particular narrow enterprise. Some live for grain farming. Others dream of hogs or dairy cows. The idol worship may not be cows, but rather the ever larger and more advanced diesel horses of today. Social status is determined not by cows or the level of earth care, but rather the total number of acres farmed and what pickup truck is parked in front of the local café.

North American farmers might do well to begin with a better understanding of the land God has granted them temporary stewardship rights over. Farmers must know both the creator and the creation. Steps must be taken to escape the trap of low cost commodity production and provide food for people instead. If farmers truly are not farming for the money they should reject farming for self and farm to please and glorify God instead. The specific path informed by God's principles will certainly be unique to each farm and farmers, but the global need to choose Godly wisdom over worldly wisdom is clear.

Responding to Structural Evil in the Agricultural Economy

Individual farmers must play a key role in the redemption of agriculture, and agricultural stewards from all over the world should respond to their calling in obedience and faithfulness. However, it is also necessary to address what might be considered a primary "structural evil" of global agribusiness. We now live with commodities and fixed prices for items that should be distinguishable and valued accordingly. The now dominant system of agribusiness is characterized by an unhealthy disconnect between farm and dinner table, with many people largely helpless in their desire to be faithful members of God's Kingdom. The challenge becomes rebuilding community relationships between agricultural producers (farmers) and agricultural consumers (primarily city folks).

Structural Evil from the Cornfield

A simple example from the cornfield can help clarify the challenge of structural evil. A North American farmer produces No. 2 yellow corn and delivers it to a local terminal for an agreed price per bushel. The grain must meet recognized standards for test weight, moisture, and purity but no other information is considered necessary to determine the correct market price. Generally the market views all corn as "equal," even though some of the grain may be "good" while some is "bad." A percentage of the farmer's corn may have been planted on land that is highly erodable and thus totally unsuitable for row crops. This "bad" corn should never have been produced on land that needs a permanent plant cover. Obviously, even the most caring of farmers will still produce a mixed harvest. In addition, each individual farm and farmer operates in a unique context. What concerned citizen would really want to encourage a farmer guilty of groundwater contamination, soil erosion, local extinction of native species, or the misuse of pesticides?

Even so, corn is corn. Reviewing the label on a box of roasted corn flake cereal highlights the challenge. Nutritional information is provided for total energy per serving, protein, fat, and essential vitamins and minerals. Another column factors in the possible addition of skim milk. A special limited time promotional even offers the chance of winning valuable merchandise. The paper packaging itself is clearly marked as "from recycled materials." The box of cereal is covered with print providing some very important and useful information. However, the primary ingredient, corn, remains simply corn. More is known regarding the origin of the expensive packaging material than of the corn itself! The conscious and concerned "consumer" is often left lamenting in the supermarket isle scanning the labels for small clues and praying to God for mercy.

The Importance of Proper Pricing

Recognizing the above, the "right price" is not simply what the market will bear, but rather an infinitely variable sum. However, it is quite impossible to vote with care in the market place if the important information is not available. Unfortunately, most food is now thoroughly laundered (washed clean) by the time it reaches the consumer. (Just like blood diamonds from war zones or drug money.) Diamonds are diamonds, money is money, and food is food. Often we simply cannot know, but economics for the good of God's larger household still requires that we differentiate. How might this look in our food system? Farmers should tend and care for soil, plants, and all creatures according to their unique needs. Consumers should have the opportunity to "vote" on products that are differentiated in truly meaningful ways. Not all corn is equal.

The important link between product differentiation, consumer preference, and pricing is widely acknowledged. Companies place a great emphasis on building up brand loyalty and convincing people to purchase their product. The producer of corn flakes is trying to swing the purchase decision in their favor with the chance to win merchandise. The corn itself fails to factor in the equation.

Fair Trade Coffee as a Model for Informed Price Discrimination

Coffee has become an important commodity in international trade, and like corn, not all coffee is "equally good." The coffee market has differentiated a great deal during that past few years with far more attention being given to unique beans and blends. Coffee is not just coffee anymore. The industry is all about creating special market niches and building brand loyalty. The important consideration for a coffee drinker with an active Christian conscience becomes "what makes a particular coffee good or bad?" Is the decision simply a matter of taste preference and price? Certainly not.

"Equal exchange coffee" provides one valuable example of how the unique attributes of the food itself can factor into the marketplace. The Christian Century magazine carried an advertisement for Equal Exchange gourmet coffee from the Interfaith Coffee Program (2001). The banner line reads: "A Crisis Brewing in Our Cup of Coffee?" The primary text follows:

> "As the second most heavily traded commodity in the world, coffee is a vital source of income for poor farmers in the developing world. But as world coffee prices have fallen to historic lows, coffee-growing communities have been plunged into a crisis. Recent news reports have detailed the tragic results- farmers abandoning their crops, unemployed farm workers crowded in shantytowns, families separated as members brave borders to find work in other countries. But across the U.S. a growing number of congregations are taking action in a simple way- by drinking fairly traded coffee. Through the Interfaith Coffee Program, your community gets a delicious cup of coffee while farmers receive a fair price- currently over double the world market price—helping them to provide for themselves and their families."

The Interfaith Coffee Program provides more valuable information on their homepage at www.equalexchange.com. Equal exchange coffee is purchased directly from smallholder cooperative groups allowing them to realize greater income. The small family farmers also have distinct advantages over larger commercial plantations in terms of land stewardship and care for God's creatures. Not all coffee is equal, and it is important for Christians to link consumptive choices to care of the global economic household. The basic assumption of the Interfaith Coffee Program is that Christians should and do care, and will in fact vote redemptively in the marketplace when given the information and opportunity to do so.

If "fair trade" is a possibility for coffee producers, why not expand the concept to other food commodities as well? The actual value of the corn in the box of cereal is just a small fraction of the total sales price. People should have the option to buy corn, or milk, or eggs or chicken or a host of other food items from farmers at a fair price with assurances that the needs of God's larger household are also being met. The small and scattered farmer/producers will find it difficult to transform the agricultural landscape without the support and commitment of the larger human community. Agricultural economics is not a field of academic study reserved for just a few, but rather the concrete living out of human values and beliefs. God is the chief economist. Humans were created in the image of God. God's economy is not about self-interest, but rather the whole. Worldview transformation and Biblical Holism remains central.

The Role of Agricultural Missionaries in Cultivating Biblical Holism

The redemption of agriculture might be understood fundamentally as a simple task. Christian agriculturists first embrace the good news of God's Kingdom, then apply Biblical principles in their calling, and finally they transform agricultural economics at both personal and structural levels. God works through His faithful and willing servants to bring Shalom. On one hand the task is simple and clear. However, we should not conclude that redemptive work is easy, or that Christian faith and commitment will automatically yield abundant fruit. As such, it is appropriate to consider more fully the nature of the agricultural missionary task and suggest a few areas for strategic engagement.

A. Plenty of work is already being done (usually with an eye to greater profit) to increase the yields of corn, rice, wheat and many other food crops. This research may be well and good in the proper context. However, if farmers take this new technology and still insist on planting every last square foot of "their" land, what real hope do we have for the wider scope of God's good creation? What hope can we offer the Fulani farmer selling peanuts to buy more cows that the land can no longer sustain? Market forces constantly push for higher production, and Christians need not add fuel to the flames. *The most important and needed development for the agriculturist is transformation of the heart and of worldviews.*

B. *Heart conversions must begin from the personal level and extend to the structural.* The path ahead depends precisely upon building a more holistic worldview that brings faith, belief, and values back to the marketplace. According to Tetsunao Yamamori (1996)

> "The Great Commission is not about the percentages of national populations that we may consider to have been 'reached' or remain 'unreached' with the gospel, important as these considerations are. Our Lord did not say, 'Go make disciples of some people or even of a large percentage of the people of the nations.' What he commanded was, 'Go make disciples of the nations, go make the nations my disciples.' The Great Commission, therefore, is about the discipline of the nations, the conversion of things that make people into nations—the shared and common processes of thinking; attitudes; world views; perspectives; languages; and the cultural, social and economic habits of thought, behavior and practice."

C. Christian missionaries have gone to the nations of the world with a message of sin, repentance, and new life in Christ. The call is for personal conversion and commitment to Jesus as Lord and Savior, with a dramatic departure from old ways of sin and a new life of righteousness by the power of God's Spirit. *Perhaps the primary work of the Christian Agriculturist is to expose the evils of economic idolatry, call for repentance, and point to the New Kingdom of heaven on earth.* How much do we know the creation that should be in our care? Is it just Corn, beans, hogs, or dairy that we study and care for? Are we ignorant regarding some key stakeholders or careless and selfish stewards? Are we ready to hear, repent, and believe?

D. Agriculturists, and perhaps especially other Christians, may be defensive when their views of farming, economics, and Biblical understanding are called into question. *As such, the work of discipleship is best undertaken in the context of vital human relationships.* We can hardly expect to confront people on "good" or "bad" coffee in the isle of the super-market. The isle or foyer of church may prove equally ineffective. A sustained conversation with people who truly desire to grow in faithfulness and obedience will be required. It is also unlikely that a pastor's 20-minute sermon, or even several messages devoted to Biblical perspectives on food and agriculture, will bring people far enough along the path of change. A more extensive and in-depth adult study class with selected reading assignments, times for reflection and discussion, and practical steps to greater Christian faithfulness will likely be more effective.

E. *Challenging the worldview of farmers is necessary but may prove difficult.* Agricultural producers are constantly searching for new possibilities to enhance their often-tenuous economic position. Practical considerations tend to dominate. Will this new crop variety put more grain in the bin? Will this piece of equipment save time and expense in the field? Farmers are also busy people, so they can only be counted on to attend short duration events that promise some economic advantage. Farmers may share some tendencies with the Israelites of the Old Testament, only looking to God for deeper direction and foundations for life when times are tough. When the Midwest agricultural economy was poor in the early to mid 1980s farmers flocked to attend Christian farmers meetings. During the difficult times much hand wringing and some soul searching took place. A few years down the road (once hog prices had moved back up some) the financial pressure was off and interest in "Christian Farming" seemed to fade. Is our concern for obedience or simply self?

F. Biblical Holism and Agriculture cannot be "sold" at a quick morning seminar or a special field day, and consumers will not be "converted" by passing comments in the super-market or church isle. As such, *effective programs for sharing the good news of God the chief economist will need to be developed for various situations.*

The Anglican Mission Farm in The Gambia organized an agricultural training program that promoted Biblical Holism as a foundation for farming activities. The seven-week residential program included both theory and practical dimensions for poultry production and agro-forestry. Technical information was part of the learning experience, but arguably not the most important dimension. Rather, foundational questions were raised concerning agricultural values, beliefs, and ethics. More emphasis was placed on Biblical/theological reflection and foundations for Holism than any other topic.

The course started from the Genesis account of creation highlighting God's delight in all he made and man's special role as caretaker. The impact of human sin and the mixed blessing or our global food system was also explored. The term "agro-forestry" first entered classroom discussion three weeks into the program- based not just on tangible benefits to people alone, but rather on obedience to God the creator of all. The trainees did eventually establish tree seedlings and "do real work in the garden," but not before they were well introduced to the expansive love and care of the Chief Steward.

G. What fruit can we expect to realize as the Good News takes root? *Faithful Christian witness will likely yield important but incremental changes of both worldview and agricultural practice.* Conversion of culture may be dramatic, but slow change with the passage of time is more likely. The rise and fall of the moldboard plow provides one example of how change occurs. This dangerous but once omnipresent tool did not make a sudden dramatic exit from the Midwestern-farming scene. Farmers never renounced their sinful plowing habit with a communal public ceremony at the scrap metal yard. (Like a public burning of evil books or charms.) Rather, the plows were traded in on new conservation tillage machinery or simply left to rust slowly in the grove of trees behind the barn. A very dramatic and positive change in farming did occur, but slowly one farmer at a time over about 40 years- the span of nearly a generation.

According to Hiebert (1985)

> "World views, therefore, tend to conserve old ways and pro-
> vide stability in cultures over long periods of time.... But world-
> views themselves do change, since none of them are fully integrat-
> ed, and there are always internal contradictions. Moreover, when
> we adopt new ideas they may challenge our fundamental assump-
> tions. Although we all live with cultural inconsistencies, when the
> internal contradictions become too great, we seek ways to reduce
> the tension. Normally, we change or let go of some of our assump-
> tions. The result is a gradual world-view transformation of which
> we ourselves may not even be aware."

Many farmers may continue to experience a slow conversion
to greater Biblical Holism. The case may now be nearly closed on
"plowing," but new issues will continue to surface in each generation. Like farmers, the larger number of consumers also live with
slowly changing worldviews. Making the choice for "good" coffee
may be a start, but such ideas must also expand slowly to include
more people and food. Little room exists for impatient prophets as
some of the important battles emerging now may not be concluded in this lifetime.

It is important to consider what kingdoms we need to uproot
and tear down yet today. A recent gathering of African missionaries in the Gambia considered this text from Jeremiah and
reflected on what it might mean in their context. Human sacrifices, the spiritual power of demons and magic charms were all
identified as evils to be overcome in Africa. Western Christians
don't much fear evil charms, and while cultic powers may exist
they are largely ignored. But, perhaps the western world does still
have powerful idols on the throne. Money and marketplace economic "realities" may be one such kingdom. As in the past, God
still appoints his faithful stewards "over nations and kingdoms to
uproot and tear down, to destroy and overthrow, to build and to
plant."

Conclusion

The Redemption of Agriculture and Economics will require a
transformation of worldview. Biblical holism can assist human
stewards in understanding their important role as God's image
bearers and provide an escape from limiting human economic per-

spectives. God's claim over the life of his earthly stewards is complete, and the prophetic and transforming message of Christ's Lordship must be lived out on the farm and in the marketplace.

My first cross-culture learning opportunity as an agricultural mission worker was with farmers on the Caribbean Island of Haiti. During my brief stay I had the privilege of meeting a Christian farmer named Eavwas. A visit to his small farm provided a memorable lesson on the vital importance of Christian Worldview. Our garden walk was prefaced with an unexpected time of Bible reading and prayer in his simple house. Eavwas said "You will not be able to understand the transformation that has taken place in my garden unless you first understand the great change God has worked in my heart." Eavwas read from Genesis explaining how God placed mankind in the garden to "tend and keep" all the good things of creation. A vision of Biblical stewardship in his mind and heart freed Eavwas to reject the dominant local sugarcane and rum economy, and create instead what was emerging as a diverse and productive "Garden of Eden." Obedient agricultural prophets are called primarily to multiply the testimony of Eavwas around the world today, with lives (and farms) transformed by a worldview that testifies to God's grace and power.

References

Booth Thomas, C.
> 2001   "Power Failure." *Time*. December 10, page 56.

Bread for the World
> 2002   www.bread.org/hungerbasics/index: Washington DC, USA

Council for Biotechnology Information
> 2001   *The Atlantic Monthly*. Oct., page 59.

Daly, H., and J. Cobb
> 1994   *For the Common Good*. Boston: Beacon Press.

DeWitt, C.
> 1991   *The Environment & the Christian: What Can We Learn from the New Testament?* Grand Rapids: Baker.

Hiebert, P.
> 1985. *Anthropological Insights for Missionaries*. Grand Rapids: Baker.

Interfaith Coffee Program
  2001   *Christian Century*, Dec. 5, page 24.

Jansen, K.
  1989   *Target Earth: The Necessity of Diversity on a Holistic Perspective on World Mission*. Kailua-Kona: University of the Nations.

Meeks, D.
  1989   *God the Economist*. Minneapolis: Fortress Press.

National Research Council
  1993   *Sustainable Agriculture and the Environment in the Humid Tropics*. Washington: National Academy Press.

Yamamori, T., B. Meyers, K. Dediako, and L. Reed, eds.
  1996   *Serving with the Poor in Africa*. Monrovia: MARC.

Conclusion

Give Us This Day Our Daily Bread:
A Prayer to the First Farmer

David J. Evans

On the final day of the May 2002 international conference on Biblical Holism and Agriculture held at Dordt College in Iowa, USA, one of the participants remarked, "We've needed this for 40 years!" Another added, "[This conference has been] an answer to my prayer to promote ministries in Biblically Holistic agriculture. You hit on a great need. Don't let up." Indeed, this conference and the ensuing discussions seem to have struck a responsive chord for many Christians interested in agriculture and creation care. According to God's mandate in Deuteronomy 8:3, people shall not live by bread alone, but by every word that comes from God. Thus, we are to live by bread, but we are also to live by the Word of God. When these two things are combined for the agriculturist in an intentional way, it leads to all kinds of exciting opportunities, discoveries, and adventures. When asked what prompted him to study the lowly peanut, George Washington Carver said, "Why, I just took a handful of peanuts and looked at them. 'Great Creator,' I said, 'Why did you make the peanut? Why?' With such knowledge as I had of chemistry and physics I set to work to take the peanut apart" (see reference in Miller's chapter).

Carver understood that agriculture and God's revelation

through His Word go hand in hand. If that is true, then what have we learned in the previous chapters of this book? Although it is somewhat risky to attempt to synthesize and categorize two hundred pages of thoughts and stories into a few concluding pages, a few key themes are nonetheless repeated throughout these chapters. They are:

1) God is the first farmer;

2) People have been mandated and entrusted by God to both develop and care for the creation; and

3) People involved in agriculture have a responsibility to love their neighbor as themselves.

God the First Farmer

"And the Lord God planted a garden toward the East, in Eden; and there he placed the man whom he had formed. And out of the ground the Lord God caused to grow every tree that is pleasing to the sight and good for food" (Genesis 2: 8-9a). The theme of God being the first gardener was repeated many times throughout this book. Although this might sound strange upon first hearing it, the scriptures clearly speak of God's care as he planted the garden of Eden and coaxed plants to grow in order to produce food for both humans and animals. This act by the Lord God lends tremendous dignity and purpose to the calling and vocation of modern-day agriculturists. As Darrow Miller wrote in his chapter, this concept of God as the first farmer brought wonder and awe to the Aymaran farmers in Bolivia when they first heard it. They had thought that farming was a dirty vocation for poor people who did not have any other viable options. But through the Word of God and the Holy Spirit, they began to realize that when they planted and tended their fields, they were doing nothing less than following in God's footsteps. Other authors echoed these thoughts by hammering home the point that people are created in God's image and as such possess tremendous potential and abilities to be good agricultural stewards. Njoka and Oye wrote from an African perspective about God's sovereignty over the created order. He sends the rain. He allows farmers to gain a good harvest. He controls all things. This led to discussions by various authors of the need for agriculturalists (indeed all people) to be in right relationship with the Creator. In order for farmers to be able to fully draw upon the wisdom and knowledge of God with regards to tending the garden, they need to be reconciled to him through the work of Jesus Christ on the cross and his subsequent resurrection.

People Have Been Mandated and Entrusted by God to Both Develop and Care for the Creation

Nearly all of the authors in this book touched upon God's mandate for humans to steward the creation (Genesis 2:15). Robb De Haan wrote, "like the rest of God's creatures, we give God praise, honor, and glory by living as He created us to live. We were created to keep creation as God keeps us. It is important to note that the word 'creation' is used in a comprehensive way in the Bible ... Creation includes everything that God has made—rocks, people, plants, fish, bacteria, water, and everything else. Nothing is left out. Nothing is to be uncared for." The Scriptures are replete with verses and stories about stewarding the creating. Leviticus speaks of caring for the land and allowing it to rest and be replenished. The Mosaic Laws also gives clear instructions for caring for one's animals. Jesus reiterated this when he spoke of rescuing one's ox from a well on the Sabbath. He also gives a tremendous word picture to us in speaking about the good shepherd who cares for his sheep and is even willing to leave the 99 in order to rescue the one that is lost. In light of these Biblical mandates, many of the authors challenged us to examine the way that we as Christians do agriculture. Is any of the care that is mentioned in the Scriptures for both land and animals exhibited on the farms of Christians throughout the world today? Or is a Christian farm today indistinguishable from that of a non-Christian? These are important questions that will mostly likely frame the debate in this area for years to come.

In addition to this area of stewardship, a few of the authors ably unpacked the Biblical mandate given to people to develop the creation. It is the God-given role of people involved in agriculture to be fruitful and to produce bounty with the resources that God has entrusted to them. Without bounty, there is an ever-decreasing resource base to steward. Conversely, without stewardship, the bounty is short-lived and eventually exhausted. Both need to happen simultaneously in order for God's creation to unfold according to His intentions. In Genesis 1, the text reads "Then God said, 'Let us make man in our image in our likeness, and let them rule over the fish of the sea and the birds of the air, over the livestock, overall the earth, and over all the creatures that move along the ground.' God blessed them and said to them, 'Be fruitful and increase in number; fill the earth and subdue it. Rule over the fish of the sea and the birds of the air and over every living creature that moves on the ground." Thus, those who practice agriculture should work hard to increase soil fertility. They should control weeds and pests. They should raise a diverse variety of crops and animals. They should be fruitful and produce bounty.

People Involved in Agriculture Have a Responsibility to Love Their Neighbor as Themselves

Several of the authors examined and reflected on the relationship between agriculturists and their neighbors. This was evident in the chapters on ethics, economics and humanity. Vos made some very interesting connections between the modernization of agriculture in the US and the growth of unhealthy competition among farmers. He wrote, "Farmers [interviewed in a book] repeatedly mentioned that they feel pressure to use cutthroat methods to beat out their neighbors by a few bushels per acre. During the farm crisis of the 1980s in North America, it was often said that farmers were more interested in their neighbor's land rather than in their neighbors as people in a community. In general, among people involved in agriculture, there is a feeling that competition is much more prevalent than it used to be." How does this cultural change among North American farmers stack up against the Biblical mandate to love one's neighbor as oneself? Other authors in these pages generated lively discussion about the prevailing economic models that drive modern agriculture. Is bio-technology (genetically modified organisms) good or bad? Does the Bible bring anything to bear on this subject? What about the poor in the land? In a figurative sense, are they able to glean in the fields following the modern-day harvest?

At the end of the day, this book will probably raise more questions than it answers. But these questions need to be raised if Christians involved in agriculture around the world are to better understand the role that they are called to play in bringing God's word and His kingdom to bear on the land, animals, and neighbors that have been entrusted to their care. The answers will probably not come easy. That said, the apostle Paul's words ring true for us when he commands us to not be conformed to this world, but to be transformed by the renewing of our minds, that we may prove what is the good, acceptable and perfect will of God.